T0073216

Clustering and Outlier Detection for Trajectory Stream Data

East China Normal University Scientific Reports
Subseries on Data Science and Engineering

ISSN: 2382-5715

Chief Editor
Weian Zheng
Changjiang Chair Professor
School of Finance and Statistics
East China Normal University, China
Email: financialmaths@gmail.com

Associate Chief Editor
Shanping Wang
Senior Editor
Journal of East China Normal University (Natural Sciences), China
Email: spwang@library.ecnu.edu.cn

This book series reports valuable research results and progress in scientific and related areas. Mainly contributed by the distinguished professors of the East China Normal University, it will cover a number of research areas in pure mathematics, financial mathematics, applied physics, computer science, environmental science, geography, estuarine and coastal science, education information technology, etc.

Published

Vol. 10   *Clustering and Outlier Detection for Trajectory Stream Data*
by Jiali Mao (East China Normal University, China),
Cheqing Jin (East China Normal University, China) and
Aoying Zhou (East China Normal University, China)

Vol. 9   *Concurrency Control and Recovery in OLTP Systems:*
High Scalability and Availability
by Peng Cai (East China Normal University, China),
Jinwei Guo (East China Normal University, China) and
Aoying Zhou (East China Normal University, China)

Vol. 8   *Network Data Mining and Analysis*
by Ming Gao (East China Normal University, China),
Ee-Peng Lim (Singapore Management University, Singapore) and
David Lo (Singapore Management University, Singapore)

More information on this series can also be found at https://www.worldscientific.com/series/ecnusr

(Continued at end of book)

East China Normal University Scientific Reports | **Vol. 10**
Subseries on Data Science and Engineering

Clustering and Outlier Detection for Trajectory Stream Data

Jiali Mao
Cheqing Jin
Aoying Zhou
East China Normal University, China

World Scientific

NEW JERSEY · LONDON · SINGAPORE · BEIJING · SHANGHAI · HONG KONG · TAIPEI · CHENNAI · TOKYO

Published by

World Scientific Publishing Co. Pte. Ltd.

5 Toh Tuck Link, Singapore 596224

USA office: 27 Warren Street, Suite 401-402, Hackensack, NJ 07601

UK office: 57 Shelton Street, Covent Garden, London WC2H 9HE

Library of Congress Cataloging-in-Publication Data
Names: Mao, Jiali, author.
Title: Clustering and outlier detection for trajectory stream data / Jiali Mao, Cheqing Jin,
    Aoying Zhou, East China Normal University, China.
Description: New Jersey : World scientific, [2020] | Series: East China Normal University
    scientific reports, 2382-5715 ; vol. 10 | Includes bibliographical references and index.
Identifiers: LCCN 2019052258 | ISBN 9789811210457 (hardcover) |
    ISBN 9789811210464 (ebook)
Subjects: LCSH: Intelligent transportation systems--Data processing. |
    Database management. | Spatial data mining.
Classification: LCC TE228.3 .M345 2020 | DDC 388.3/1--dc23
LC record available at https://lccn.loc.gov/2019052258

British Library Cataloguing-in-Publication Data
A catalogue record for this book is available from the British Library.

For any available supplementary material, please visit
https://www.worldscientific.com/worldscibooks/10.1142/11555#t=suppl

Desk Editors: Herbert Moses/Amanda Yun

Typeset by Stallion Press
Email: enquiries@stallionpress.com

East China Normal University Scientific Reports

Jianpan Wang (Professor, Department of Mathematics, East China Normal University)
Rongming Wang (Professor, School of Financial and Statistics, East China Normal University)
Wei-Ning Xiang (Zijiang Chair Professor, Department of Environmental Science, East China Normal University; Professor, Department of Geography and Earth Science, University of North Carolina at Charlotte)
Danping Yang (Professor, Department of Mathematics, East China Normal University)
Kai Yang (Professor, Department of Environmental Science, East China Normal University)
Shuyi Zhang (Zijiang Chair Professor, School of Life Sciences, East China Normal University)
Weiping Zhang (Changjiang Chair Professor, Department of Physics, East China Normal University)
Xiangming Zheng(Professor, Department of Geography, East China Normal University)
Aoying Zhou (Changjiang Chair Professor, School of Data Science and Engineering, East China Normal University)

Subseries on Data Science and Engineering

Chief Editor
Aoying Zhou
Changjiang Chair Professor
School of Data Science and Engineering
East China Normal University, China
Email: ayzhou@sei.ecnu.edu.cn

Associate Editors
Rakesh Agrawal (Technical Fellow, Microsoft Research in Silicon Valley)
Michael Franklin (University of California at Berkeley)
H. V, Jagadish (University of Michigan in Ann Arbor)
Christian S. Jensen (University of Aalborg)
Masaru Kitsuregawa (University of Tokyo, National Institute of Informatics (NII))
Volker Markl (Technische Universität Berlin (TUBerlin))
Gerhard Weikum (Max Planck Institute for Informatics)
Ruqian Lu (Academy of Mathematics and Systems Science, Chinese Academy of Sciences)

Subseries on Educational Information Technology

Chief Editors
Ren Youqun
East China Normal University, China

Gu Xiaoqing
East China Normal University, China

Editorial Board
J Michael Spector (University of North Texas)
Charles Crook (University of Nottingham)
David Gibson (Curtin University)
Yong Zhao (University of Kansas)
Jan Elen (University of Leuven)
Barbara Wasson (University of Bergen)
Maggie Minhong Wang (University of Hong Kong)
Hua Hua Chang (University of Illinois at Urbana-Champaign)
Tristan Jonson (Northeastern University)

Preface

Urban transportation plays a critical role in the city and has significant influence in the development of urbanization. But in recent years, cities face a series of issues such as traffic jams, energy wastage, severe air pollution, etc. Developing smart transportation helps to improve the efficiency, safety, and environmental sustainability of urban transportation. To provide urban residents faster, cheaper, and greener ways to travel in cities, it is necessary to provide appropriate solutions for transport planning, traffic management, and control. With the widespread applications of modern mobile devices and the vigorous development of location acquisition technologies, numerous moving objects relay their locations continuously through longitude and latitude coordinates, speed, direction, timestamps, etc. Correspondingly, a tremendous amount of positional information is accumulated in the form of trajectory data streams. This enables us to develop smart transportation through systematic research and the development of analyzing technologies upon trajectory streams. By analyzing the trajectory streams in a timely and effective manner, we can gain insights about evolutionary moving behaviors as well as the movement trends of the entities. This will further facilitate the control and management of traffic.

Although there are many books on spatio-temporal databases, mobile computing and data mining and so on, this is a unique book dedicated to enabling smart transportation applications using trajectory stream analyzing techniques like clustering and outlier detection, where a broad spectrum of coverage and an authoritative overview will also be provided. The clustering analysis and outlier detection are two typical moving pattern discovery techniques for mining the trajectory stream data. As an unsupervised approach, clustering aims to group a large amount of trajectories into numerous comparatively homogeneous clusters to extract the representative paths or the common moving trends shared by various objects. Conversely, the main task of the outlier detection is to identify a few trajectories that appear to be significantly distinct from the remaining data, and to reveal abnormal events. Designing efficient mechanisms for clustering and outlier detection upon trajectory streams can facilitate a broad range of time-critical applications, such as intelligent transportation management, route planning, road infrastructure optimization, etc.

A trajectory stream can be viewed as a continuous and infinite sequence of positions accompanied and ordered by the explicit timestamps. Recently, effort has been devoted to clustering and outlier detection upon streaming trajectories. The main challenge comes from the strict space- and time-complexities of processing continuously arriving trajectory data, combined with the difficulty of coping with the concept drift. Moreover, due to constraint factors like skewness distribution and the evolving nature of trajectory data, it is challenging to put forward the highly-effective methods for clustering and outlier detection upon trajectory streams. It is even more difficult to exploit the high-precision solutions for the distributed streams generated by geographically dispersed equipments, to meet the requirement of on-the-fly execution with minimal transferring overheads among the nodes. To tackle the above mentioned issues, we are committed to developing clustering and outlier detection techniques upon trajectory streams, to facilitate various transportation applications such as cloned vehicle detection and identifying changes to the road topological structure.

This book covers the major topics that shape the field of clustering and outlier detection upon trajectory streams, and is aimed at advanced undergraduates, graduate students, researchers, and professionals. It will also provide researchers and application developers a comprehensive overview of the general concepts, techniques, and applications on analyzing using trajectory stream data, and help them to explore this new field and develop more valuable methods and applications. It may also serve as a general introduction to recent developments in this promising research area, and will be very useful to interested readers. Here is a brief introduction to the topics that will be covered in each chapter.

Chapter 1 introduces the concepts and technologies for solving issues in trajectory stream analyzing that newcomers will be faced with when exploring this field. These issues include: characteristics of trajectory stream data and the existing analysis techniques, and the trajectory analysis framework. In addition, this chapter emphasizes the challenges as well as research issues pertaining to analyzing trajectory streams, and ends with some fundamental techniques for analyzing trajectory streams efficiently, such as similarity measurement, the index technique, distributed framework, etc.

Chapter 2 addresses the issue of clustering upon trajectory streams. It designs two synopses to maintain the characteristics of trajectory stream data incrementally, and presents a framework — called OCluwin — to cluster the evolving streaming trajectories. More specifically, it contains a *micro-clustering* component to cluster and summarize the most recent sets of trajectory line segments at each time instant, and a *macro-clustering* component to build large macro-clusters based on the micro-clusters over a specified time horizon. Next, we present two methods — TSCluWin and OCluST — based on two defined synopsis structures (EF_o as well as EF), which can extract the spatio-temporal clustering characteristics of the stream data in memory and track the latest cluster changes of the trajectory streams in real time. Theoretical analysis and experimental results on the real trajectory data sets showed that our proposal could achieve the superior performance in clustering streaming trajectories.

Chapter 3 proposes an outlier detection framework to discover the outliers from trajectory streams. Initially, a feature grouping-based mechanism is presented to divide all the features of trajectory data into two groups called the *Spatial Similarity Feature* and *Movement Difference Feature*. For trajectory fragments that are obtained by trajectory simplifying, the local neighbors for each trajectory fragment is searched according to the *Spatial Similarity Feature*. The outliers are then identified within the local neighborhood in terms of the *Movement Difference Feature*. Based on the feature differences among local adjacent objects in one or more time intervals, two outlier definitions are provided — the local anomaly trajectory fragment (TF-*outlier*) and the evolutionary anomaly moving object (MO-*outlier*). Furthermore, we devise a basic solution and then an optimized algorithm to detect both types of outliers. Experimental results on three real data sets validated our proposal for effectiveness and efficiency.

Chapter 4 first puts forward a two-phase distributed framework to tackle the issue of efficiently analyzing the trajectory streams derived by multiple disperse nodes. Initially, a synopsis data structure is presented to extract clustering characteristics of distributed trajectory streams. Then, in combination with a sliding-window model, we design a two-layer distributed framework and then develop an incremental algorithm for online clustering over distributed trajectory streams called OCluDTS. It contains a parallel local clustering component to cluster and summarize the most recent sets of trajectories on each remote site, and a global clustering component of the coordinator to build the global clusters on the received local synopsis structures. Moreover, the pruning mechanism of similarity calculation and the optimization strategy of "testing first and transferring later" enabled the OCluDTS algorithm to boost the efficiency.

Subsequently, in order to capture the outliers upon the distributed streams, we present trajectory outlier definitions to characterize the anomaly trajectory fragment, the anomaly fragment cluster, and the evolutionary anomaly object in distributed trajectory streams. On the basis of that, we propose the first scalable decentralized outlier detection algorithm over distributed trajectory streams, called ODDTS. With the aim of continuously providing feature grouping-based outliers detection over distributed trajectory streams, it consists of remote site processing (F-*outlier* and FC-*outlier* detection) and coordinator processing (EO-*outlier* detection). ODDTS can achieve obvious performance gains through a parallel outlier detection mechanism with the minimal transmission overhead among the nodes. Extensive experiments over real trajectory data demonstrated high detecting validity, less communication cost, and linear scalability of our proposals upon distributed trajectory streams.

Chapter 5 proposes a transportation safety management application that uses a trajectory outlier detection technique, i.e., cloned vehicle detection. The ubiquitous inspection spots deployed in the city first collect information from passing vehicles and then turns this information into the trajectories of these vehicles, which opens up a new opportunity for cloned vehicle detection. Existing detection methods using trajectory data cannot pinpoint the cloned vehicle effectively because they are using the fixed speed threshold. In this chapter, we propose a two-phase framework, called CVDF, to detect the cloned vehicles and discriminate behavior patterns of vehicles that use the same plate number. In the detection phase, cloned vehicles are identified based on speed thresholds extracted from historical trajectory and behavior abnormality analysis within the local neighborhood. In the behavior analysis phase, we aim to differentiate the trajectories by matching degree-based clustering before extracting the frequent temporal behavior patterns. We considered and mixed the traces of vehicles that use the same license plate. The experimental results on real-world data show that the CVDF framework has high detection precision and could effectively reveal the behavior of cloned vehicles. Our proposal would provide a scientific basis for solving cloned vehicle crimes.

Chapter 6 provides a few road map updating applications through trajectory clustering analysis, which includes inferring missing roads, identifying underground roads, and detecting road intersections. First, to discover the missing roads in the road network, a two-phase hybrid framework, called HyMU, is proposed to update the digital map with inferred roads. It takes advantage of *line-based* and *point-based* strategies. Through inferring road candidates during consecutive time windows and merging the road candidates to generate missing roads, HyMU can even discover newly built roads in sparse trajectory areas. Second, a three-step underground road discovery framework is proposed, which includes an incremental clustering phase, a sub-trajectory detecting phase, and a cluster filtering phase. It can effectively discover underpasses from walking trajectories and tunnels from vehicular trajectories. Finally, an effective two-phase road intersection detection framework is presented, which comprises trajectory quality improving and intersection extracting.

More importantly, our approach of using an hybrid clustering strategy can effectively detect different-sized road intersections by extracting candidate cells based on direction statistic analysis and refining the locations of intersections.

All in all, this book focuses on the clustering analysis and anomaly detection technology upon trajectory streams, and conducts a detailed analysis around a series of basic issues. As the sliding-window model is one of the basis models for processing trajectory streams and can eliminate the effects of obsolete data, knowing how to incrementally cluster on the continuously arriving trajectory stream data over sliding windows becomes a basis issue. In the actual applications, a trajectory outlier usually has significant behavioral differences with its local spatial–temporal neighbors. In view of this, measuring the moving behavioral outlierness of each trajectory based upon the local spatial–temporal neighborhoods, and further identifying the abnormal trajectory and abnormal objects becomes a basic issue.

Additionally, the trajectory streams are collected by distributed nodes in more and more applications. Extending the existing clustering analysis technique of the centralized trajectory streams and designing an appropriate clustering method for handling distributed trajectory streams becomes another basis issue. This issue not only needs to take into account obtaining high quality clustering results, it also must guarantee high efficiency. Also, another basic problem to be solved is being able to design an effective outlier detection technique upon the distributed trajectory streams. Solutions to this problem must be capable of identifying the abnormal trajectory (or trajectory cluster) that has obvious behavioral difference within its local spatial–temporal neighborhoods on each node, and then detecting abnormal evolving moving objects in the distributed scenarios. To address the above mentioned basis issues, this book develops basic and optimized approaches to provide the solutions.

Furthermore, this book attempts to leverage trajectory clustering and trajectory outlier detection to solve the problems in traffic safety management, such as cloned vehicle detection, detecting road intersections and updating road maps with information on missing roads and underground roads. Theoretic analysis and extensive experimental results on the real data showed that our proposals could solve the aforementioned issues efficiently, and significantly improve result quality and execution efficiency. The last chapter (Chapter 7) is devoted specifically to the summary for this book and the discussion for future trends. The latter includes improving analysis accuracy, fusing more data to provide in-depth insight, and customizing an appropriate analysis method for varieties of real application scenarios, etc.

Jiali Mao
Cheqing Jin
Aoying Zhou
Shanghai, China

About the Authors

Jiali Mao is currently a research professor with the School of Data Science and Engineering, East China Normal University. She received doctoral degree in Software Engineering from East China Normal University. She has played critical roles in scientific projects of the National Natural Science Foundation of China and has worked on industrial projects cooperating with enterprises such as Didi. She has published over 40 articles, which include papers in international journals such as *TKDE*, and has presented papers in top conferences such as ICDE and SDM. She has served as an external reviewer for journals such as *KAIS*, *TKDE*, *TKDD*, *FCS*, and the *Journal of Software*. Her research interests include text mining, spatial–temporal/contextual data management, and intelligent service for smart city applications.

Cheqing Jin is a professor with the School of Data Science and Engineering, East China Normal University. He is a member of the China Computer Federation Technical Committee on Databases. His research interests include data stream management, location-based services, uncertain data management, blockchain, and so on. He was the PI for a number of projects of the

National Natural Science Foundation. He has co-authored one monograph and published more than 100 papers, some of which received awards, such as *Chinese Journal of Computers* Best Paper Award and Best Paper Run-up Award of WAIM 2011. He also received the Fok Ying Tung Education Foundation's Young Teachers Award.

 **Aoying Zhou** is currently the Vice President of the East China Normal University (ECNU) and the founding Dean and Professor of School of Data Science and Engineering. He received his bachelor's and master's degrees in Computer Science from the Chengdu University of Science and Technology, China, in 1985 and 1988, respectively, and his PhD from Fudan University, China, in 1993. Before joining ECNU in 2008, Aoying worked for Fudan University in the Computer Science Department for 15 years. He is the winner of the National Science Fund for Distinguished Young Scholars supported by the National Natural Science Foundation of China (NSFC) as well as the professorship appointment under the Changjiang Scholars Program of the Ministry of Education, China. He is now the Vice Director of Database Technology Committee of the China Computer Federation. Aoying is serving as a member of the editorial boards of journals such as *Chinese Journal of Computer*, *Data Science and Engineering*, and *World Wide Web Journal*, among others. His research interests include database, data management, and data-driven applications.

Acknowledgments

This research was supported by the Development Program of China (2016YFB1000905) and the National Science Foundation of China (Nos. 61702423, 61370101, 61532021, U1501252, U1401256, and 61402180).

We thank all our friends: Qiuge Song, Tao Wang, Minxi Li, He Chen, Min Pu, and Pengda Sun. Without their technical contributions, this book would not have been possible.

We would also like to express our sincere thanks and appreciation to the people at Springer (US) for their generous help throughout the publication preparation process.

Contents

Chapter 1

Introduction

1.1 Background

With the vigorous development and increasing maturity of wireless sensor network technology, transmission technology, and location acquisition technology, the positions of moving objects (e.g., vehicle, ship, and human, etc.) have been collected in real time on a large scale. This type of temporal positional data records information like the geographic coordinates and velocity of any object at each timestamp while moving. They are continuously accumulated and updated rapidly, which form massive amounts of trajectory streams. This provides us unprecedented opportunities to gain insights about movement behavior and trends of moving objects such as humans and vehicles. More importantly, leveraging mega-scale trajectory stream data to extract valuable movement patterns has enabled a wide spectrum of traffic applications, such as route planning [Liu *et al.*, 2016], anomaly detection [Mao *et al.*, 2017b], road infrastructure optimization [Wang *et al.*, 2017b], and other intelligent traffic management [Duan *et al.*, 2016], etc.

For instance, as one of the most important means of transport in the city, taxis are widely found distributed across the urban road network. Through GPS sensors, they relay their respective location information to a central server at intervals like 30 seconds to 2 minutes. Such a continuous, infinite sequence of positions accompanied and ordered by explicit timestamps form a trajectory stream. This enables taxi

1

companies to process taxi-hailing requests timely. In addition, more and more users are using GPS-enabled smartphones to continuously share their positional data in travel through popular online social platforms like Weibo and Twitter. Positional streams that are generated by such users in the movement process enable them to participate in solving complicated issues like route planning and detour detection on the trip in a distributed manner. In another example, the surveillance inspection spots that are deployed in city traffic crossroads record the movement information of passing vehicles (e.g., real-time location, velocity and turning behavior) and transmit them through the leased lines to the servers of the traffic control centers in their respective regions. Hence, the sequences of positions that are received continuously by the servers of various regions have formed into their independent trajectory streams. Analyzing these distributed trajectory streams can help detect abnormal traffic events, such as speeding vehicles or vehicles that use fake license plates.

1.1.1 *Characteristics of trajectory data*

(1) Noise interference

The GPS positioning equipments are most likely to be affected by building shielding, external electromagnetic interference, equipment failure, and other factors, which result in the collected position data having large positional deviation from the true value. In addition, the human factor (e.g., taxi drivers temporarily turning off the on-board GPS devices to save energy) may also cause positional information to disappear during certain time periods. As a result, problems such as data loss and numerical anomaly usually exist in the collected trajectory data, which seriously affects the accuracy of analysis results. This necessitates effective pre-processing strategies like filtering, calibration, and interpolation methods to improve the quality of trajectory data.

(2) Massive and real time

Location information in any trajectory stream is different from any static trajectory data set and is generated by any moving object in real time and continues to increase. Hence, the trajectory stream data has the characteristics of being *massive* and in *real time*. In the aforementioned examples, because massive position data continuously arrives at a high rate from single or multiple data sources, an efficient processing mechanism becomes a necessity to gain timely insights about moving behavior patterns, in order to keep up the pace of data volume and velocity. This requires effective methods like trajectory resampling, trajectory simplification, trajectory compressing, online analysis, etc.

(3) Skewed distribution

In actual applications, the trajectory data distribution is always *skewed*. For instance, in a road network, some roads only have a small number of vehicles driving over a long period of time, while a few main roads have a large number of vehicles passing in a short time. This results in a sparse and uneven distribution of trajectory data. This necessitates the development of an analysis method with self-adapting strategies to fit different distribution density of data, e.g., dynamically adjusting thresholds of mining methods with the variation of distribution density of data.

(4) Time-varying evolution

A trajectory stream continuously arrives and produces, which means that as long as the moving object is in an active state, the time sequence position information it generates will change continuously over time. Accordingly, the moving behavior patterns extracted from the data will evolve dynamically with time. This requires us to have the ability of tracking the movement behavior, i.e., from its appearance, evolution or variation, to its disappearance of behavior. Most of all, through tracking, we are capable of detecting abnormal behavior of objects as early as possible and allowing us time to provide the necessary support for urban emergency management.

(5) Concept drifting

For analysis tasks like clustering, trajectory clusters will gradually increase in size due to the continuous growth of data. Correspondingly, the centers of such trajectory clusters will gradually shift and deviate from their true centers, which is called concept drifting. This greatly influences the accuracy of clustering results. To tackle this issue, it is necessary to design a mechanism to integrate with the sliding-window model or time-decaying model, which can remove the outdated data or lessen the influences of obsolete data while receiving the incoming data.

1.1.2 *Analysis techniques for trajectory data*

Since trajectory data records the position of any moving object at each timestamp and reflects the movement trend of the moving object over a long period of time, it can provide strong support for various management decisions, including those relating to urban traffic. As a result, trajectory data analysis has become an important research hotspot, which has attracted widespread attentions in many fields, including data science, sociology, and geography. There have been considerable methodologies and algorithms on analyzing trajectories as well as moving objects. These mainly focus on several typical tasks, including spatio-temporal pattern discovery of moving objects and mining for trajectories, e.g., trajectory clustering, trajectory classification, trajectory outlier detection, etc.

(1) Spatio-temporal pattern discovery of moving objects

The spatio-temporal patterns of moving objects can be mined from trajectory data in terms of different types of application requirements. *Frequent pattern* extraction aims to detect the spatio-temporal behaviors that moving objects frequently occur at, e.g., the routes visited by moving objects frequently. *Periodic pattern* is viewed as a strict time-related frequent pattern, which needs to detect the movement periodicity of moving objects, e.g., the weekly commuting pattern of urban residents. The *Grouping pattern* extraction aims to discover similar behaviors of moving objects in groups, according to a certain temporal and spatial constraint, such as a *moving cluster, flock, convoy, swarm*, etc.

(2) Trajectory mining

The typical mining techniques for trajectory data include classification, clustering, and outlier detection. The goal of trajectory classification [Lee *et al.*, 2008b] is to construct the classification model to predict the class labels of moving objects based on their generated trajectories and discriminative features. Trajectory clustering aims to group a large number of trajectories into comparatively homogeneous clusters based on the predefined spatio–temporal proximity, to extract the representative paths or common moving trends shared by various objects [Lee *et al.*, 2007; Ester *et al.*, 1996; Gaffney and Smyth, 1999; Wang *et al.*, 1997; Jensen *et al.*, 2007; Li *et al.*, 2004, 2010]. For instance, in hurricane landfall forecast application, discovering common landfall trends of hurricanes helps to improve the forecasting accuracy. In animal migration analyzing application, extracting common behaviors of animals can assist in revealing the cause of animal migration.

Outlier detection, as a special trajectory analysis technique, has attracted more attention in academic and industrial circles. Distinct from its former two kinds, trajectory outliers aim to identify a few trajectories that are obviously dissimilar with the majority of the others, according to a certain similarity criterion, such as vessels whose movement behaviors are significantly different from others [Lei, 2016], hurricanes that suddenly change wind direction [Lee *et al.*, 2008a], taxis with detour behaviors [Ge *et al.*, 2011; Liu *et al.*, 2014] unexpected road changes in road networks [Wu *et al.*, 2015; Zhu *et al.*, 2015], etc.

Recently, clustering and outlier detection on trajectory data have become more and more important in various applications, such as intelligent transportation management [Pan *et al.*, 2013], route planning [Liu *et al.*, 2016; Chen *et al.*, 2017], road infrastructure optimization [Wu *et al.*, 2015], etc. The two types of analysis techniques enable us to understand the moving behaviors of objects. For instance, trajectory clusters can be utilized for a better understanding of homogeneous behavioral population groups, which can help with transportation infrastructures management and optimization. In addition, outlier detection can be leveraged for screening abnormal moving behaviors, even for exceptional events in inhabitant trips, e.g., the dangerous driving behaviors that will cause traffic accidents. Thus, in this book, we are primarily concerned with clustering and outlier detection upon trajectory streams.

1.2 Framework of Trajectory Analysis

As illustrated in Figure 1.1, a system infrastructure of trajectory analysis consists of data pre-processing, data management, pattern extraction,

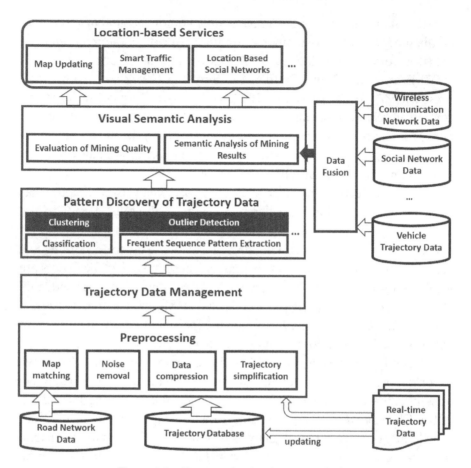

Figure 1.1. Framework of trajectory analysis.

semantic analysis of mining results, etc. When processing continuously arrived and rapidly updated trajectory stream data, it is first necessary to eliminate noise trajectories, correct the position deviation, and reduce the processing scale of data to proliferate the quality of analysis. Secondly, to satisfy the demands of query and analysis in real time, trajectory stream data is required to be stored and managed efficiently. Thirdly, pattern extraction from trajectory data is implemented on the basis of the previous two stages. The moving behavior patterns or moving trends of entities are needed to be extracted by analysis tasks such as trajectory classification, clustering, frequent pattern discovery, and anomaly detection. Finally, the quality of the extracted pattern needs to be assessed. Meanwhile, semantic analysis can be executed on mining results to give a reasonable interpretation of the patterns and further reveal the important events behind the patterns.

1.2.1 *Pre-processing trajectory data*

GPS positioning equipments easily generate position data with large deviations from the truth value due to the influences of shielding by buildings, external electromagnet interference, and equipment failure. In addition, the location information collected by the acquisition equipment will be missed during some time periods due to human factors, e.g., taxi drivers temporarily shutting down their GPS equipment embedded in cars to save energy. As a result, there exists the issue of uncertainty or inaccuracy in collected trajectory data, such as longitude/latitude out-of-boundary, data loss, numerical anomaly, etc. This will seriously affect the accuracy of analyzing results on trajectory data.

To reduce the impact of noise data on mining performance, trajectory data should initially be cleaned by methods like data exception filtering and threshold filtering. Then, the data needs to be verified for accuracy by determining whether it is missing, contains error information or has been modified by combining with historical movement trend data. Besides this, the trajectory data needs to be smoothed by denoising methods like the mean–median filter, Kalman filter, and particle filter. In order to reduce the scale of real-time processing of trajectory data, online data compression technology, sampling technology, and trajectory segmentation technology based on time interval/trajectory shape can be used. These techniques can approximately represent the trajectory data under the premise of ensuring the spatio-temporal characteristics of the data. In the field of transportation and the other specific applications, map-matching technology can be harnessed to correct the deviation of trajectory data, thus further improving the accuracy of mining results.

1.2.2 *Trajectory data management*

One of the key characteristics of a trajectory stream is that large-scale data arrives continuously in the form of a high-speed stream. In view of the time-varying evolution of a trajectory stream, it is impossible to quickly establish any prior knowledge of any data from the newly arrived trajectory data. Likewise, due to the strict response time requirements of stream processing, it is useless to carry out the processing operation after the permanent storage. Therefore, processing incoming trajectory data is mainly dependent on memory processing capability. This can be achieved by designing an appropriate synopsis data structure.

Moreover, in addition to the standalone data management system, the distributed data stream management system should be taken into account for managing trajectory stream data. Although the single-machine data stream management system can process a certain scale of data, in the context of massive data, the amount of continuously arriving trajectory data may far exceed the computing and processing capacity of a single physical machine. Distributed computing architecture can be leveraged to ensure the real-time acquisition of mining results. The representative distributed stream data processing systems include *Storm*, *S4*, *Samza*, and *Spark*. When storing and managing the continuously arriving trajectory data, the latest arriving trajectory stream data can be synchronously written to the trajectory database on the disk to finish the updating of the data.

1.2.3 *Pattern extraction from trajectory data*

The existing methods of trajectory pattern discovery include trajectory classification, cluster analysis, anomaly detection, frequent sequence pattern extraction, and so on. In order to efficiently extract the moving behavior patterns from trajectory streams, it is necessary to design lightweight online mining methods suitable for limited system resources. For such mining tasks like trajectory classification, anomaly detection, and frequent sequence pattern discovery, one not only needs to consider the movement behavior pattern based on the extraction of historical trajectory data, but also has to identify new movement behavior characteristics based upon the latest arrived trajectory data.

Furthermore, for the distributed trajectory streams generated by geographically distributed positioning devices, it is imperative to design high-performance distributed mining algorithms to minimize the costs of parallel computing and transmission under the resource-constrained environment. Therefore, in view of inherent characteristics of trajectory stream data (such as massive, real-time, time-varying evolution as well as skewness distribution) and to solve the resulting conceptual drift problem, efficient clustering analysis and anomaly detection methods for centralized and distributed trajectory streams need to be urgently designed to serve a wide range of real-time location services.

1.2.4 *Semantic analysis of mining results*

In order to improve the interpretation ability of trajectory data and realize the timely display and feedback of mining results, appropriate visual interactive analysis technology should be harnessed according to specific mining application requirements. On one hand, human–computer interaction technology can be applied to provide the setting interface of parameters, thresholds and other parameters, as well as the functional interface for the selection of mining methods, so as to guide users to gradually conduct trajectory data analysis and participate in the specific interactive analysis process. On the other hand, the mining results can be clearly displayed with charts, animations, and other forms to help users understand.

Based on this, extracted mobile behavior patterns can be analyzed semantically by combining with other relevant data sources, e.g., social network data from Weibo and Twitter, Internet data, telecom data, POI data, weather data, house-price data, air pollution data, etc., to reveal the cause of their emergence and further assist in the discovery of their hidden special events. For semantic analysis results, specific colors and levels of brightness can be used to highlight the connections between the behavioral patterns. It is helpful to determine the trend of mobile behavior development and the spatial–temporal scope of its influence, which will help decision makers to formulate control strategies as early as possible.

1.3 Challenges and Research Issues

1.3.1 *Real-time analysis*

Massive, fast, and time-varying positional sequences arrive continuously in the form of data streams, but there is no fixed uniform pattern of data distribution. Conventional trajectory clustering techniques adopt the *first store then process* strategy, which requires them to perform multiple data scans. Therefore, such methods are not suitable for processing trajectory streams online. There is an urgent need to establish and maintain an efficient synopsis data structure with a limited memory space, to extract and store the spatio-temporal characteristics of different trajectory clusters arriving in each time interval. For instance, the synopsis data structure can include the linear (or quadratic) sum of the center position, angular and average velocity, as well as the number of trajectories and the time of the latest arrival trajectory, etc. Such synopsis data structure can be leveraged to effectively reduce the storage space and computing overhead while maintaining the clustering characteristics of the incoming trajectory data. It helps to process the ever-increasing trajectory stream data with limited system resources, and hence proliferate the efficiency of online trajectory analysis.

In addition, for the task of trajectory outlier detection, in view of the skewness distribution of trajectory data, it is imperative to design online outlier detection mechanism based on local neighbor behavior differences. It may conduct single-pass scanning analysis of the "infinite" position data stream in the limited memory space, and can discern abnormal trajectories that are distinct from noise data.

1.3.2   *Evolutionary analysis*

Under the time-varying evolution of trajectory stream data's influence, a trajectory outlier is not always constant. In other words, even if the trajectory data has similar movement behavior with its local neighbors, it may still evolve into a behavioral anomaly relative to its neighborhood in the next time periods. Evaluating the evolving trend of trajectory anomaly from appearing, growing, changing to disappearing is a difficulty of outlier detection upon trajectory streams. This requires the trajectory anomaly detection method to be able to distinguish the anomalies from noise data and detect anomalies that are different from the adjacent position sequence, and also to track the evolution of abnormal trajectory over a period of time to further identify abnormal moving objects. In the pursuit of this general aim, and based on the combination of the sliding-window model, time decay window model and other technologies, the historical trajectories of moving objects and the outlierness of the latest incoming trajectories shall be integrated to help identify the evolving trajectory anomalies.

Moreover, when processing large-scale distributed trajectory streams, it will involve high overheads of trajectory data transmission and storage as well as computing to transfer these distributed trajectory streams to the the central server for centralized storage and analysis. But such a method cannot satisfy the real-time analysis requirement with high processing delay. Therefore, the limitedness of system resources and the real-time response demand of trajectory analysis make the online clustering and anomaly detection upon distributed trajectory streams more challenging.

1.3.3 *High accuracy of analysis result*

In actual scenarios, the trajectory streams are skewed and time-varying evolutionary. For clustering analysis upon distributed trajectory streams, although adopting the strategy of parallel clustering for the local trajectory stream by multiple nodes can effectively improve the execution efficiency, the clustering result on the respective local streams cannot reflect the global movement pattern of the moving objects. Thus, it is necessary to design a two-stage processing strategy of implementing local clustering, then global clustering.

While in the process of anomaly detection upon distributed trajectory streams, the abnormal behaviors of the objects extracted from the trajectory streams by different nodes (e.g., the servers in various regions) are different. In addition, the outlierness of the moving behavior of the objects may be determined by more than one node due to those objects traveling across multiple nodes. In the meantime, the normal object can gradually evolve into the outlier over time. As a result, after each node implements parallel detection processing on its local trajectory stream, it should be considered to perform evolutionary anomaly detection processing by the coordinator site, based on the local anomaly detection results to detect abnormal moving objects as early as possible.

1.3.4 *Minimal transmission overheads*

Distinct from the analysis for the single trajectory stream, the overheads of data transmission between the nodes will become the bottleneck of the distributed trajectory streams analysis. In order to minimize the transmission overheads among the nodes and improve the execution efficiency and scalability of the algorithm, the data transmission between the remote sites and the coordinator site should be reduced by as much as possible. For online clustering analysis of distributed trajectory streams, it needs to design an appropriate synopsis data structure that is suitable for distributed clustering by various remote sites, to extract the clustering characteristics of incoming trajectories in real time.

As compared with transferring local trajectory stream data to the coordinator site for centralized clustering analysis, leveraging the strategy of transferring local clustering results in the form of synopsis data structure between the remote site and the coordinator site can greatly reduce the transmission overhead. Similarly, for online anomaly detection upon distributed trajectory streams, transmitting local anomaly detection results of each remote site (such as the ID of the trajectory or ID of the moving object) to the coordinator site, can significantly enhance detection performance.

1.4 Fundamental Techniques for Efficient Analyzing

1.4.1 *Similarity measurement*

Designing the trajectory similarity measure (also known as distance function) is a key problem for trajectory clustering and anomaly detection. The similarity between trajectories is generally used for measuring the distances between trajectory points or trajectory segments. As a special kind of time series in multidimensional space, the similarity criterion function suitable for time series data can generally be applied to the similarity measurement for trajectory data, e.g., Euclidean distance [Nanni and Pedreschi, 2006], DTW [Yi *et al.*, 1998], LCSS [Vlachos *et al.*, 2002, 2006], ERP [Chen and Ng, 2004], EDR [Chen *et al.*, 2005], etc.

However, the aforementioned measurement methods pay more attention to the global similarity between trajectories and do not consider the local similarity between sub-trajectories in a short time, which is exactly the problem that needs to be solved for online clustering and online anomaly detection upon trajectory streams. In addition, due to the high computational complexity of these distance measurement methods, they cannot be directly used for trajectory clustering and trajectory outlier detection in space-constrained applications (e.g., road networks).

To this end, Lee *et al.* (2007) proposed an improved *Hausdorff* method to measure the similarity between sub-trajectories, which describes the distance between any two sub-trajectories as a weighted sum of vertical distance, parallel distance, and angle distance. *Hausdorff* distance is originally used to measure the maximum value of the shortest distance between the nearest data points in two data sets. Because it takes direction into account when measuring distance between the data, it is also used by Roh and Hwang (2010) and Han *et al.* (2015) to evaluate the similarity of trajectories that have different directions in the road network and is represented as the longest distance between road sections.

1.4.2 *Indexing technique*

To support efficient querying and analysis of trajectory data, it is imperative to choose or design the appropriate index strategy. Trajectory data is distinct from the other types of data due to its inherent spatio-temporal characteristic. Therefore, designing a specialized index technique is more suitable for the demand of trajectory analyzing.

The existing trajectory index techniques mainly include: (1) incorporating a time dimension into the traditional multi-dimension index like the *R-tree* and obtaining the improved index, e.g., three-dimensional *R-tree* and *STR-tree* [Pfoser *et al.*, 2000]; (2) building a single tree according to each timestamp and sharing the common portions for two consecutive trees to reduce the redundancy, hence deriving the multi-version index, e.g., *HR-tree* [Nascimento and Silva, 1998], *HR+tree* [Tao and Papadias, 2001a], and *MV3R-tree* [Tao and Papadias, 2001b]; and (3) dividing the spatial dimension into lattices and building an index for each lattice in terms of the time dimension, e.g., SETI [Chakka *et al.*, 2003] and *MTSB-tree* [Zhou *et al.*, 2005].

Most of the above mentioned techniques aim to meet the analysis requirements for a static trajectory data set. In order to handle ever increasing data, a few researches strive for improving the *R-tree* index, e.g., *SEB-tree* [Song and Roussopoulos, 2003].

1.4.3 *Distributed framework*

In recent decades, with the wide applications of open source data processing systems such as Hadoop, OpenStack, and Spark, we have the ability to efficiently analyze the trajectory data that arrive from disparate sources. To support real-time and high-throughput analysis of distributed trajectory streams, a number of spatial data management systems based on distributed memory have emerged that can provide spatial query services, e.g., SpatialSpark [You *et al.*, 2015], GeoSpark [Yu *et al.*, 2015], LocationSpark [Tang *et al.*, 2016], and Simba [Xie *et al.*, 2016].

Moreover, a few systems that aim to process trajectory data have appeared, e.g., STORM [Christensen *et al.*, 2015] and OceanST [Yuan *et al.*, 2014]. STORM focuses on coping with interactive approximate queries, which can constantly provide query results with a certain degree of confidence by gradually increasing the sampling data. Likewise, OceanST employs the sampling technique to get approximate query results. But OceanST is more suitable for the stream case of continuously increasing data, and provides many query interfaces that can respond to all kinds of query requests.

1.5 Organization

The rest of this book is organized this way: in Chapter 2, we study the problem of clustering upon trajectory streams by using the sliding-window model; in Chapter 3, we analytically explore the problem of *feature grouping-based* outlier detection upon trajectory stream; in Chapter 4, we show how to track the trajectory clusters and estimate the outlierness of trajectories upon distributed streams; in Chapter 5, we lay a strong emphasis on the application of outlier detection in the traffic security management field, i.e., Cloned Vehicle Detection; in Chapter 6, we give the solutions of inferencing different types of road changing, which includes discovering missing roads, identifying underground roads, and detecting road intersections.

Chapter 2

Clustering Analysis upon Trajectory Streams

2.1 Introduction

As a typical class of a moving pattern discovery approach, clustering aims to group a large amount of trajectories into comparatively homogeneous clusters to extract the representative paths (or common moving trend) shared by various objects [Lee *et al.*, 2007; Ester *et al.*, 1996; Gaffney and Smyth, 1999; Wang *et al.*, 1997; Jensen *et al.*, 2007; Li *et al.*, 2004, 2010]. For instance, in an hurricane landfall forecast application, discovering the common behavior of hurricanes can improve forecasting accuracy. In an animal migration analyzing application, extracting the common behaviors of animals can reveal the cause of animal migration.

An important observation is that the trajectory of one moving object may belong to different clusters with the progression of stream. That is, the clustering result may evolve with time. For example, traffic is highly dynamic in a road network scenario; trajectory stream generated by vehicles may evolve more dramatically over shorter time horizons. Figure 2.1 illustrates a small example of the trajectories of four taxis, from time instant, t_0 to t_2. Obviously, during $[t_0, t_1]$, four trajectories construct one cluster, while in $[t_1, t_2]$ they form two clusters due to different moving directions.

To estimate real-time traffic road conditions, we need to keep up with the continuously evolutionary streaming trajectories. This requires clustering to be performed on a recent subset of the streaming data.

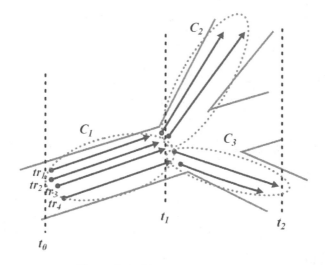

Figure 2.1. Evolution of clusters.

The sliding-window model that keeps most recent W tuples in a limited time window is suitable to describe the evolution of clustering result. In other words, any tuple outside the current time window has no effect on the current clustering result. On the basis of the sliding-window model, we can focus on the traces of vehicles in the recent time horizon, and generate clusters based on them. Through extracting the moving behavior of each cluster at each time instant, we are able to estimate the real-time traffic condition of the road that each cluster is located on. Such traffic information can be provided to road users and applied to real-time routing planning and traffic management.

To the best of our knowledge, the problem of online clustering trajectory data stream over the sliding-window model has not been addressed. The challenges come from the limited system resources, huge stream volume, high arrival rate, and real-time response requirements, combined with the difficulty of concept drift. Furthermore, the existing work cannot be adopted to deal with this issue directly. First, any existing work on trajectory data stream clustering does not consider removing the influence of outdated tuples [Li *et al.*, 2010]. Along with incrementally clustering incoming trajectory data, the expired records cannot be discarded upon any arbitrary arrival of new ones. The size of micro-clusters continuously increases with the drifts of the cluster centers, which leads to the concept drift and thus degrades the clustering performance. Secondly, the existing data stream clustering upon the sliding-window model treats each tuple a *"full"* entry [Aggarwal *et al.*, 2003], while each tuple in the trajectory data stream is only a *"part"* of an entry.

In this chapter, we develop an online approach to deal with this issue, including the line segment *micro-clustering* component and the *macro-clustering* component. During the micro-clustering phase, a number of micro-clusters, each represented by a compact synopsis data structure, are maintained incrementally. During the macro-clustering phase, a small number of macro-clusters are built upon the micro-clusters according to a clustering request within a specified time horizon. The core innovation in this framework is exploiting a novel compact synopsis data structure to represent each micro-cluster. Distinct from trajectory simplification [Lee *et al.*, 2007] or trajectory compression [Hönle *et al.*, 2010] technologies, such a synopsis can preserve the spatio-temporal charac-teristic of a trajectory in memory, while removing the influence of obsolete tuples. The experimental results demonstrate the applicability of a new proposal for online clustering streaming trajectories. It also shows better clustering performance than the congeneric algorithms.

This chapter is organized as follows. First, the preliminary concepts of clustering upon trajectory streams are presented in Section 2.2. Then, we outline and analytically study the scheme for clustering streaming trajectories in Section 2.3. Section 2.4 presents the effectiveness and efficiency evaluations. Section 2.5 illustrates some real-traffic situation evaluation cases using trajectory clustering technique. The latest works are described in Section 2.6. Finally, in Section 2.7, we conclude this chapter.

2.2 Preliminaries

In this section, we define some notations formally and then formalize the problem of online clustering of streaming trajectories.

Definition 2.1 (Trajectory Stream). A trajectory stream that consists of a series of positional records of M moving objects is denoted as $S = \{(o^{(1)}, p_1^{(1)}), (o^{(2)}, p_1^{(2)}), \ldots, (o^{(M)}, p_1^{(M)}), (o^{(1)}, p_2^{(1)}), \ldots\}$, where

$p_i^{(j)}$ is the location of an object, $o^{(j)}$, at the time instant, t_i, in 2D space (i.e., $p_i^{(j)} = (x_i^{(j)}, y_i^{(j)})$).

A trajectory stream is commonly assumed unboundedness. Hence, it is common to use a window to limit an infinite stream to a specified finite set of records within a given time horizon. We adopt the idea of the sliding tuple-based window model, which is commonly used for discounting obsolete data. Only the latest W records in the window are valid at the point in time of the clustering.

Definition 2.2 (Sliding Tuple-based Window). Given a stream, S, a window size, W, a starting time instant, t_s, and a ending time instant, t_e, a sliding tuple-based window over S at t_e is a finite multiset of stream elements with $S_W = \{(o^{(1)}, p_s^{(1)}), (o^{(2)}, p_s^{(2)}),$ $\ldots, (o^{(M)}, p_s^{(M)}), \ldots, (o^{(1)}, p_e^{(1)}), \ldots, (o^{(M)}, p_e^{(M)})\}$. Whenever the window slides forward, the number of positional elements received in S_W is W.

In general, the positional record (represented as trajectory) of one object is defined as follows:

Definition 2.3 (Trajectory). A trajectory of an object, o, denoted as $\text{tr}_o = \{(p_1, t_1), (p_2, t_2), \ldots\}$, is a sub-sequence of S affiliated to o. Such records arrive in chronological order, i.e., $\forall i < j, t_i < t_j$. Two temporal adjacent points are connected into a line segment, L_i, i.e., L_i is denoted as (p_i, p_{i+1}). Correspondingly, the trajectory of an object, o, is also denoted as $\text{tr}_o = \{(L_1, t_1), (L_2, t_2), \ldots\}$.

Due to the infeasibility of keeping massive trajectory data in memory, original data needs to be summarized and clustering results need to be approximated. We summarized this original data by using a compact synopsis data structure called the Exponential Histogram of Temporal Trajectory Cluster Feature (EF_o). Each bucket in an EF_o is a Temporal Trajectory Cluster Feature (TF_o), which attempts to summarize the features of incoming trajectory line segments at each time instant. Accordingly, we use the Minimum Bounding Rectangle (MBR) to represent the spatial range of all line segments contained in a TF_o.

Definition 2.4 (Temporal Trajectory Cluster Feature, TF_o). Given a set of consecutive line segments $\{L_1, L_2, \ldots, L_n\}$ at each time instant, group them into clusters, and use TF_o to represent the cluster, Feature, of each cluster, TF is of the form $(LS_{cen}, LS_A, BL, TR, n, t)$.

- LS_{cen}: The linear sum of the line segments' center points;
- LS_A: The linear sum of the line segments' angles;
- BL: The bottom left corner of the MBR (minimal bounding rectangle);
- TR: The top right corner of the MBR;
- n: The number of line segments;
- t: The timestamp of the most recent line segment.

Note that the MBR is the minimal bounding rectangle of all the line segments contained in a TF_o. Figure 2.2(a) illustrates an example of the MBR for two black polylines, where we can draw a line segment to represent the moving pattern of all the line segments in TF_o. Firstly, we obtain the central point (denoted as TF_o.cen) and the angle (denoted as θ) of that line segment by calculating them with $\frac{LS_{cen}}{n}$ and $\frac{LS_A}{n}$, respectively. Then, we plot a line across the central point along that angle and finally extend it to reach the borders of the MBR. The intersection points are treated as the starting and ending points of the representative line segment. For example, the black thick line segment with the starting point (denoted as TF_o.rp_s) and the ending point (denoted as TF_o.rp_e) are regarded as the representative line segment in Figure 2.2(a).

As a TF_o may consist of multiple line segments (and they will go out of the window one by one in the future), which necessitates a structure to deal with the expired line segments. An Exponential Histogram (EH) is

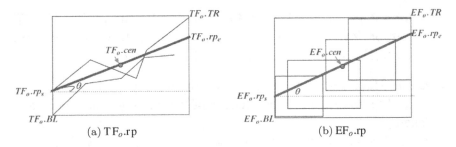

(a) TF_o.rp   (b) EF_o.rp

Figure 2.2.   The representative trajectory line segment of TF_o and EF_o.

a well-known tool to deal with the sliding-window model, where all the tuples in the data stream are divided into a number of buckets according to the arrival time [Datar *et al.*, 2002]. Inspired by the EH, we devise a novel structure called the Exponential Histogram of Temporal Trajectory Cluster Feature (denoted as EF_o) as shown in the following.

Definition 2.5 (Exponential Histogram of Temporal Trajectory Cluster Feature (EF_o)). Given a user-defined parameter, ε, EF_o is a collection of TF_os on some sets of line segments $\{C_1, C_2, \ldots C_i, C_j \ldots\}(1 \le i < j)$ with the following constraints:

1. $\forall i, j$, any line segment in C_i arrives earlier than that in C_j;
2. $|C_1| = 1$. $\forall i > 1$, $|C_i| = |C_{i-1}|$ or $|C_i| = 2 \cdot |C_{i-1}|$;
3. At most $\lceil \frac{1}{\varepsilon} \rceil + 1$ TF_os are placed in each level.

Likewise, we obtain a representative line segment for an EF_o. The central point (denoted as $EF_o.cen$) and the angle (denoted as θ) of the representative line segment are the weighted mean of all TF_os, respectively, i.e., $\frac{\sum_i TF_{oi}.cen \times TF_{oi}.n}{\sum_i TF_{oi}.n}$ and $\frac{\sum_i TF_{oi}.\theta \times TF_{oi}.n}{\sum_i TF_{oi}.n}$. The corners of EF_o can also be computed based on the corners of all TF_os involved directly. Figure 2.2(b) illustrates an example about the MBRs for a group of TF_os contained in an EF_o, and the generated thick representative line segment ($EF_o.rp_s$, $EF_o.rp_e$).

Through further experimental observation, it is found that the angle of the trajectory cluster is more easily affected by the longer segment within the cluster. In view of this, a new temporal trajectory cluster feature is proposed by considering the linear sum of the trajectory line segments' length within the same cluster.

Definition 2.6 (Temporal Trajectory Cluster Feature, TF). The TF of a set of line segments, $C = \{L_1, L_2, \ldots, L_n\}$, is of the form $(LS_{cen}, LS_A, LS_{len}, SS_{len}, \max_{len}, \min_{len}, BL, TR, n, t)$.

- LS_{cen}: The linear sum of the line segments' center points;
- LS_A: The linear sum of the product of the line segments' angle and length;
- LS_{len}: The linear sum of the line segments' length;
- SS_{len}: The squared sum of the line segments' length;

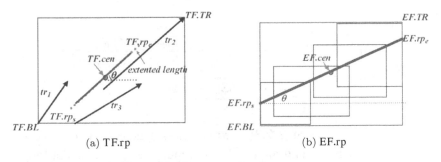

(a) TF.rp   (b) EF.rp

Figure 2.3.   Representative line segment.

- $\max_{\text{len}}$: The maximum of the line segments' length;
- $\min_{\text{len}}$: The minimum of the line segments' length;
- BL: The bottom left corner of MBR;
- TR: The top right corner of MBR;
- n: The number of line segments;
- t: The timestamp of the last line segment.

Figure 2.3(a) illustrates an example of an MBR that contains three black lines. We use a line (denoted as TF.rp(s, e), where s and e are the starting and ending points, respectively) to represent the moving pattern of all the line segments in TF in terms of the central point (denoted as TF.cen) and angle (denoted as TF.θ). Specifically, for angle calculation, as the longer line segment is intrinsically more important than a shorter line segment, we take the line segment's length into account in obtaining the angle of representative line segment, i.e., $\frac{\text{LS}_A}{\text{LS}_{\text{len}}}$.

In addition, it is easy to derive a shorter representative trajectory line segment due to the effects of a few short line segments that are absorbed in a cluster. Hence, we attempt to extend the average length of line segments to make representative line segments conform better to original data distribution. We extend the average length of line segments with the product of the standard deviation (denoted as σ) and the ratio of $\max_{\text{len}}$ to $\min_{\text{len}}$. Then, we derive TF.rp(s, e) by the following formula.

$$s = \left((\text{cen})^{(1)} - \frac{\text{len}}{2} \cos \theta, (\text{cen})^{(2)} - \frac{\text{len}}{2} \sin \theta \right),$$

$$e = \left((\text{cen})^{(1)} + \frac{\text{len}}{2} \cos \theta, (\text{cen})^{(2)} + \frac{\text{len}}{2} \sin \theta \right),$$

where

$$cen = \frac{LS_{cen}}{n}, \theta = \frac{LS_A}{LS_{len}}, len = \frac{LS_{len}}{n} + \frac{max_{len}}{min_{len}} \cdot \sigma,$$

$$\sigma = \frac{\sqrt{n \cdot SS_{len} - LS_{len}^2}}{n}.$$

As illustrated in Figure 2.3(a), three line segments (tr_1, tr_2, and tr_3) have different lengths and angles. We compute the central point, angle, and average length of three line segments to obtain a representative line segment, namely, a thick line with a dashed part (denoted as ($TF.rp_s$, $TF.rp_e$)).

Property 2.1 (Additive Property). Let $TF(C_1)$ and $TF(C_2)$ denote the TF structures for two sets C_1 and C_2, respectively, $C_1 \cap C_2 = \emptyset$. $TF(C_1 \cup C_2)$ is constructed on $TF(C_1)$ and $TF(C_2)$. The new entries, LS_{cen}, LS_A, LS_{len}, SS_{len}, and n are equal to the sum of the corresponding entries in $TF(C_1)$ and $TF(C_2)$. The new entries, max_{len} and t, are computed as the maximum of the corresponding entries in $TF(C_1)$ and $TF(C_2)$. The new entry, min_{len}, is computed as $min(TF(C_1).min_{len}, TF(C_2).min_{len})$. Moreover, the corners of the new TF can be directly computed based on the two original corners.

As a collection of multi-level TFs on the sets of trajectory line segments $C_1, C_2, \ldots$, the EF's definition is similar with EF_o.

Lemma 2.1. *Given an EF that contains n_i tuples and an error threshold, ε, the amount of obsolete tuples is within $[0, \varepsilon n_i]$, and the number of TFs is at most $(\frac{1}{\varepsilon} + 1)(\log(\varepsilon n_i + 1) + 1)$.*

Proof. Only the last TF (namely, the oldest TF in the highest level of TFs) in EF may contain the expired records. Let n_s denote the number of tuples in the last TF, according to Definition 2.5, we have $\frac{1}{\varepsilon}(1 + 2 + 4 + \ldots + n_s) \leq n_i$. Then, $n_s \leq \varepsilon n_i$ holds. Moreover, an EH structure with the window size, n_i, and the parameter, ε, can be constructed. Each TF maps to a bucket in the EH structure. According to Datar *et al.* (2002), an EH structure computes an ε-deficient synopsis using at most $(\frac{1}{\varepsilon} + 1)(\log(\varepsilon W + 1) + 1)$ buckets, where W represents

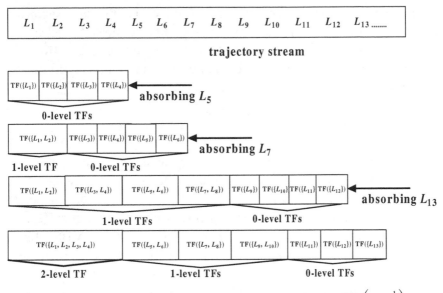

Figure 2.4. Process of incorporating line segments into an EF $\left(\varepsilon = \frac{1}{3}\right)$.

the window size. Thus, there exists at most $\left(\frac{1}{\varepsilon} + 1\right) (\log(\varepsilon n_i + 1) + 1)$ TFs in an EF. □

We maintain EF in the following way. When a new line segment is incorporated into an existing EF, a new 0-level TF will be generated for it at first. After absorbing more and more line segments, once the number of 0-level TFs in EF exceeds the threshold $\left(\lceil \frac{1}{\varepsilon} \rceil + 1\right)$, two oldest 0-level TFs are merged to generate a 1-level TF. Such a merge operation may propagate from the lowest level toward the higher levels until there are less than $\lceil \frac{1}{\varepsilon} \rceil + 1$ TFs at a certain level.

Figure 2.4 exemplifies how an EF can be maintained when $\varepsilon = \frac{1}{3}$. It means that at most four TFs are kept at each level. As we can see, when L_5 arrives, a new 0-level TF (TF($\{L_5\}$)) is generated, which results in five 0-level TFs. Then, a 1-level TF (TF($\{L_1, L_2\}$)) is generated by merging TF($\{L_1\}$) and TF($\{L_2\}$). A similar merging operation occurs when L_7 arrives. Furthermore, the arrival of L_{13} triggers the merging of TF($\{L_9\}$) and TF($\{L_{10}\}$), which further triggers the merging of TF($\{L_1, L_2\}$) and TF($\{L_3, L_4\}$).

Likewise, to extract the moving pattern of all the line segments absorbed in EF, we derive a representative line segment for each EF. The central point (denoted as EF.cen) and the angle (denoted as EF.θ) of the representative line segment are computed by the following formulas, respectively.

$$\text{EF.cen} = \frac{\sum_i \text{TF}_i.\text{LS}_{\text{cen}} \times \text{TF}_i.n}{\sum_i \text{TF}_i.n}, \quad \text{EF.}\theta = \frac{\sum_i \text{TF}_i.\text{LS}_A}{\sum_i \text{TF}_i.\text{LS}_{\text{len}}}.$$

The corners of the MBR that describe EF are computed based on all the TFs' MBR. Then, we plot a line across EF.cen, along EF.θ, and finally extend it to the borders of MBR. The intersection points are treated as the starting and ending points of the representative line segment. Figure 2.3(b) illustrates an example about the MBRs for a group of TFs contained in an EF, and the black thick line segment (EF.rp$_s$, EF.rp$_e$) is the derived representative line segment.

The TF and EF synopsis structures allow us to effectively extract and maintain the spatio-temporal characteristics of clusters at different intervals. In addition, an EF synopsis can promptly remove the obsolete records when clustering trajectories, which prevents the size of each cluster from getting larger and larger, and hence avoids the shifting of cluster's center.

Figure 2.5 illustrates the evolutions of three clusters (represented by EF$_1$, EF$_2$ and EF$_3$, respectively) in the current window (including seven time instants). Owing to the elimination of obsolete data as time goes by, the boundary of each cluster does not become larger and larger, and hence avoids a concept shift. Meanwhile, since each EF maintains its histogram, the EF synopsis can adjust the frequency of generating a new TF adaptively, which reduces space consumption. Specifically, a new EF that contains a TF will be created only when the incoming trajectory segment cannot be absorbed into any existing cluster. If such a segment is an outlier, only one TF will be created for it in a new EF, and the EF that contains the outlier will be removed when it gets outdated.

Our goal is to divide all the trajectory line segments into clusters in terms of the similarity measurement. Essentially, whether the similarity between a trajectory line segment and an EF, or that among EFs (EF is represented by its representative line segment), is translated to measure the similarity between trajectory line segments. Note that two

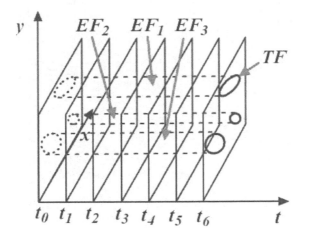

Figure 2.5. An example of EF in the current window.

trajectory line segments close to each other but generated at different time intervals are actually not similar. In view of that, we define similarity as the combination of the spatial proximity and temporal closeness between line segments. For spatial proximity measurement, although the Euclidean distance-based schemes are commonly used in the spacial data management field, including DTW (Dynamic Time Warping Distance [Chu *et al.*, 2002]), LCSS (Longest Common Subsequences [Vlachos *et al.*, 2002]), ERP (Edit Distance with Real Penalty [Chen and Ng, 2004]), and EDR (Edit Distance in Real Sequence [Chen *et al.*, 2005]), they are not suitable for measuring spatial proximity in certain scenarios with bidirectional property.

For instance, as illustrated in Figure 2.6, there are three trajectories (tr_1, tr_2, and tr_3) on two separate roads. According to Euclidean distance-based schemes, tr_1 is closer to tr_2. Nevertheless, in a real-road network, there exists no route between tr_1 and tr_2, and accordingly tr_2 is closer to tr_3. Hence, we leverage the adapted *Hausdorff distance* in Roh and Hwang (2010) to measure spatial proximity. The distance between two trajectory line segments is regarded as the maximal distance between two line segments after alignment, i.e., $\mathrm{DL}(L', L'') = \max(\mathrm{dl}(L', L''), \mathrm{dl}(L'', L'))$, where

$$\mathrm{dl}(L', L'') = \max(\min(\|p'_s, p''_s\|, \|p'_s, p''_e\|),$$
$$\min(\|p'_e, p''_s\|, \|p'_e, p''_e\|)).$$

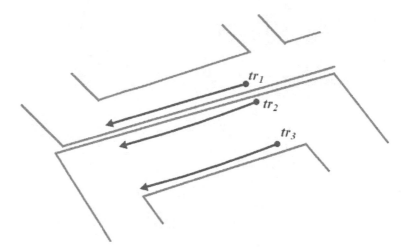

Figure 2.6. Spacial proximity in a road network scenario.

Here, p_s' (or p_s'') and p_e' (or p_e'') denote the starting and ending positions of two line segments separately, and $||p_s', p_s''||$ denotes the length of the shortest path between p_s' and p_s''.

On the basis of spatial proximity measurement, we define the difference between two trajectory line segments as follows.

Definition 2.7 (Difference Measurement). Given a temporal closeness threshold, ρ ($0 < \rho \le \frac{1}{2}$), a spatial proximity threshold, γ ($\gamma \le 1$), a spatial proximity weight, λ ($0 \le \lambda \le 1$), a window size, W, the arrival time instant of line segment, t, and the length of two line segments (denoted as L' and L'') is denoted as $||L'||$ and $||L''||$ separately. Let $\text{sig}(\cdot)$ denote the normalization function (here $\text{sig}(\cdot) = \frac{1}{1+e^{-(\cdot)}}$), which is used to normalize the spatial distance and temporal distance. Iff $\frac{\text{DL}(L',L'')}{||L'||+||L''||} \le \gamma$ and ($L'.t - L''.t < \rho W$), the difference between L' and L'' is defined as

$$\text{Diff}(L', L'') = \lambda \cdot \text{sig}\left(\frac{\text{DL}(L', L'')}{||L'|| + ||L''||}\right) + (1 - \lambda) \cdot \text{sig}(|L'.t - L''.t|).$$

We usually put more weights on spatial proximity by setting $\lambda > \frac{1}{2}$. Generally, a smaller Diff value means there is a high similarity between the line segments, namely, the line segments are closer to each other in a recent time interval.

Finally, we summarize the problem definition here as follows.

Given a time horizon of length, len, the current time instant, t_c, and a trajectory stream portion that flows into the current time window (depicted as a multiset of trajectory segments), our goal is to discover the micro-clusters (represented as the set of EFs) at each time instant, and the macro-clusters according to the clustering request within the specific time interval $[t_c - \text{len}, t_c]$.

In the following section, on the basis of the TF and EF synopsis, we proceed to study the problem of online clustering streaming trajectories over the sliding-window model.

2.3 General Framework

In this section, we propose a framework to cluster trajectory streams using the sliding-window model, called Online Trajectory Stream Clustering over Sliding Window (or OCluWin for short). Since a trajectory is referred to as a set of consecutive line segments (Definition 2.3), our scheme is essentially a line segment clustering algorithm. As illustrated in Algorithm 1, OCluWin is comprised of two components: a line segment micro-clustering phase (line 1) and an EF's macro-clustering phase (line 2).

Algorithm 1: OCluWin

Input: S: Stream of trajectory line segments; W: window size; ε: error threshold; ρ: time tolerance threshold; k: maximum number of EFs; len: time horizon of length, and t_c: current time instant;

Output: Z': Set of all generated EFs;

1 $Z \leftarrow MicroClu(S, W, \varepsilon, \rho, k)$;
2 Execute *macro-clustering on Z within* $[t_c - \text{len}, t_c]$;
3 *Get a set Z' using the macro-clustering result;*
4 **return** Z';

During the first phase, on the basis of the aforementioned synopsis data structures, appropriate statistical information of the micro-clusters in the current time window is extracted and maintained incrementally, as shown in Algorithm 2. Each micro-cluster is represented by an EF (or EF_o) structure, and each bucket in an EF (or EF_o) is a TF (or TF_o) that represents the summary statistics of a set of trajectory segments at each time instant.

During the second phase, given a time horizon, a small number of macro-clusters are derived on EFs (or EF_os) by invoking traditional density-based clustering techniques. In this way, the cluster characteristics of streaming trajectories can be preserved with continuity in time and contiguity in space.

2.3.1 *Line segment micro-clustering*

The micro-clustering phase aims to cluster the continuously arriving trajectory line segments at each time instant while discarding expired ones. Algorithm 2 shows the main framework to generate and maintain EFs for trajectory line segments. It executes two algorithms to achieve the subtasks separately (lines 7 and 17). Let Z represent the set of EFs generated during the micro-clustering phase. Initially, Z is emptied, and subsequently, k EFs are generated one after another and added to Z when continuously receiving k line segments. Specifically, we create an EF that contains a TF for each incoming line segment through an initialization process, and regard the line segment itself as the representative line segment of such an EF (line 2). Instead of the original trajectory data being kept in the memory, k EFs are at most kept in the memory at any time.

When a line segment, L_x, arrives, we attempt to find its most similar EF from the existing EFs. According to Definition 2.7, only EF (denoted as h) with the greatest spatial proximity over a recent time interval is deemed as the appropriate EF to absorb L_x, and the entries of it are accordingly adjusted based on L_x. If L_x cannot find its most similar EF, a new EF, h_n, that only contains $TF(\{L_x\})$ will be created (line 19) on the condition that the number of EFs is less than k.

Algorithm 2: MicroClu($S, W, \varepsilon, \rho, k$)

  Input: S: Trajectory stream; W: window size; ε: error threshold;
              ρ: time tolerance threshold, and k: Maximum number of
              EFs;

  Output: Z: Set of all generated EFs;

1 $Z \leftarrow \emptyset$; $Z_{\text{list}} \leftarrow \emptyset$;

2 Initialize Z;

3 **foreach** *line segment, L_x, in S* **do**

4 | find the most similar EF, h, and the second most similar EF,
    | h_s, for L_x;

5 | **if** $\text{Diff}(h.rp, L_x) < d_{\min}$ **then**

6 | | /*$d_{\min}$ denotes the minimum difference threshold of
    | | absorbing trajectory segments into an EF*/;

7 | | $Insertline(L_x, h, h_s, \varepsilon)$;

8 | **else**

9 | | **if** $|Z| = k$ **then**

10 | | | **if** $\exists h_e \in Z, \left(\left(|t_c - h_e.t| \geq W \right) \vee \right.$
                           $\left. \left(\left(|t_c - h_e.t| \geq \rho W \right) \wedge \left(h_e.n_i \leq \frac{\sum_{i=1}^{k} n_i}{k} \right) \right) \right)$ **then**

11 | | | | /* n_i denotes the number of an EF */;

12 | | | | $Z \leftarrow Z \setminus \{h_e\}$;

13 | | | | /*Z_{list} denotes a set of influenced EFs owing to the
    | | | | deleting, merging, and creation of some EFs; */ ;

14 | | | | $Z_{\text{list}} \leftarrow Z_{\text{list}} \cup$ the EFs where the most similar EF is h_e;

15 | | **else**

16 | | | find the most similar EF pair (h_i, h_j);

17 | | | $MergeEF(h_i, h_j, \varepsilon, Z)$;

18 | | | $Z_{\text{list}} \leftarrow Z_{\text{list}} \cup$ the EFs where the most similar EF is h_i
    | | | or h_j;

19 | | $h_n \leftarrow new\ \text{EF}(\text{TF}(\{L_x\}))$;

20 | | $Z \leftarrow Z \cup h_n$;

21 | | $Z_{\text{list}} \leftarrow Z_{\text{list}} \cup h_n$;

22 | | $Maintain(Z_{\text{list}})$;

23 **return** Z;

Algorithm 3: Insertline(L_x, h, h_s, ε)

Input: L_x: Newly arrived line segment; h: most similar EF of
        L_x; h_s: second most similar EF of L_x, and ε: and error
        threshold;

Output: h;

1   $h \leftarrow h \cup \{TF_0(\{L_x\})\}$;

2   $h.t \leftarrow L_x.t$;

3   $l \leftarrow 0$;

4 **while** *true* **do**

5   **if** $n_l \leq \lceil \frac{1}{\varepsilon} \rceil + 1$ **then**

6   /* n_l denotes the number of l-level TFs */;

7   break;

8   **else**

9   Merge two oldest l-level TFs of h into an $(l + 1)$-level TF;

10    $l \leftarrow l + 1$;

11 **if** *the oldest* TF *of* h, TF_{1st}, *expires* **then**

12   Drop TF_{1st} from h;

13 **if** $(\text{Diff}(h.rp, h_s.rp) < h.ds)$ **then**

14    $h.ds \leftarrow \text{Diff}(h.rp, h_s.rp)$;

15    $h.c \leftarrow h_s$;

16 **return** h;

When the number of EFs exceeds k, we need to take into account eliminating the expired EFs (lines 10–12) or merging EFs (lines 16–17) to make room for the newly created EF. The detailed procedure for inserting L_x into h is shown in Algorithm 3. A $TF_0(\{L_x\})$ is generated first and is added to h (line 1). Subsequently, once the number of 0-level TFs in h exceeds $\lceil \frac{1}{\varepsilon} \rceil + 1$, the two oldest 0-level TFs are merged to generate a 1-level TF. Such a merge operation is repeated several times for higher levels until the number of a certain level of TFs is lower than $\lceil \frac{1}{\varepsilon} \rceil + 1$ (lines 4–10).

In the following, we describe the process of individual subroutines such as eliminating obsolete records and merging EFs.

2.3.1.1 *Expired records elimination*

In essence, the significance of each position in a trajectory stream is time-decaying, until it finally becomes outdated and negligible. To eliminate the adverse effect of expired records on the micro-clustering results (e.g., concept drift), we consider removing the insignificant records including obsolete EFs, and a few EFs with the earlier updated time will no longer absorb tuples in the current window. More specifically, when a line segment, L_x, is incorporated into its most similar EF h, h must be checked to see if it contains obsolete TFs, and then be discarded (lines 11–12 in Algorithm 3).

Furthermore, when the number of EFs exceeds the specified threshold, k, we not only remove the expired EFs but also filter out those with the earlier updated time and an insufficient amount of participating trajectory segments. Let t_i represent the time instant of the latest updated TF in an EF h_i, and t_c represent the current time instant. Then, we can obtain the updated period of h_i by $(t_c - t_i + 1)$. If the updated period is beyond more than half (e.g., $\frac{2}{3}$) of the current window size, h_i is deemed as an EF that has not been updated for a long time. Furthermore, we filter out such EFs with longer updated periods and participating records smaller than the average participating records of all EFs in the current window (lines 10–12 in Algorithm 2).

2.3.1.2 EF *merging*

If no EF is deleted, that is, none of the aforementioned eliminating criteria are met, we attempt to find the most similar EF pair to merge until the size of the existing EFs meets the space constraints, as shown in Algorithm 4. Only the most similar EF pair will be merged into a new EF according to Definition 2.7. However, even the two most similar EFs face the problem of an inconsistent time instant of corresponding level TFs. Therefore, for any two most similar EFs, h_i and h_j, we first align all level TFs of them in terms of the time range of each level of TFs (line 1). To be specific, we obtain a set of time instants of all levels of TFs in h_i and h_j, and insert h_i or h_j with the empty level of the missing time range to ensure one-to-one correspondence between all levels of TFs of h_i and h_j.

Algorithm 4: Merge EF(h_i, h_j, ε, Z)

Input: h_i, h_j: Two EFs that need to be merged; ε: error
  threshold, and Z: a set of all generated EFs;

Output: Z;

1 Align all level TFs of h_i and h_j in terms of their time range;
2 $l \leftarrow 0$;
3 **while** ($h_i.n_l + h_j.n_l + h_{\text{new}}.n_l > 0$) **do**
4   /* n_l denotes the number of l-level TFs */;
5   **if** ($h_i.n_l + h_j.n_l + h_{\text{new}}.n_l > \lceil \frac{1}{\varepsilon} \rceil + 1$) **then**
6   Merge the oldest l-level TFs from h_i and h_j into new
      $(l + 1)$-level TFs of h_{new};

7   **else**
8   Insert into h_{new} with l-level TFs of h_i and h_j;

9    $l \leftarrow l + 1$;
10 $Z \leftarrow Z \setminus \{h_i, h_j\} \cup \{h_{\text{new}}\}$;
11 **return** Z;

Later, the merging process is akin to the process of incorporating the line segments into an EF. If the number of corresponding l-level TFs in two EFs exceeds $\lceil \frac{1}{\varepsilon} \rceil + 1$, the oldest l-level TFs are merged into $(l + 1)$-level TFs (lines 5–6). Otherwise, l-level TFs in two EFs are directly combined into l-level TFs of new EF (lines 7–8). Such operations will cascade to a higher level $l = 0, 1, 2, \ldots$, until the sum of the number of a certain level of TFs is 0.

However, the computation overhead of finding the most similar EF pair is costly, especially when the number of EFs (k) is too large. A nested loop used for calculating and comparing the similarity between all pairs of EFs is inevitable, and costs $O(k^2)$ (k is the number of EFs). Owing to the evolving properties and high updating cost of a data stream, tree-based indexes cannot be applied well to cluster trajectory streams. We opt for a heuristic strategy to speed up this process. For each EF, we maintain its most similar EF (denoted as c) as well as the difference (denoted as ds) between its most similar EF and itself. In particular,

---

Algorithm 5: Maintain(Z_{list})

Input: Z_{list}: Set of influenced EFs;

Output: $Z_{\text{list}}.c$: Most similar EFs for Z_{list};

1 **foreach** EF, h_i *in* Z_{list} **do**
2   **foreach** EF, h_j *in* Z **do**
3   **if** $(\text{Diff}(h_i.rp, h_j.rp) < h_i.ds)$ **then**
4             $h_i.ds \leftarrow \text{Diff}(h_i.rp, h_j.rp)$;
5             $h_i.c \leftarrow h_j$;
6   **if** $(\text{Diff}(h_i.rp, h_j.rp) < h_j.ds)$ **then**
7             $h_j.ds \leftarrow \text{Diff}(h_i.rp, h_j.rp)$;
8             $h_j.c \leftarrow h_i$;

9 **return** $Z_{\text{list}}.c$;

---

when receiving a line segment L_x, we attempt to search its most similar EF h and the second most similar EF h_s (lines 3–4 in Algorithm 2).

During the process of absorbing L_x into h, the difference between h and h_s (denoted as $\text{Diff}(h.rp, h_s.rp)$) is computed and compared with $h.ds$. If $\text{Diff}(h.rp, h_s.rp) \leq h.ds$, the original most similar EF of h ($h.c$) is replaced with h_s (lines 13–15 in Algorithm 3). Only when a new EF is created for L_x, and the most similar EF of h is eliminated or merged into the other EF, we need to search the most similar EF for the influenced EFs (denoted as Z_{list}) by the difference measurement between the representative trajectory line segments of the EFs. Hence, we derive Z_{list} after newly creating, deleting, and merging the EFs (lines 14, 18, and 21 in Algorithm 2), and implementing the maintenance of the most similar EFs for Z_{list} (line 22 in Algorithm 2).

The maintaining details are illustrated in Algorithm 5. For each EF h_i in Z_{list}, we re-find the most similar EF for it by comparing the difference between h_i and every existing EF h_j (lines 1–5). At the same time, we accordingly update h_j's most similar EF via a difference comparing process (lines 6–8).

In this way, when searching for the most similar EF pair to merge, we simply need to traverse the most similar EF lists of all EFs to find the EF pair with the least difference. As a result, the cost of searching for the most similar EF pair to merge in the best case can be reduced to $O(k)$. Only when the deleted or merged EF is the most similar EF of all EFs, the cost of searching for the most similar EF pair to merge is $O(k^2)$. Actually, this extreme case rarely occurs. Moreover, keeping the most similar EF for each EF does not require much extra space, which additionally needs to store the index of the most similar EF, the value of ds, and a list of indexes of the inverse most similar EFs for each EF. As compared to the memory consumption of TFs that are included in each EF, such extra space consumption is negligible if $n \gg k$.

2.3.2 EFs *macro-clustering*

Given a clustering request over a time horizon of length, len, and a current time instant, t_c, we can further derive larger macro-clusters based on previously generated micro-clusters. As micro-clusters are line segment clusters of arbitrary shape, and density-based clustering methods are suitable for discovering such types of clusters, we implement macro-clustering using the DBSCAN method. As mentioned in Section 2.2, the micro-clusters are represented by the representative trajectory line segments of the EFs. Hence, EFs in $[t_c - \text{len}, t_c]$ are treated as pseudo line segments, and they are re-clustered to produce macro-clusters using a variant of the DBSCAN algorithm [Lee *et al.*, 2007; Li *et al.*, 2010]. The approach of generating a representative trajectory for a macro-cluster is the same as that for a set of trajectory partitions in Lee *et al.* (2007). Specifically, a representative trajectory of a macro-cluster is a small sequence of points generated by using a sweep line approach and a smoothing technique, which can better capture the spatial characteristics of a macro-cluster.

If the given time horizon exceeds the current window size, in addition to the latest EFs that are maintained in the main memory, the historical EFs stored on the disk within the specific period will also be used for macro-clustering. At this point, the representative trajectory line segments of such EFs can be clustered offline to generate the macro-clusters by executing the DBSCAN algorithm. Intuitively, larger macro-clusters tend to indicate more valuable patterns in contiguous regions during continuous periods. For instance, in the scenario of hot region identification, the road regions that the macro-clusters cover exhibit similar mobile behaviors (e.g., maintain a similar low speed) at consecutive intervals, which can be further identified as hot areas (e.g., traffic congestion).

2.3.3 *Time and space complexity*

The goal of OCluWin is to continuously cluster arriving trajectory line segments. The cost of incorporating a new line segment, L_x, into its most similar EF mainly involves lines 4, 9, and 16 in Algorithm 2. The cost of line 4 (finding the most similar EF for L_x) is simply $O(k)$. At line 9, when the number of EF exceeds k, the cost of removing obsolete EFs is $O(k)$. At line 16, the cost of calculating the difference between EFs and merging a similar pair of EFs is $O(k^2)$ for the worst-case scenario. Consequently, the per-record processing cost is at most $O(k^2)$. However, in essence, the merging process seldom occurs because the eliminating criteria ensure that some EFs are deleted to make enough room for the newly created EF.

Concerning space complexity, given an error threshold, ε, the maximal number of EF, k, window size, W, and number of line segments absorbed in the i-th micro-cluster, n_i, then $\sum_{i=1}^{k} n_i = W$, and the number of obsolete records is within $[0, \varepsilon W]$. There are at most $(\frac{1}{\varepsilon} + 1)(\log(\varepsilon n_i + 1) + 1)$ TFs in an EF [Datar *et al.*, 2002]. The total number of TFs in k EFs is at most $\sum_{i=1}^{k} (\frac{1}{\varepsilon} + 1)(\log(\varepsilon n_i + 1) + 1)$. In addition, the number of TFs required by merging two EFs is $(\frac{1}{\varepsilon} + 1)(\log(\varepsilon(n_i + n_j)) + 1)$. As a consequence, the total required memory (the total number of TFs) of clustering streaming trajectories using the sliding-window model is $O\left(\frac{k}{\varepsilon} \log(\varepsilon \lceil \frac{W}{k} \rceil)\right)$.

2.4 **Experimental Evaluation**

In this section, we conduct extensive experiments to evaluate the clustering performance and efficiency of our proposal. Based on the OCluWin framework, two approaches using two different synopsis structures (EF_o and EF) are named OCluST and TSCluWin.

First, we utilize TRACLUS [Lee *et al.*, 2007] as the baseline approach to compare against OCluST. OCluST extracts spatio-temporal characteristics of trajectories at different intervals with very little information loss. TRACLUS clusters over the original trajectory data set, and is regarded as the most effective trajectory clustering algorithm available for a static trajectory data set. Therefore, we choose the clustering result of TRACLUS as a precision evaluation standard.

To better perform an accuracy comparison against TRACLUS, we fit a hurricane data set and deer movement data set in a single window. Second, in order to verify the effectiveness and efficiency of OCluST on streaming trajectories, we compare OCluST against two algorithms (TCMM [Li *et al.*, 2010] and TSCluWin) on a trajectory data set for taxis. TCMM is a representative incremental trajectory clustering approach that employs a micro- and macro-clustering framework to cluster trajectory data. Unlike OCluST, TCMM does not take the temporal aspects of the trajectories into account, and cannot eliminate obsolete trajectories. Finally, we evaluate traffic conditions on-the-fly by executing the OCluST algorithm on a trajectory data set for taxis.

All code, written in Java, is run on a PC with an Intel Core CPU at 3.1 GHz and 8 GB of RAM. The operating system is Windows 8.1. Unless mentioned, the parameters are set here as follows:

$$\varepsilon = 0.5, \quad \gamma = 0.75 \quad \text{and} \quad \rho = 0.5.$$

Data sets

We use four real-world trajectory data sets, including a hurricane track data set,[1] a deer movement data set,[2] and two taxi trajectory data sets. The former two are derived in free space and the latter two are obtained on a restricted road network.

Just like Lee *et al.* (2007), we choose the *Atlantic hurricane track data* within the period 1950–2004 and extract the latitude and longitude information of hurricanes for the experiment. The deer movement data set contains the radio-telemetry locations of deer in 1995. We extract the x and y coordinates from *Deer*1995 for the experiment.

The taxis' trajectory data sets contain the GPS logs of taxis over a period of three months from October to December 2013, covering the

---

[1] http://weather.unisys.com/hurricane/atlantic/.
[2] http://www.fs.fed.us/pnw/starkey/data/tables/.

main road networks of Shanghai and Beijing. Each GPS log is represented by a sequence of timestamped points (latitude and longitude positions).

2.4.1 *Effectiveness evaluation*

Results for hurricane track data. To verify the accuracy of our proposal, we first implement TRACLUS and OCluST on the hurricane track data. Both algorithms use the DBSCAN algorithm in different phases. minLns and ε are important parameters for DBSCAN and ε is a neighbor threshold. To differentiate it from the error threshold in our proposal, we use d to denote the neighbor threshold for DBSCAN. Figure 2.7 shows the clustering result of TRACLUS and the macro-clustering result of OCluST using the optimal parameter values (TRACLUS: minLns = 9, $d = 130,000$, OCluST: $k = 1000$, minLns = 30, $d = 320,000$). Thin lines depict raw trajectories and thick lines with arrows represent the extracted clusters (directions marked using arrows), specifically, macro-clusters for OCluST.

The clustering results of both algorithms are similar except for a few minor differences. They all capture the moving trends of hurricanes accurately, that is, moving from east to west first and then moving from west to east, occasionally mixed with south-to-north movement. As we can see, four clusters (see Figure 2.7(a)) are identified by TRACLUS and three macro-clusters (see Figure 2.7(b)) are identified by OCluST.

In addition, the lengths and locations of the representative line segments in both algorithms exist with very few deviations. This is mainly because OCluST executes macro-clustering using the DBSCAN algorithm

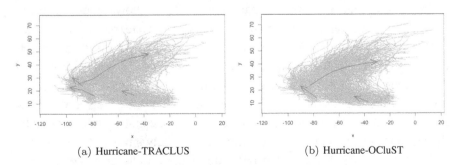

(a) Hurricane-TRACLUS   (b) Hurricane-OCluST

Figure 2.7. Clustering result for the hurricane track data.

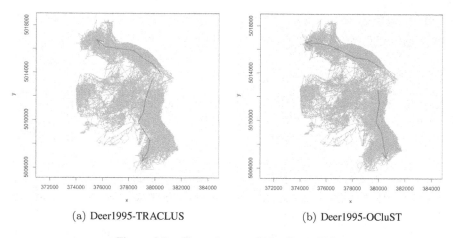

(a) Deer1995-TRACLUS   (b) Deer1995-OCluST

Figure 2.8.   Clustering result for Deer1995.

on a set of representative trajectory segments of micro-clusters, which summarizes the trajectories with very little information loss. TRACLUS executes clustering on trajectory partitions of original trajectories by using the DBSCAN algorithm and derives the representative trajectories. It is noted that the clusters obtained by the DBSCAN algorithm are easily affected by the direction and length of core line segments and border line segments. Since the direction and length of the representative line segments in OCluST are different from those of trajectory partitions in TRACLUS, the clustering results in Figure 2.7 are quite reasonable.

Results for deer movements in 1995. In the subsequent effectiveness experiment, we report on the clustering results of TRACLUS and OCluST on deer movements data. Figure 2.8 shows the clustering results for both algorithms by using the appropriate parameter values (TRACLUS: minLns = 8, $d = 149$, OCluST: $k = 300$, minLns = 100 and $d = 750$). Also, we use thin lines to depict raw trajectories and thick lines to represent the extracted clusters (directions marked using arrows). Like the results for the hurricane track data, save for very few differences in the lengths and locations of representative line segments, the clustering results of both algorithms are broadly similar. As illustrated in Figure 2.8(a) and (b), on the left side of the middle area, we observe that deer move in different directions though the movement data is not dense enough to form a cluster. Hence, we derive two clusters in the two most dense regions, which match the intuitive clusters.

Results for Shanghai taxi trajectory data. For effectiveness validation purpose, in addition to comparing our proposal with TRACLUS in free space, we conduct evaluations by comparing OCluST with two algorithms (TCMM and TSCluWin) on a restricted road network. These three approaches maintain the same number of micro-clusters. As for the important parameter, d_{max}, of TCMM, we set the same value as Li *et al.* (2010) did, i.e., $d_{max} = 800$.

Here, we consider the sum of the square distance (SSQ) used by Aggarwal *et al.* (2003) and Li *et al.* (2010) as the criterion to evaluate the quality of the clustering results (micro-clusters or macro-clusters). For each cluster, c_i, we first obtain the SSQ by computing the sum of the square distance between each line segment in c_i (denoted as L_j^i, $0 < j \leq n_i$) and the representative line segment of c_i (denoted as $c_i.rp$), and then derive the average SSQ by calculating the ratio of SSQ to the number of trajectory line segments (denoted as n). Therefore, the average SSQ can be calculated as

$$\text{Average SSQ} = \frac{1}{n} \sum_{i=1}^{k} \sum_{j=1}^{n_i} \text{DL}^2(L_j^i, c_i.rp),$$

where k denotes the number of clusters (micro-clusters or macro-clusters). Generally, a smaller average SSQ value means a higher clustering quality.

First, to validate the effectiveness of our proposal, we compare the micro-clustering results obtained by three algorithms (OCluST, TSCluWin and TCMM) under different window sizes. In terms of the reported average SSQ value, we conclude that OCluST and TSCluWin cluster the streaming trajectories more effectively than TCMM, while OCluST obtains the best clustering results.

Figure 2.9 shows the average SSQ obtained by three approaches (OCluST, TSCluWin, and TCMM) as time progresses, when the window size is set to 160,000 and 330,000, respectively. We observe that in all cases, OCluST and TSCluWin behave better (with a smaller average SSQ value) than TCMM because obsolete records are promptly eliminated, and the clustering changes in the most recent records in the current

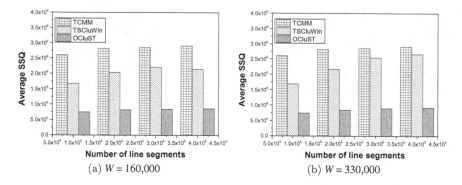

Figure 2.9.   Quality comparison.

window can be precisely captured by OCluST and TSCluWin. Thus, the micro-clusters are kept relatively compact with fewer records whenever the cluster center drifts. Conversely, since TCMM does not consider eliminating the influence of the expired records, a micro-cluster may continuously increase on the boundary rather than be split into multiple small micro-clusters.

In addition, OCluST invariably obtains better outcomes than TSCluWin, as illustrated in Figure 2.9. With the dramatic increase of positional data, TSCluWin easily obtains larger micro-clusters than OCluST because longer representative line segments are easily derived by TSCluWin's approach when the positional data had great distances between corresponding starting positions or ending positions. As a result, uneven clustering results drastically degrade the overall performance of micro-clustering, as illustrated in Figure 2.9(a). Furthermore, as data continues to flow in, OCluST's approach shows better clustering efficacy with the use of more effective methods for extracting representative line segments. At the same time, the clustering efficacy is less influenced by larger window sizes, as illustrated in Figure 2.9(b).

2.4.2 *Efficiency evaluation*

Execution time evaluation. We assess the efficiency of our proposal by comparing OCluST and TSCluWin with TCMM when dealing with streaming trajectories. Figure 2.10 shows a per-record processing time comparison (expressed in seconds) among the three methods. The OCluST

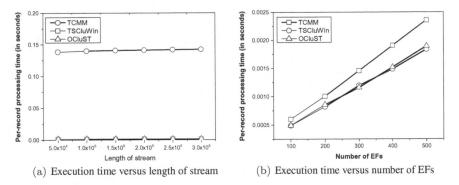

(a) Execution time versus length of stream   (b) Execution time versus number of EFs

Figure 2.10.   Execution time comparison.

curves nearly overlap the TSCluWin curves. As shown in Figure 2.10(b), the per-record processing time of OCluST and TSCluWin fluctuates smoothly and is superior to that processed by TCMM with the progression of a trajectory stream.

TCMM takes 0.13 seconds to obtain a cluster, while OCluST and TSCluWin only take around 0.008 seconds. The faster processing rate in our proposal is because micro-clustering is executed on the original trajectory data (without disregarding any trajectory points). By contrast, TCMM needs to partition trajectories using the MDL method before the micro-clustering phase, which consumes additional waiting time for partitioning accumulated trajectory data into sub-trajectories.

In addition, to test the algorithm's robustness in the presence of uncertainty, we study the sensitivity of our proposal to parameter k. Figure 2.10(b) shows the per-record processing time when the number of micro-clusters is varied. Since the distance computation cost of finding the most similar micro-cluster for an incoming line segment keeps growing as the number of clusters increases, all the approaches scale linearly with the number of micro-clusters. Nevertheless, with an increase in the class number, the execution overheads of OCluST and TSCluWin grow more slowly than that of TCMM, and are less affected by the parameter k.

Memory usage evaluation. One important efficiency characteristic for the streaming algorithms is its memory usage. As previously mentioned, TF and EF synopsis structures extract and maintain the spatio-temporal characteristics of micro-clusters at different intervals, which effectively

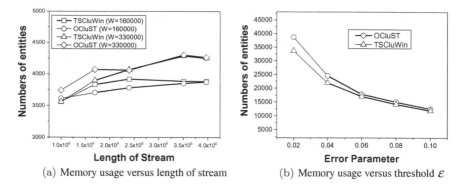

(a) Memory usage versus length of stream   (b) Memory usage versus threshold ε

Figure 2.11. Memory usage comparison.

compresses the size of the data needed to be stored. Therefore, we evaluate the memory usage of two algorithms by using the memory space usage of the synopsis structures (TF), without taking into account other issues. Since this type of entity (TF synopsis structure) defined in the OCluST and TSCluWin methods needs almost the same memory space, we utilize the number of entities (TF) to estimate the memory usage of both algorithms.

Figure 2.11(a) shows the memory footprint (in the number of entities) of OCluST and TSCluWin when the window size, W, is set to 160,000 and 330,000, respectively. For $W = 160,000$, as the number of trajectories increases from 100,000 to 400,000, the memory usage of both methods fluctuates with the progression of the trajectory stream, and OCluST requires less memory than TSCluWin. This is based on the fact that a more balanced clustering result is easily obtained by OCluST than TSCluWin.

By contrast, for $W = 330,000$, the memory usage of TSCluWin outperforms OCluST at first, and then equals OCluST when the number of incoming records is beyond 240,000. This is because the maintenance of the most similar EF for Z_{list} in OCluST is more complicated than that in TSCluWin. A larger window size leads to more influenced EFs needing to update their most similar EFs. However, when the number of trajectories is larger than 240,000, the number of TFs drops with the elimination of expired records. Both methods require almost the same memory usage.

Moreover, we study the effect of input parameter, ε, on memory usage. Figure 2.11(b) shows the memory usage of OCluST and TSCluWin when the window size is set to 250,000 by tuning the value of parameter, ε. OCluST maintains a slightly larger memory footprint than TSCluWin. In addition, when the value of ε increases from 0.02 to 0.1, the memory usage of both approaches decreases significantly. This is because ε determines the number of expired records within the time window. Specifically, in the current window, with the increment of ε, more obsolete records are eliminated, and fewer TFs are stored in the memory.

2.5 Application to Real-World Problem: Real-Time Traffic Information Evaluation

In order to further assess the performance of our proposal on real-world problems, we apply it to the taxi trajectory data set (*Taxi Shanghai13* and *TaxiBeijing13*) to derive real-time traffic information for an urban road network. Although there are specific pervasive techniques and on-road (fixed) sensors for estimating traffic situations, e.g., magnetometers, visual cameras, and inductive loops built into the road surface, these are prone to error and are limited to critical portions of the arterial network, owing to their high costs of implementation and maintenance. This requires some new ways to collect traffic data for evaluating road situations.

Since taxis with in-vehicle GPS devices travel along the entire road network, their trajectories typically cover much wider areas and hence they can be treated as mobile probes to measure traffic states. As a complementary solution to fixed sensors, this opens the door for our proposal to be used to deeply understand road network traffic, especially in areas where no sufficient infrastructure to estimate traffic has or can be deployed.

Among the existing traffic estimation methods, the aggregate-based method [Zhang *et al.*, 2013; Castro *et al.*, 2012] is widely used to estimate the road conditions of each link (i.e., a unidirectional road segment) owing to its simplicity. However, it aims to generate the aggregate values (e.g., average speed and maximum speed) of each road link, and cannot reveal similar moving behavior of objects that drive on each road segment or on wider road regions. Thus, to indicate the roads where vehicular traffic is most concentrated, and to estimate the mean speed of each road segment in real time, we use our proposal instead of the aggregate-based method to cluster and discover the common behavior of each cluster.

2.5.1　*Indicate high-vehicular-density route distribution*

We first implement our proposal on *Taxi Shanghai13* to indicate the roads where vehicular traffic is most concentrated during a specified time period. The clustering result of trajectories on a randomly selected region is visualized in Figure 2.12. Figure 2.12(a) shows the movement distribution of taxi traces during the period (from 10:00 to 10:30 a.m.) on 7 October, which involves 477,810 trajectory line segments (highlighted in dark lines). We implement our proposal on trajectories within the intervals [10:00, 10:10] and [10:10, 10:20] separately. These are portions of data shown in Figure 2.12(a).

Then, we derive 300 clusters (highlighted in thick line segments) on trajectory segments within each interval, as shown in Figure 2.12(b) and (c). It is observed that the clustering results within the two intervals can capture most traffic flows in Figure 2.12(a), but with a few differences, which is consistent with the actual dynamic traffic conditions. In addition, since clustering is maintained on raw trajectory line segments, the obtained representative trajectory of each cluster behaves in a short route form, and hence the derived clusters are discrete on the map. The clustering result indicates the road segments where vehicular traffic is the most concentrated. The real-time traffic information for high-vehicular-density route distribution can be delivered to road users for traffic management.

2.5.2　*Estimating the speeds of the road segments*

We also attempt to implement our proposal on *TaxiBeijing13* to estimate the traffic situation in Beijing on 9 October. As mentioned earlier, the clustering of streaming trajectories is more flexible in evaluating real-time traffic conditions than the aggregate-based method. For instance, we can estimate a varied range of road region traffic situations by using different distance thresholds in clustering. In our experiment, the average speed is employed to estimate the traffic situation because other information can

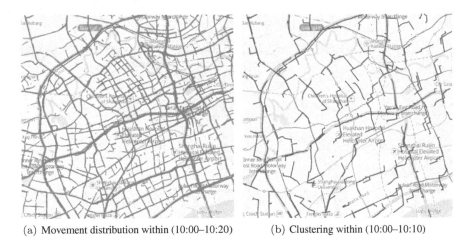

(a) Movement distribution within (10:00–10:20)   (b) Clustering within (10:00–10:10)

(c) Clustering within (10:10–10:20)

Figure 2.12. Indications of high-vehicular-density route distribution in Shanghai.

be derived by speed (e.g., estimated travel time). We treat the average speed of each cluster as the mean speed of a road segment where a cluster is located on. By setting speed thresholds, we empirically divide the traffic conditions into three classes: traffic jams with speeds lower than 28.8 km/h (highlighted in dark line segment), less congested traffic with speeds within a range [28.8 km/h, 54 km/h] (highlighted in light line segment), and smooth traffic with speeds beyond 54 km/h.

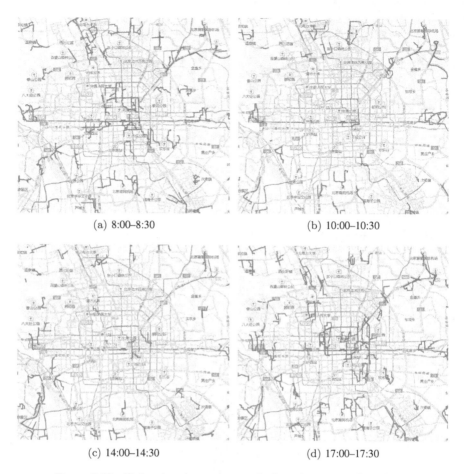

(a) 8:00–8:30

(b) 10:00–10:30

(c) 14:00–14:30

(d) 17:00–17:30

Figure 2.13. Estimating the mean speed of road segments in Beijing.

Figure 2.13 shows the clustering results for four intervals (8:00–8:30, 10:00–10:30, 14:00–14:30, and 17:00–17:30) on 9 October 2013. As shown in Figure 2.13(a), for [8:00–8:30], the congestion distribution is from the outside to the inside of the city. Congested roads are mainly concentrated in the south and north directions of East 2nd Ring Road, West 2nd Ring Road, East 3rd Ring Road, and on most highways entering Beijing (dark line segments on the map). Traffic moves slowly in the Zhongguancun Bridge area, Hangtianqiao area, Yongding Road, Wanquanhe Road, and Yuanmingyuan West Road (light line segments on the map).

During the interval [17:00–17:30], as illustrated in Figure 2.13(d), there is serious congestion in the north-to-south direction of East and West Second Ring Roads, as well as the north-to-south directions of East and West Third Ring Roads. Vehicle travel is more concentrated in the famous business circles and surrounding Catering areas, e.g., the Dongzhimen, Xizhimen, CBD, Financial Street, and Zhongguancun regions (in dark lines on the map). Moreover, the traffic crawls in the regions near Beijing West Railway Station and Beijing South Railway Station (in light lines on the map). During the other two intervals (10:00–10:30 and 14:00–14:30), congestion is not serious and traffic is relatively smooth. The vehicle velocity changes that were derived from taxi trajectories can exhibit peaks in the morning and afternoon rush hours, and basic impartial traffic pressure during off-peak hours. As a result, the clustering results of our proposal can effectively evaluate traffic conditions in real time.

2.6 Relative Works

In this section, we review existing work on data stream clustering and trajectory clustering, and then cover continuous querying over trajectory stream. We end by introducing a few researches devoted to the clustering of streaming trajectories.

2.6.1 *Clustering upon data stream*

Traditional clustering approaches either contain a partition-based method (e.g., K-means [Lloyd, 1982]), hierarchical-based method (e.g., BIRCH [Zhang *et al.*, 1996]), density-based method (e.g., DBSCAN [Ester *et al.*, 1996]), or a grid-based method (e.g., STING [Wang *et al.*, 1997]). All of the above approaches need to visit the data set more than once, so they are not suitable for a streaming scenario that requires real-time responses. Babcock *et al.* (2003) studied the clustering issue over the sliding-window model with a focus on the theoretical bound analysis. Aggarwal *et al.* (2003) developed the CluStream algorithm to cluster large evolving data streams based on the pyramid model. They further proposed a UMicro algorithm to deal with uncertain data streams [Aggarwal and Yu, 2008]. Zhou *et al.* (2008) presented the SWClustering algorithm to track the evolution of clusters over the sliding-window model by using a novel synopsis data structure called the EHCF. Jin *et al.* (2014) proposed the cluUS algorithm to cluster uncertain data streams upon the sliding-window model. However, none of the above methods can deal with trajectory data directly due to the different scenarios. In such a scenario, each tuple in the data stream is an entry, while each tuple in streaming trajectories is only a part of an entry.

2.6.2 *Clustering on static trajectory data*

There exist salient accomplishments on a clustering static trajectory data set, including road-network unaware [Gaffney and Smyth, 1999; Lee *et al.*, 2007] aware ones [Won *et al.*, 2009; Roh and Hwang, 2010; Han *et al.*, 2015]. Gaffney *et al.* (1999) treated the whole trajectory as a basic unit and introduced the fundamental principles of clustering trajectory based on the probabilistic mixture regression model. Lee *et al.* (2007) presented a partition-and-group framework (TRACLUS) to derive common sub-trajectories. Since the MDL method used in partitioning the trajectory suffers from high computation overhead, it is not suited for online clustering trajectories with limited memory resource.

Quite a few researches address the road-network scenarios [Won *et al.*, 2009; Lee *et al.*, 2010; Han *et al.*, 2015]. Won *et al.* (2009) presented a similarity measurement by considering the total length of matched road segments and proposed a clustering algorithm by adjusting the FastMap and hierarchical clustering schemes. Roh and Hwang (2010) proposed a distance measure that considers the spatial proximity of vehicle trajectories on the road network and presented a neighbor-based clustering approach called NNCluster. Han *et al.* (2015) proposed a road-network aware clustering method, called NEAT, which considers the traffic locality characterized by the spatial constraints of the road network, the traffic flow among consecutive road segments, and the flow-based density. Nevertheless, the above mentioned work require clustering on stored trajectory data, so they cannot be directly applied to streaming trajectories.

2.6.3 *Continuous query over trajectory stream*

There are approaches that are to some degree orthogonal to our work but deserve to be mentioned. Various techniques about trajectory simplification

[Lee *et al.*, 2007] or trajectory compression [Hönle *et al.*, 2010] have been studied in real-time trajectory tracking [Lange *et al.*, 2011], but they refer to the problem of minimizing the amount of the position data that are communicated and stored. Due to a high computational overhead to attain the optimal results, they are unsuitable to online cluster the rapidly changing stream data in the limited memory. In addition, more recent achievements have been reported for continuous query processing over trajectory stream [Nehme and Rundensteiner, 2006; Sacharidis *et al.*, 2008; Zheng *et al.*, 2013; Tang *et al.*, 2012; Li *et al.*, 2013]. Nehme and Rundensteiner (2006) proposed SCUBA to optimize the execution of continuous queries on spatio-temporal data streams by utilizing motion clustering. Sacharidis *et al.* (2008) proposed a framework for online maintenance of hot motion paths in order to detect frequently traveled trails of numerous moving objects. Zheng *et al.* (2013) presented a method to discover closed gathering patterns from a large trajectory data set. Tang *et al.* (2012) studied the problem of incremental discovering traveling companions from streaming trajectories by a data structure termed a "traveling buddy". Li *et al.* (2013) proposed a group discovery framework that satisfies the requirements, which include sampling independence, density-connectedness, trajectory approximation, and online processing.

2.6.4 *Clustering upon trajectory stream*

Trajectory clustering for static data sets [Lee *et al.*, 2007] scarcely considers maintaining clusters incrementally. Jensen *et al.* (2007) exploited an incrementally maintained clustering feature CF, and proposed a scheme for the continuous clustering of moving objects. Li *et al.* (2004) presented the concept of Moving Micro-Cluster to catch the regularities of moving objects. Nevertheless, they highlighted incrementally clustering moving objects rather than trajectories. Li *et al.* (2010) proposed an incremental trajectory clustering framework, called TCMM, which includes micro-clusters maintenance by simplifying new trajectories into directed line segments, and macro-clusters generated by clustering the micro-clusters. While in the micro-clustering phase, TCMM has to accumulate sufficient incoming positional data to obtain the simplified sub-trajectories by using the MDL method. In addition, due to the effect of obsolete data, along with the process of continuously absorbing more records and merging the most similar pair of micro-clusters, the centers of micro-clusters will gradually shift, which leads to concept drift and thus degrades the effectiveness of the resulting clusters. In general, incremental clustering approaches barely consider the temporal aspects of the trajectories and cannot scale up to mine massive trajectory streams.

Targeting the requirement of clustering trajectory big data, Deng *et al.* (2015) presented a scalable density-based clustering algorithm, called Tra-POPTICS, and parallelized it with the Hyper-Q feature of Kelper GPU and massive GPU threads. Costa *et al.* (2014) proposed a framework (Lifting and Fourier Transforms) that pre-elaborates original trajectories by using non-separable Fourier transforms. Yu *et al.* (2013) proposed CTraStream for clustering trajectory data stream, including online line segment stream clustering and the update process of closed trajectory clusters based on the TC-Tree index. It attempts to extract patterns that are similar to a convoy pattern [Jeung *et al.*, 2008].

2.7 Conclusion

In this chapter, we proposed a framework to cluster evolving streaming trajectories using the sliding-window model, called Online Trajectory Stream Clustering over Sliding Window (or OCluWin for short). It consists of two components: a micro-clustering component that summarizes trajectory line segments in the current window and a macro-clustering component that reclusters the previously extracted summaries according to the user's request. Then we presented two methods (named TSCluWin and OCluST, respectively) based on two different defined synopsis structures (i.e., TF_o and EF_o, as well as TF and EF), which can extract the spatio-temporal clustering characteristics of the stream data in memory, and track the latest cluster changes of the trajectory stream in real time. By conducting extensive experiments on real-world data sets, we compare our proposed approaches to the other algorithms (TRACLUS and TCMM) in terms of effectiveness and efficiency. A theoretical analysis and comprehensive experimental results demonstrate that our proposal is of high quality, requires little memory, has a fast processing rate in coping with streaming trajectories, and outperforms the baseline approach.

Chapter 3

Outlier Detection upon Trajectory Streams

3.1 Background

Hawkins (1980) has intuitively defined outlier in an observation that deviated so much from other observations that it aroused suspicion that it had been generated by a different mechanism. On the other hand, Barnett (1994) states that an outlier is an observation (or subset of observations) which appears to be inconsistent with the remainder of that set of data. To some extent, the phrase "deviates from other observations" or "inconsistent with the remainder of that set of data" is subjective and context-based. A trajectory outlier is usually regarded as an abnormal trajectory that is obviously distinct from the majority of trajectories according to a certain similarity criterion, such as sea vessels whose movement behaviors are significantly different from others in the same area [Lei, 2016], hurricanes that suddenly change wind direction [Lee et al., 2008a], taxis with detour behaviors [Ge et al., 2011; Liu et al., 2014], unexpected road changes [Wu et al., 2015; Zhu et al., 2015], etc.

Considerable efforts have been invested toward defining an appropriate similarity criterion to measure the closeness among trajectories. First of all, an indispensable step is to extract representative features of each trajectory, based on which a function is utilized to measure the pairwise similarity (or distance) among them. Although the weighted linear sum of the distances for all features is widely adopted as the overall function

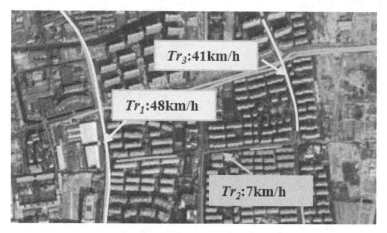

(a) Speed-based outlier.

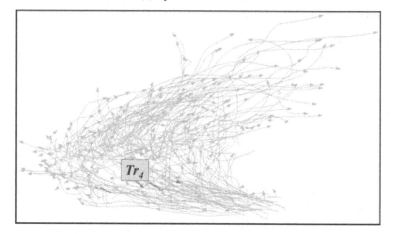

(b) Direction-based outlier.

Figure 3.1. Examples of trajectory outliers.

[Lee *et al.*, 2007; 2008a], it is insensitive to the situation where trajectories are similar in some features, but significantly different in others.

Figure 3.1(a) illustrates a small example of three trajectories derived by taxis at some time interval, denoted as Tr_1, Tr_2 and Tr_3, respectively. They are close to one another, among which Tr_2 (highlighted in dark broken line) with the speed of 7 km/h is most likely to be an outlier, since the average speed of its neighbors, Tr_1 and Tr_3, is about 44 km/h. Such an outlier may indicate a traffic jam. However, whether it is an outlier (or not) depends on the weight of the speed feature. It will not be identified as an outlier accurately if the weight of the speed feature is small and the weighted linear sum of the distances for all the features is not large enough to make it different from most of the other trajectories.

Similarly, in a hurricane landfall forecast scenario, as depicted in Figure 3.1(b), Tr_4 (highlighted in short dark line) is located in a very dense region, but its moving direction is opposite to its neighbors (move from east to west). Tr_4 is an outlier, indicating a hurricane whose wind direction changes suddenly. But whether it is an outlier depends on the weight setting of the direction feature. For Tr_4 to be identified as an outlier, the weight of the direction feature needs to be large and the weighted linear sum of the distances for all the features must also be large enough to make it distinct from most of the others.

In order to address the aforementioned issue, we put forward a novel feature grouping-based mechanism, where all features are divided into two groups, and our goal is to find outliers from a set of objects that are close to one another by the first group of features, but obviously different from the rest of the features. According to the new scenario, Tr_2 and Tr_4 are regarded as outlier because Tr_2 is close to its neighbors (Tr_1 and Tr_3) by spatial proximity (but with a different speed), while Tr_4 is close to its neighbors by spatial proximity, but is different in the direction feature.

It is challenging to detect outliers upon trajectory data streams due to strict time- and space-complexities. Aside from the aforementioned problem of feature selection, other key considerations could and should be taken into account when devising an outlier detection method for a trajectory stream. To deal with a stream of infinite positional point series, the outlier detection technique must satisfy the requirements such as real-time response, lightweight execution, noise-tolerance and tracking the evolutionary property of the outlier.

Specifically, trajectory position information must first be transient. An outlier should be determined immediately once it occurs, which requires one to handle the streaming data efficiently. Secondly, noise that is alike to an outlier should become the barrier of anomaly detection, and thus outlier detection techniques should be able to discern noise from any true anomaly to improve detection precision. Finally, a trajectory stream may evolve dynamically, while an abnormal moving property of trajectory should evolve gradually. Therefore, the outlier detection technique should have the ability to identify the evolutionary trajectory outlier as quickly as possible.

In a bid to solve the above issues, we will introduce a novel framework in this chapter, which will identify local anomaly trajectory fragments and evolutionary anomaly moving objects in streaming scenarios. It is comprised of two components, including the trajectory simplification phase and the outlier detection phase. During the simplification phase, appropriate fragments of raw trajectories at each timebin (including m timestamps, $m \geq 1$) are derived and the features of trajectory fragments are classified into two groups.

During the detection phase, to estimate the degree of outlierness for trajectory fragments with regard to their neighboring fragments at each timebin, we firstly search local neighbors for each trajectory fragment by computing the similarity in the first group of features. Subsequently, we assign a local anomaly factor for every trajectory fragment in terms of the difference in the second group of features between its neighbors and itself, and identify local anomaly trajectory fragments by comparing with a given local anomaly threshold. Finally, considering the evolving nature of streaming trajectories, the local anomaly factor of a moving object's trajectory fragment at each timebin is accumulated with a historical local anomaly factor of its older trajectory fragments multiplied by a decay function, to generate its evolving anomaly factor. When the evolving anomaly factor of a moving object exceeds a given evolutionary anomaly threshold, it is regarded as a moving object outlier.

The remainder of this chapter is structured as follows. In Section 3.2, the preliminary concepts are introduced and the problem is formally defined. In Section 3.3, we outline the scheme and elaborate on the details of two outlier detection algorithms. In Section 3.4, a series of performance evaluations on three data sets are given. Section 3.5 reviews the related work in literature. Finally, we succinctly conclude this chapter in Section 3.6.

3.2 Preliminaries

In this section, we introduce some preliminary concepts and formalize the problem of outlier detection upon trajectory streams. Table 3.1 summarizes major notations used in the rest of this chapter.

Table 3.1. List of notations.

Notation	Definition
S	The trajectory stream
T_c	The current timebin in a trajectory stream
N	The window size
p_i	The location of an object at the timestamp, t_i
tf	A trajectory fragment
TF_c	The set of trajectory fragments at the current timebin
M	The number of features per trajectory
d	The distance threshold
d_a	The ally threshold
ρ	The local outlier threshold
ι	The evolutionary anomaly threshold

Definition 3.1 (Trajectory Stream). A trajectory stream refers to sequences of positional records of multiple moving objects, which is denoted as $S = \{p_1^{(1)}, p_1^{(2)}, \ldots, p_2^{(1)}, p_2^{(2)}, \ldots\}$, where $p_i^{(j)}$ is the location of an object, $o^{(j)}$, at timestamp, t_i, in 2D space, i.e., $p_i^{(j)} = (x_i^{(j)}, y_i^{(j)})$.

Due to different sampling rates of various moving objects, to guarantee that each moving object reports its location at least once in a time interval, we utilize the term "timebin" (denoted as T) to describe a basic time interval. One timebin includes m timestamps ($m \geq 1$). Correspondingly, a trajectory stream is regarded as an infinite sequence of trajectory points ordered by timebins. In order to limit the infinite trajectory stream to a specified finite set of records within a given time horizon, we employ the concept of a time-based sliding window. It can be the stream elements that arrived within the most recent timebins, e.g., an hour. It is commonly used for discounting obsolete data as new ones come in, which keeps the window fresh. Let N represent the window size. Whenever the window slides forward, it moves forward by 1 timebin, as shown in Figure 3.2.

Definition 3.2 (Trajectory). The trajectory of an object, o, denoted as $Tr_o = \{(p_1, t_1), (p_2, t_2), \ldots (p_n, t_n)\}$, is a sub-sequence of S affiliated to o. Such records arrive in chronological order, where p_i is the location of o at timestamp, t_i, $\forall i < j$, $t_i < t_j$.

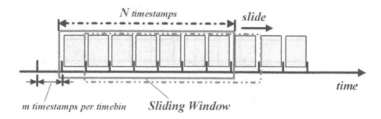

Figure 3.2. Example of a sliding window with size of N timestamps.

It is space-efficient to summarize each trajectory by reserving a small number of samples. For example, $\{p_1, p_2, \ldots, p_{100}\}$ can be summarized by $\{p_1, p_{11}, p_{21}, \ldots p_{91}\}$. However, selecting appropriate samples is challenging. We provide a trajectory simplification method in this chapter (see Section 3.3.1), where each trajectory is simplified by a set of characteristic points, and every two consecutive characteristic points are connected into a trajectory fragment.

Definition 3.3 (Trajectory Fragment). The fragment of a trajectory, Tr_o, denoted as $\text{tf} = \{(p_i, t_i), (p_j, t_j)\}$ $(i < j)$, is a line segment connecting two consecutive characteristic points, (p_i, p_j).

Henceforth, we use $\text{TF}_c(\text{tf}_1, \text{tf}_2, \ldots)$ to represent the set of trajectory fragments derived by simplifying the trajectory stream at the current timebin. Let $F = f_1, \ldots, f_M$ denote M features of a trajectory fragment. We divide all features into two groups. The first group, $(f_1, \ldots, f_b)$, called *Similarity Feature* (SF), is used to find the spatial neighbors of each trajectory fragment, and the second group $(f_{b+1}, \ldots, f_M)$, called *Difference Feature* (DF), is used to identify the trajectory fragment, which is obviously distinct from its spatial neighbors.

For instance, in hurricane landfall forecast application, the track information of an hurricane involves the hurricane's position in latitude and longitude, maximum surface wind speed, and minimum central pressure within a certain period. To discover the abnormal behaviors of hurricanes that are significantly different from their neighboring trajectories with respect to wind speed and central pressure, we regard latitude and longitude as an SF, and choose the maximum surface wind speed and minimum central pressure as the DF.

Let $w_1, \ldots, w_M$ denote the weight of each feature, respectively, $\sum_{l=1}^{M} w_l = 1$, and $\text{dis}_l(\text{tf}_i, \text{tf}_j)$ denote the distance between two trajectory fragments (tf_i and tf_j) by feature, f_l. Note that $\text{dis}_l(\text{tf}_i, \text{tf}_j)$ can be any typical distance metric, such as the Euclidean distance, DTW distance, Hausdorff distance, etc. Furthermore, Diff_1 and Diff_2 denote the distance between tf_i and tf_j by SF or DF, respectively.

$$\text{Diff}_1(\text{tf}_i, \text{tf}_j) = \sum_{l=1}^{b} w_l \cdot \text{dis}_l(\text{tf}_i, \text{tf}_j), \tag{3.1}$$

$$\text{Diff}_2(\text{tf}_i, \text{tf}_j) = \sum_{l=b+1}^{M} w_l \cdot \text{dis}_l(\text{tf}_i, \text{tf}_j). \tag{3.2}$$

To identify anomaly trajectory fragment at each timebin, we search the neighbors for each trajectory fragment in terms of SF, and then estimate the anomaly degree of each trajectory fragment within its similar neighborhood according to DF.

Definition 3.4 (Neighborhood of Trajectory Fragment). Given a threshold, d, the neighborhood of trajectory fragment, tf_i, at timebin, T_c, contains all the fragments whose distance from tf_i are not larger than d by SF, i.e.,

$$N_{T_c}(\text{tf}_i) = \{\text{tf}_j \in \text{TF}_c | \text{Diff}_1(\text{tf}_i, \text{tf}_j) \leq d\}.$$

We adopt the Local Outlier Factor (LOF) [Breunig *et al.*, 2000] to measure the outlierness of a trajectory fragment. LOF, a density-based outlier detection technique by considering the neighborhood density of each element relative to that of its nearest neighbors, does not need to learn data distribution in advance and is capable of detecting outliers with respect to the density of its local neighbors. Based on the idea of LOF, we introduce the concept of the local difference density to measure the difference in DF between each trajectory fragment and its adjacent trajectory fragments and the local anomaly factor (LAF) to estimate the anomaly degree of a trajectory fragment.

Definition 3.5 (Local Difference Density). The local difference density of tf_i at timebin, T_c, is defined as

$$\text{ldd}_{T_c}(tf_i) = \frac{|N_{T_c}(tf_i)|}{\sum_{tf_j \in N_{T_c}(tf_i)} \text{Diff}_2(tf_i, tf_j)}.$$

Definition 3.6 (Local Anomaly Factor). The local anomaly factor of a trajectory fragment, tf_i, at timebin, T_c, is defined as

$$\text{LAF}_{T_c}(tf_i) = \frac{\sum_{tf_j \in N_{T_c}(tf_i)} \frac{\text{ldd}_{T_c}(tf_j)}{\text{ldd}_{T_c}(tf_i)}}{|N_{T_c}(tf_i)|}.$$

In general, a larger LAF indicates that a trajectory fragment is more likely to be an outlier candidate. Therefore, a local anomaly trajectory fragment is a trajectory fragment with an LAF above a given threshold; see the definition here as follows:

Definition 3.7 (Local Anomaly Trajectory Fragment). Given a local outlier threshold, ρ, trajectory fragment, tf_i, at timebin, T_c, is called a local anomaly trajectory fragment, or in short, TF-*outlier*, iff $\text{LAF}_{T_c}(tf_i) > \rho$.

A TF-*outlier* is a fragment with DF that is significantly different from its neighborhood at its current timebin. For instance, reconsidering that trajectory (tr_2) with a velocity of 7 km/h in Figure 3.1, it is obviously a local outlier with regard to its neighbors in other roads with an average velocity of 44 km/h.

However, due to noise disturbance, a trajectory fragment with a larger LAF may be a false TF-*outlier* if not given an appropriate local anomaly threshold. We take into account the evolving nature of trajectory stream in solving this problem. The moving behaviors of objects keep evolving in streaming scenarios. An object which has a normal trajectory fragment at the current timebin may evolve into an outlier in the future. Distinct from anomaly detection of trajectory fragments at each timebin, we shall continuously capture the evolving trajectory outlier from the beginning of the trajectory stream via an evolving outlierness measurement. Note that this evolving outlierness measurement should not only consider the local anomaly factor of the object's trajectory fragment at the current timebin, but also take into account the influence of the historical outlierness of an object's older trajectory fragment.

That the sliding window model completely eliminates the historical data is undesirable for this issue. An alternative approach is to employ time decay to reduce the importance of historical outlierness. Specifically, for each moving object at each timebin, we accumulate the products of all the local anomaly factor of its historical trajectory fragments and a forward time decay function [Cormode *et al.*, 2009], and add the local anomaly factor of its trajectory fragment at the current timebin to obtain its evolutionary anomaly factor. The forward decay is computed on the amount of time between the arrival timebin of each historical trajectory fragment of the object and a landmark, where the arrival timebin of the oldest trajectory fragment of each object, denoted as T_s, is used as the landmark for each object.

Definition 3.8 (Evolutionary Anomaly Factor). Given the oldest timebin, T_s, the current timebin, T_c ($T_s \leq T_c$), and a monotone non-decreasing function, g, the evolutionary anomaly factor of a moving object, o, is defined as

$$\text{EAF}_{T_c}(o) = \sum_{T_k=T_s}^{T_c} \frac{g(T_k - T_s)\text{LAF}_{T_k}(\text{tf}_i)}{g(T_c - T_s)}.$$

Definition 3.9 (Evolutionary Anomaly Moving Object). Given an evolutionary anomaly threshold, ι, a moving object, o, at timebin, T_c, is an outlier, or in short, (MO-*outlier*), iff $\text{EAF}_{T_c}(o) > \iota$.

Finally, we summarize the problem definition here as follows:

Problem statement. Given a local outlier threshold, ρ, and evolutionary anomaly threshold, ι, our goal is to continuously discover all the local anomaly trajectory fragments (TF-*outlier*) and the evolutionary anomaly moving objects (MO-*outlier*) upon trajectory streams.

3.2.1 *Special cases*

3.2.1.1 *Driving in reverse*

A vehicle that drives in reverse reflects in its trajectory whose moving direction is opposite to its vicinities. As exemplified in Figure 3.3, the direction of trajectory, Tr_2, is opposite to its neighbors (Tr_1 and Tr_3) at

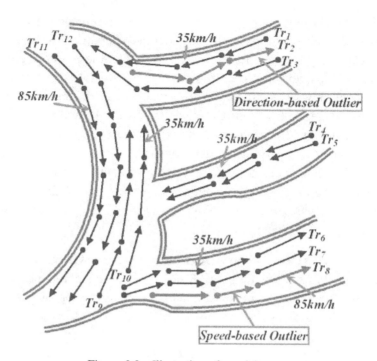

Figure 3.3.   Illustration of special cases.

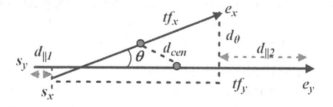

Figure 3.4.   Difference measurement of a direction-based outlier.

the current timebin. To find the behavior of reverse driving, we choose latitude and longitude as the SF and the direction (calculated by latitude and longitude) as the DF. Based on SF, we first look for the neighbors of each trajectory fragment using Diff_1, which is the weighted sum of the center point distance (denoted as d_{cen}) and parallel distance (denoted as $d_{\parallel}$).

For any two trajectory fragments, tf_x and tf_y, as shown in Figure 3.4, tf_y is longer than tf_x without any loss of generality, where $d_{\text{cen}} = \|\text{cen}_x - \text{cen}_y\|$; $d_{\|} = \frac{d_{\|1} + d_{\|2}}{2}$. Then we use Diff$_2$ (Euclidean distance) to measure the local difference density as well as the local anomaly degree of each trajectory fragment on DF between its neighbors and it. Here, Diff$_2$ refers to the angle distance (denoted as d_θ) computed on DF. Let $\|\text{tf}_x\|$ denote the length of tf_x, and if we assign θ the smaller intersecting angle between tf_x and tf_y, then d_θ is defined as follows:

$$d_\theta = \begin{cases} \|\text{tf}_x\| \times \sin(\theta), & 0° \leq \theta < 90° \\ \|\text{tf}_x\|, & 90° \leq \theta < 180°. \end{cases}$$

Finally, we identify TF-*outlier*, Tr$_2$, at the current timebin, as illustrated in Figure 3.3, which indicates a car is driving along the wrong way.

3.2.1.2 *Overspeeding*

Overspeeding is a severe road traffic violation and easily leads to the occurrence of heavy traffic accidents. As illustrated in Figure 3.3, the speeding behavior of a vehicle can be depicted as a trajectory, Tr$_8$, with high speed (85 km/h), whereas its neighbors (Tr$_6$ and Tr$_7$) keep to a slow speed (35 km/h). To find the overspeeding behavior, we choose latitude, longitude and direction (calculated by latitude and longitude) as SF, and then the speed as DF.

To begin, we find neighboring trajectories with the same direction by using Diff$_1$ on SF, which is the weighted sum of d_{cen}, $d_{\|}$ and d_θ in Figure 3.4. Then, we use Diff$_2$ (Euclidean distance) to measure the local difference density and local anomaly degree of each trajectory fragment on DF between its neighbors and it, based on which TF-*outlier* (Tr$_8$) is identified. Over the next several timebins, we proceed to measure the local anomaly degree and evolutionary anomaly factor of trajectory fragments. When the evolutionary anomaly factor of the moving object that Tr$_8$ belongs to exceeds ι, we detect it as the MO-*outlier*, which indicates that it is a speeding car.

Algorithm 6: Local and Evolutionary Outlier Detection upon Trajectory Stream

---

Input: S: a trajectory stream

Output: (1) A_{st}: A set of local anomaly trajectory fragments;

(2) A_o: A set of evolutionary anomaly moving objects;

1 **foreach** *trajectory, Tr, at incoming timebin, T_c, of S* **do**

2 $\quad$ $Tr_{simp} \leftarrow TraSimp(Tr)$;

3 $\quad$ $Tr_{all} \leftarrow Tr_{all} \cup Tr_{simp}$;

4 Generate sets of trajectory fragments from Tr_{all};

5 **foreach** *set of trajectory fragments, TF_c, at incoming timebin, T_c, of S* **do**

6 $\quad$ $(A_{st}, A_o) \leftarrow TODS(TF_c)$ (or $(A_{st}, A_o) \leftarrow OTODS(TF_c)$);

7 **return** A_{st} and A_o;

3.3 Framework: Local and Evolutionary Outlier Detection in Trajectory Stream

In this section, we propose a framework to identify local anomaly trajectory fragments and evolutionary anomaly moving objects upon streaming trajectories. In our framework, each incoming trajectory will be split into a set of consecutive trajectory fragments. As illustrated in Algorithm 6, our framework comprises two phases — the trajectory simplification phase (lines 1–4) and the outlier detection phase (lines 5–7). During the first phase, appropriate fragments of raw trajectories at each timebin are derived and the pseudocode of trajectory simplification function is presented in Algorithm 7. During the second phase, the local anomaly factor and evolutionary anomaly factor of each trajectory fragment are computed at each timebin. Based on whichever local anomaly, trajectory fragments as well as evolutionary anomaly moving objects are detected.

3.3.1 *Trajectory simplification*

To accelerate the trajectory outlier detection, each trajectory is simplified into a small number of characteristic points with the least information loss.

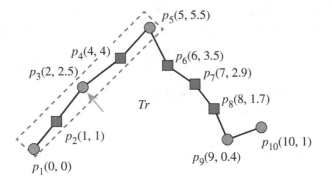

Figure 3.5. A trajectory and its characteristic points.

Specifically, when the behavior of one positional point is very different from its previous points, this point is determined as a characteristic point. For a trajectory, $\text{Tr} = \{p_1, p_2, \ldots p_n\}$, it can be simplified with k characteristic points, namely, $\text{Tr}_{\text{simp}} = \{p_{l_1}, p_{l_2}, \ldots p_{l_k}\}$ $(1 \leq l_1 < l_2 < \ldots < l_k \leq n)$. Each two adjacent characteristics points are connected to form a trajectory fragment (denoted as $\text{tf}(p_{l_i}, p_{l_{i+1}})$, $1 \leq i < k$).

Figure 3.5 illustrates an example trajectory, $\text{Tr} = \{p_1, p_2, \ldots p_{10}\}$, and its characteristic points (highlighted in solid circles) after simplification, i.e., $\text{Tr}_{\text{simp}} = \{p_1, p_3, p_5, p_9, p_{10}\}$. An appropriate simplification method must ensure that the number of characteristic points is as little as possible (conciseness), and the difference between the original trajectory and its simplified edition is as small as possible (preciseness). However, conciseness and preciseness are conflicting properties. This needs an optimal trade-off between them.

Trajectory simplification (or segmentation) techniques include the temporal interval-based method [Pelekis *et al.*, 2009], distance based-method [Anagnostopoulos *et al.*, 2006], representativeness-based method [Panagiotakis *et al.*, 2012] and the trajectory shape-based method [Lee *et al.*, 2007]. In our trajectory simplification phase, we employ the MDL principle and adapt the approximate method in Lee *et al.* (2007). The cost of the MDL is represented as the sum of $L(H)$ and $L(D|H)$ (both encoded in bits), where $L(H)$ (conciseness measurement) denotes the sum of the length of all trajectory fragments, and $L(D|H)$ (preciseness measurement) represents the sum of the differences between a trajectory and its derived trajectory fragments. We utilize Diff_1 by SF (i.e., coordinate information of positional point) to measure the difference. Formally, we have

$$L(H) = \sum_{j=1}^{m-1} \log_2(\text{Diff}_1(p_{l_j} p_{l_{j+1}})),$$

$$L(D|H) = \sum_{j=1}^{m-1} \sum_{k=l_j}^{l_{j+1}-1} \log_2(\text{Diff}_1(p_{l_j} p_{l_{j+1}}, p_k p_{k+1})).$$

An optimal simplification is achieved by minimizing the cost of the MDL. In Lee *et al.* (2007), an approximate solution is to achieve local optima on the MDL cost of each trajectory fragment. Let $\text{MDL}_{np}(p_i, p_j)$ denote the MDL cost when there is no simplification between p_i and p_j, and $\text{MDL}_p(p_i, p_j)$ denote the MDL cost when treating p_i and p_j as two characteristic points, then

$$\text{MDL}_p(p_i, p_j) = L(H) + L(D|H)$$

and

$$\text{MDL}_{np}(p_i, p_j) = L(H).$$

Intuitively, the goal of the local optimum is to find a long trajectory fragment (p_i, p_j). It ensures that no point (e.g., p_k) between p_i and p_j satisfies $\text{MDL}_p(p_i, p_k) \geq \text{MDL}_{np}(p_i, p_k)$. If $\text{MDL}_p(p_i, p_{j+1}) \geq \text{MDL}_{np}(p_i, p_{j+1})$, point p_j is chosen as a characteristic point. Though this characteristic selection method guarantees good time complexity, it cannot ensure p_j as the point to minimize the cost of MDL.

In view of this, as shown in Algorithm 7, when we calculate MDL_p and MDL_{np} for each point in a trajectory, we record two values: the maximal difference (denoted as $D_{\max}$) between MDL_p and MDL_{np}, and the index of that point (denoted as $I_{\max}$) with maximal difference in the traversed points so far (lines 5–10). Each time a point is traversed, we compare the difference (denoted as DIFF) between its MDL_p and MDL_{np} with $D_{\max}$, and set $D_{\max}$ to whichever is larger, and then update the value of $I_{\max}$. When DIFF < 0, we choose $p_{I_{\max}}$ rather than the

---

Algorithm 7: TraSimp (Trajectory Simplification)

Input: Tr: A trajectory $\{p_1, p_2, \ldots p_n\}$ in trajectory stream;

Output: Tr_{simp}: A set of all extracted characteristic points;

1   $\text{Tr}_{\text{simp}} \leftarrow \{p_1\}, s \leftarrow 1$;

2   /*s denotes the starting index and c denotes the current index*/;

3   $\text{len} \leftarrow 1, D_{\max} \leftarrow 0, I_{\max} \leftarrow s$;

4   /*len denotes the length of trajectory fragment*/;

5   **while** $(s + \text{len} \leq n)$ **do**

6     $c \leftarrow s + \text{len}$;

7     $\text{DIFF} \leftarrow \text{MDL}_{np}(p_s, p_c) - \text{MDL}_p(p_s, p_c)$;

8   **if** $\text{DIFF} > D_{\max}$ **then**

9       $D_{\max} \leftarrow \text{DIFF}$;

10      $I_{\max} \leftarrow c$;

11   **if** $\text{DIFF} < 0$ **then**

12       $\text{Tr}_{\text{simp}} \leftarrow \text{Tr}_{\text{simp}} \cup \{p_{I_{\max}}\}$;

13       $s \leftarrow I_{\max} + 1$;

14       $\text{len} \leftarrow 1, D_{\max} \leftarrow 0, I_{\max} \leftarrow s$;

15   **else**

16       $\text{len} \leftarrow \text{len} + 1$;

17   $\text{Tr}_{\text{simp}} \leftarrow \text{Tr}_{\text{simp}} \cup \{p_n\}$;

18   **return** Tr_{simp};

---

immediate previous point as a characteristic point, and look for the next characteristic point start with $p_{I_{\max}+1}$ (lines 11–14).

Example 1. Let us consider a trajectory Tr of 10 points in Figure 3.5. When we traverse point p_5 in Tr, because $\text{MDL}_p(p_1, p_5) \geq \text{MDL}_{np}(p_1, p_5)$, p_4 (the previous point of p_5) is chosen as a characteristic point by Lee *et al.* (2007). Distinct from that, because the difference between $\text{MDL}_{np}(p_1, p_4)$ and $\text{MDL}_p(p_1, p_4)$ is 1.17, the difference between $\text{MDL}_{np}(p_1, p_2)$ and $\text{MDL}_p(p_1, p_2)$ is 0, the difference between $\text{MDL}_{np}(p_1, p_3)$ and $\text{MDL}_p(p_1, p_3)$ is 3.03, $D_{\max} = 3.03$, $I_{\max} = 3$. So we choose p_3 instead of p_4 as a characteristic point. In this way, we simplify the rest points of Tr. This characteristic point selecting method can achieve a local optima better, which is demonstrated in Section 3.4 (as shown in Figure 3.7).

3.3.2 *TF*-outlier *and MO*-outlier *detection*

After the trajectory fragments are obtained by trajectory simplification at per timebin, we need to identify the TF-*outlier* and MO-*outlier* with respect to their local neighborhood. The detailed description of the TODS (short for $\underline{T}$F-outlier and M$\underline{O}$-outlier $\underline{D}$etection upon Trajectory $\underline{S}$tream) algorithm is presented in Algorithm 8.

At each timebin, the neighborhood of each trajectory fragment is determined by a distance threshold, d (Definition 3.4). However, a fixed value of d is not well suited to search for neighbors in the regions of different density. The intuition is that the trajectory fragments are closer to each other in the dense region, but depart from each other in sparse region. Therefore, setting a smaller distance threshold empowers the trajectory fragments that have no neighbors in sparse regions.

Algorithm 8: TODS ($\underline{T}$F-*outlier* and M$\underline{O}$-*outlier* $\underline{D}$etection upon Trajectory $\underline{S}$tream)

Input: TF_c: A set of trajectory fragments at timebin, T_c;
Output: (1) A_{st}: A set of local anomaly trajectory fragments;
          (2) A_o: A set of evolutionary anomaly moving objects;

1 **for** *each trajectory fragment* tf_i *of each object o at* TF_c **do**
2   find the local neighbors $N_{T_c}(tf_i)$ for tf_i;
3    $LAF_{T_c}(tf_i) \leftarrow \frac{\sum_{tf_j \in N_{T_c}(tf_i)} \frac{ldd_{T_c}(tf_j)}{ldd_{T_c}(tf_i)}}{|N_{T_c}(tf_i)|}$;
4   **if** $LAF_{T_c}(tf_i) > \rho$ **then**
5       $A_{st} \leftarrow A_{st} \cup \{tf_i\}$;
6    $EAF_{T_c}(o) \leftarrow EAF_{T_{c-1}}(o) \frac{g(T_{c-1}-T_s)}{g(T_c-T_s)} + LAF_{T_c}(tf_i)$;
7   **if** $EAF_{T_c}(o) > \iota$ **then**
8       $A_o \leftarrow A_o \cup \{o\}$;

9 **return** A_{st} *and* A_o;

To solve this problem, we take density into account in the distance threshold setting. The density of a trajectory fragment at T_c is determined by the amount of trajectory fragments within the distance from it, and such a distance can be calculated by the standard deviation (denoted as σ) of pairwise distances between the trajectory fragments arrived at T_c, i.e., $\text{Density}_{T_c}(\text{tf}_i) = |N_{T_c}(\text{tf}_i)|$ in terms of distance, σ. Accordingly, the value of d can be adjusted by multiplying the ratio of the average density of trajectory fragments arrived at T_c with its local density, namely,

$$d \cdot \frac{\frac{1}{|\text{TF}_c|} \sum_{\text{tf}_j \in \text{TF}_c} \text{Density}_{T_c}(\text{tf}_j)}{\text{Density}_{T_c}(\text{tf}_i)}.$$

Through adaptive adjustment of d, the value of d rises in the sparse region and decreases in a dense region. In this way, we guarantee that the trajectory fragments have neighbors in sparse regions and that they will not miss any outlier detection.

Subsequently, to identify TF-*outliers* at T_c, we compute the local difference density and local anomaly factor for each trajectory fragment (line 3). By comparing the difference of DF between each trajectory fragment and its vicinity, we derive the local anomaly degree of each element at T_c. Generally, if a trajectory fragment differs greatly from its neighbors on DF, the local anomaly factor attains a higher value. Trajectory fragments are identified as TF-*outliers* when their local anomaly factors exceed a given local anomaly threshold ρ (lines 4–5).

A trajectory fragment is identified as a TF-*outlier* at one timebin, according to the difference of DF between it and its adjacent elements. But due to the disturbance of noise data, it is difficult to specify an appropriate local outlier threshold to identify TF-*outlier* accurately and reduce the false alarms. In addition, with the evolution of trajectories, the phenomenon where a moving object has anomaly trajectory fragments in multiple timebins (maybe discontinuous) indicates the exceptional behaviors of this moving object. Thus, an effective detection approach is desirable to capture the evolving abnormal behaviors of moving objects. By employing the idea of strengthening the influence of newly arrived trajectory data while lessening the influence of outdated data (which may be noisy data), we derive the evolving anomaly factor of each moving object based on the local anomaly factors of its trajectory fragments at different timebins.

Since the evolving outlierness of a moving object is more affected by recent abnormal behaviors than by historical abnormal behaviors, a decay function is utilized to calculate the evolutionary anomaly factor (Definition 3.8). To be specific, LAFs of trajectory fragments of each moving object at the previous timebins are multiplied by a decay function, and accumulated together with LAFs at the current timebin to derive the evolutionary anomaly factor. Because the backward decay mechanism requires calculating the age of each item with respect to the current timebin, which varies over time. Additionally, every item must be revisited to compute its contribution for decayed LAF computation. As a result, we adopt the notion of forward time decay [Cormode *et al.*, 2009] based on measuring forward from a previous fixed point in time (called a *landmark*). To attain a slower decay on historical abnormality, we apply polynomial decay, specifically, $g(n) = n^2$. According to Definition 3.8, we have

$$\text{EAF}_{T_c}(o) = \sum_{T_k=T_s}^{T_c} \frac{g(T_k - T_s)\text{LAF}_{T_k}(\text{tf}_i)}{g(T_c - T_s)},$$

$$= \sum_{T_k=T_s}^{T_{c-1}} \frac{g(T_k - T_s)\text{LAF}_{T_k}(\text{tf}_i)}{g(T_c - T_s)} + \text{LAF}_{T_c}(\text{tf}_i),$$

$$= \frac{1}{g(T_c - T_s)} \sum_{T_k=T_s}^{T_{c-1}} g(T_k - T_s)\text{LAF}_{T_k}(\text{tf}_i) + \text{LAF}_{T_c}(\text{tf}_i),$$

$$= \text{EAFT}_{c-1}(o) \frac{g(T_{c-1} - T_s)}{g(T_c - T_s)} + \text{LAF}_{T_c}(\text{tf}_i).$$

Hence, the value of $\text{EAF}_{T_c}(o)$ can be calculated by multiplying $\text{EAF}_{T_{c-1}}(o)$ with the ratio of $g(T_{c-1} - T_s)$ to $g(T_c - T_s)$, and adding it with $\text{LAF}_{T_c}(\text{tf}_i)$ (line 6). When the evolving anomaly factor of the moving object, o, grows beyond threshold. ι, o would be reported as an evolutionary anomaly moving object (lines 7–8).

Time complexity analysis. For the trajectory fragments that have arrived at the current timebin, the time complexity of the TODS algorithm is $O(n \log n)$ using the $STR\text{-}tree$ index technique. Here, n is the maximum number of trajectory fragments that have arrived at the current timebin. Therefore, after the insertion of t timebins, the total time complexity of the iterated TODS algorithm is $O(tn \log n)$.

Actually, the trajectory data arrives very quickly, and searching neighbors for each trajectory fragment accordingly becomes the computational bottleneck. Whenever new trajectory data is received at every timebin, both the local outlier factor calculation and the evolutionary anomaly factor calculation are required to execute iteratively for each trajectory fragment. This involves a comparatively high computational overhead, especially when a massive amount of trajectory data arrives at one timebin. To further improve the efficiency of TODS algorithm, a high-quality but significantly less costly technique is desirable to accelerate the neighbor search and reduce the number of updates.

3.3.3 *Optimized TF-outlier and MO-outlier detection*

Although trajectories are time-varying and evolutionary in a streaming scenario, it is observed that the neighbor relationship among trajectory fragments may be retained for one or more timebins. Motivated by this, we combine this with the clustering technique and exploit a new structure to store and maintain the neighbor relationship of trajectory fragments along the trajectory stream. To be specific, we characterize a micro-group of trajectory fragments within a specified proximity threshold as *Ally Fragment* (AF for short). Here, we utilize a representative trajectory fragment (denoted as AF_{rp}) to depict the overall characteristic of an *Ally Fragment*.

Definition 3.10 (*Ally Fragment*). Given an threshold d_a $(d_a < d)$, an AF is defined as a set of trajectory fragments that for any trajectory fragment, $tf_i \in AF$, the distance between tf_i and AF_{rp} by SF is not more than d_a, i.e., $\text{Diff}_1(tf_i, AFrp) \leq d_a$.

The trajectory fragments in one AF are tightly bound to one another. The maintenance of an AF is triggered only when newly arrived trajectory fragments are inserted or obsolete trajectory fragments are deleted. Based on the structure of an AF we present an optimized TODS algorithm, denoted as OTODS. The detailed algorithmic description of OTODS is given in Algorithm 9. Initially, a trajectory fragment is randomly

---

Algorithm 9: OTODS (Optimized $\underline{T}F$-outlier and $M\underline{O}$-outlier $\underline{D}$etection upon Trajectory $\underline{S}$tream)

Input: TF_c: A set of newly arrived trajectory fragments at timebin, T_c;

Output: (1) A_{st}: A set of local anomaly trajectory fragments;

             (2) A_o: A set of evolutionary anomaly moving objects;

1 Initialize the set of ally fragments Z;

2 **foreach** *trajectory fragment* tf_i *of object* o *in* TF_c **do**

3   **if** $\exists AF$, $\text{Diff}_1(tf_i, AF) \le d_a$ **then**

4   Insert tf_i into AF;

5        $Z_{\text{INF}} \leftarrow Z_{\text{INF}} \cup \{AF\}$;

6   /* Z_{INF} denotes the influenced set of ally fragments on insertion or deletion of new trajectories */;

7   **else**

8   Create AF_{new} for tf_i; Update Z and Z_{INF};

9   Assign the closest micro-cluster to AF_{new} using clustering method;

10 **foreach** *outdated trajectory fragment* tf_e **do**

11   Remove tf_e from the corresponding AF; Update Z and Z_{INF};

12 **foreach** *ally fragment* AF *in* Z_{INF} **do**

13   Find the influenced local micro-cluster LC_m for AF;

14 **foreach** *ally fragment* AFj *in* LC_m **do**

15     $\text{LAF}_{T_c}(AFj) \leftarrow \dfrac{\sum_{AFy \in LC_m} \frac{\text{ldd}_{T_c}(AFy)}{\text{ldd}_{T_c}(AFj)}}{|LC_m|}$;

16   **if** $(\text{LAF}_{T_c}(AFj) > \rho)$ **then**

17   **foreach** *fragment* tf_i *in* AFj **do**

18           $A_{st} \leftarrow A_{st} \cup \{tf_i\}$;

19   **foreach** *fragment* tf_i *in* AFj **do**

20        $\text{EAF}_{T_c}(o) \leftarrow \text{EAF}_{T_{c-1}}(o)\dfrac{g(T_{c-1} - T_s)}{g(T_c - T_s)} + \text{LAF}_{T_c}(tf_i)$;

21   **if** $\text{EAF}_{T_c}(o) > \iota$ **then**

22           $A_o \leftarrow A_o \cup \{o\}$;

23 **return** A_{st} *and* A_o;

---

selected from newly arrived ones as a seed. Then, it is merged with its nearest trajectory fragments to generate one AF in terms of an ally threshold, d_a (lines 2–4). If its nearest AF cannot be found, a new one will be created (lines 7–8). This select-and-merge process iterates until all the arrived trajectory fragments at one timebin are absorbed into different AFs.

The representative trajectory fragment (whose computing method is similar to the one in Chapter 2) is required to be derived for all the AFs. Also, as steam progresses, it is critical to eliminate the influence of obsolete trajectory fragments from the existing AFs. It mainly involves the updates of representative trajectory fragments for influenced AFs with the insertion and deletion of trajectory fragments. That we regard AFs instead of a trajectory fragment as a basic unit when calculating ldd and LAF can drastically reduce the amount of calculation.

To further reduce the cost of the local anomaly factor calculation, our solution builds a *Local Micro-cluster* (LC for short) on AFs via hierarchical clustering (line 9), instead of searching for neighbors for each AF. As illustrated in Figure 3.6, four AFs (denoted as AF_1, AF_2,

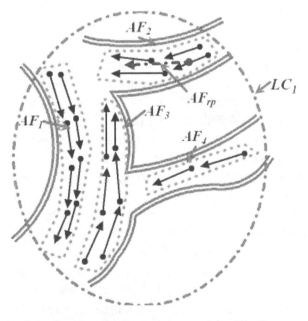

Figure 3.6. One *Local Micro-cluster* and its *Ally Fragments*.

AF_3 and AF_4, respectively) are clustered into a *Local Micro-cluster* (denoted as LC_1). The representative trajectory fragment of AF_2 is AF_{rp}. Here the *Local Micro-cluster* is distinct from temporal partitioning (defined as *Local cluster*) over a trajectory stream in Bu *et al.* (2009), where it intuitively extends the neighbor relationship of the AFs.

According to Definition 4.6, the trajectory fragments in an AF are tightly bound to each other and thus local anomaly factors of the trajectory fragments in an AF are approximately the same. Henceforth, evaluating the local anomaly factor for each trajectory fragment is transformed into estimating the local anomaly factor of an AF in a LC. The structure of an the AF simply allows it to store the neighbor relationship between objects rather than their spatial coordinates. The size of an AF is much smaller than that of a LC. Therefore, the structures of an AF and a LC can significantly accelerate the execution of the TODS algorithm.

Essentially, the insertion of new trajectory fragments or the elimination of obsolete trajectory fragments only influences the updates of LAFs for the relevant elements, including (1) the AFs that newly inserted trajectory fragments belong to, (2) the AFs that outdated trajectory fragments are deleted from, and (3) the other AFs in the LCs that newly inserted or deleted trajectory fragments belong to. We use Z_{INF} to denote the influenced set of AFs on insertion or deletion of trajectory fragments (lines 5, 8 and 11). So the updates of LAFs after each insertion or elimination are limited on AFs in Z_{INF} and do not require any recalculating of LAFs for all the AFs (lines 14–15). In the following we proceed to describe the details of updating an LAF when inserting or eliminating trajectory fragments as time goes by.

Insertion of new trajectory fragments. The main work for inserting new trajectory fragments involves the updates of ldds, LAFs and EAFs for newly inserted AFs as well as affected existing ones. On one hand, whenever new trajectory fragments are absorbed into existing or newly created AFs, ldds, LAFs and EAFs need to be calculated for the new records. On the other hand, with the insertion of new records into existing AFs, the other AFs in the same LC that the new records belong to shall accordingly update their ldds. In addition, new records and affected records need to reassign the degree of outlierness for each element, i.e., LAF and EAF (lines 14–22).

Elimination of obsolete trajectory fragments. A certain amount of trajectory fragments will be eliminated due to their obsoleteness of each timebin, which would even leads to the need for some AFs to be deleted. Similar to the insertion of new records, ldds, LAFs and EAFs of the affected trajectory fragments are required to be updated. Meanwhile, for all the LCs that deleted trajectory fragments belong to, ldds, LAFs and EAFs of the other AFs in the same LCs must be correspondingly updated.

Time complexity analysis. After inserting t timebins, the time complexity of the OTODS algorithm is $O(n \log n + (t - 1)n_A \log n_A)$ using a $STR\text{-}tree$ index technique, where n is the maximum number of arrived trajectory fragments at a timebin, n_A is the maximum number of AFs, and $n_A \ll n$. Thereby, the efficiency of the OTODS algorithm is significantly improved as compared to the TODS algorithm.

3.4 Experimental Study

In this section, we conduct extensive experiments to assess the effectiveness and efficiency of TODS and OTODS. Initially, to evaluate the effectiveness of TODS on the static trajectory data set, we utilize TRAOD [Lee *et al.*, 2008a] as the baseline approach to compare against TODS based upon the real data set. Furthermore, we execute TODS and OTODS algorithms on two real data sets to verify the effectiveness of both algorithms over streaming trajectories. Finally, we compare the efficiency of the TODS and OTODS algorithms on a real data set and then evaluate the influence of the key parameters on each algorithm.

TRAOD is the most effective distance-based trajectory outlier detection algorithm reported so far for the static trajectory data set. It partitions each trajectory into a set of line segments (denoted as t-partition), and then detects outlying t-partitions and trajectory outliers. In the detection phase, TRAOD determines the abnormity of a t-partition according to its insufficient number of close trajectories relative to the whole trajectory data set. Note that a close trajectory defined in Lee *et al.* (2008a) not only needs to meet a given distance threshold, but also ensures that sufficient portions of it are close to a t-partition. Namely, the length of the close portion of a close trajectory is not less than that of comparing a t-partition.

In addition, TRAOD identifies the trajectory outliers according to the ratio of the sum of its outlying t-partitions' lengths to its total length. As a result, outlying t-partitions and trajectory outliers detected by TRAOD are probably very long. Distinct from TRAOD, our proposal aims to detect the TF-*outlier* and MO-*outlier*. We initially find a similar neighborhood for each trajectory fragment in terms of the specified distance threshold rather than the length limit of a close trajectory. Then, we detect outliers within their local neighborhood. The rationale is that finding outliers locally is more accurate than doing so globally.

3.4.1 *Experimental setting*

We utilize three real trajectory data sets to evaluate our proposed methods, including the Atlantic hurricane track data set (hereafter termed *Best Track*[1]), taxi operational data set of 2015 in Shanghai (hereafter termed *Taxi Shanghai* 15), and the taxi trajectory data set of 2013 in Shanghai (hereafter termed *Taxi Shanghai* 13). The former data set is derived in the Euclidean space, while the latter two are derived on a restricted road network.

Best Track records a wealth of hurricane's track information between the year 1959 and 2010. It contains features such as the hurricane's position in latitude and longitude, maximum surface wind speed, as well as minimum central pressure. We choose a portion (1990–2010) of the data set, which involves 221 trajectories and 6541 points.

Taxi Shanghai15 contains about 410k trajectories derived by 13,600 taxis of Shanghai in a period from 1 to 30 April 2015. Each GPS log is received at the rate of around once every minute. It has about 13,660 trajectories per day (about 114 million points) with six attributes of vehicle ID, time, longitude and latitude, speed and taxi status (free/occupied).

Taxi Shanghai13 contains about 4,800k trajectories generated by 13,400 taxis in Shanghai for three months, from October to December in 2013. We select a test area consisting of 19 road segments (from Wuzhou Avenue, through Shenjiang road and Jufeng Road, to North Zhang Yang Road), and each road segment has one lane in each direction. It has

---

[1] http://weather.unisys.com/hurricane/atlantic/

about 53,356 trajectories per day (about 107 million points) with four attributes of timestamp, velocity, longitude and latitude coordinates. These positional records experience the periods of free-flow and congestion alternately throughout the day, and compose a real-time trajectory stream. The ground truth outlier set is manually verified through comparative velocity analysis for each trajectory fragment and its neighbors at each timebin by the volunteers. It involves a few trajectories with exceptional speed on some road segments, and the road segments that have obviously different speed from their neighbors. The labeling of the TF-*outlier* (or MO-*outlier*) is determined by the majority of the volunteers.

All codes, written in Java, are conducted on a PC with an Intel Core CPU 3.6 GHz Intel i7 processor and 16 GB of memory. The operating system is Windows 10. Unless mentioned otherwise, the parameters are: the window size $N = 30$ minutes and $timebin = 2$ minutes.

3.4.2 *Effectiveness evaluation*

Results for *Best* Track. To verify the accuracy of TODS on the static data set, we first implement TRAOD and TODS on *Best* Track. We fit *Best* Track in a time window, which enables TODS to handle the static data set just like TRAOD. Figure 3.7 visualizes the detection results of TRAOD and TODS. We choose latitude and longitude as SF and regard direction (calculated by position information), minimum central pressure and wind speed as DF. To detect the angular outlier, in the experiment of [Lee *et al.* (2008a)], more weights are put on the angular distance. Accordingly, we put more weights on the direction feature and fewer weights on the other features in DF.

Parameters of the TRAOD algorithm are set the same as Lee *et al.* (2008a) and the parameters of TODS are empirically set as follows: $d = 40$, $\rho = 1.5$ and $\iota = 1.276$. As shown in Figure 3.7, light thin lines represent normal trajectory partitions (or fragments), black thick lines represent anomaly trajectory *t*-partitions (TRAOD) or TF-*outliers* (TODS), and black thin lines represent trajectory outliers (TRAOD) or MO-*outliers* (TODS). Owing to the advantage of our improved simplified method, the trajectory simplification result of TODS is smoother than that of TRAOD, as illustrated in Figure 3.7.

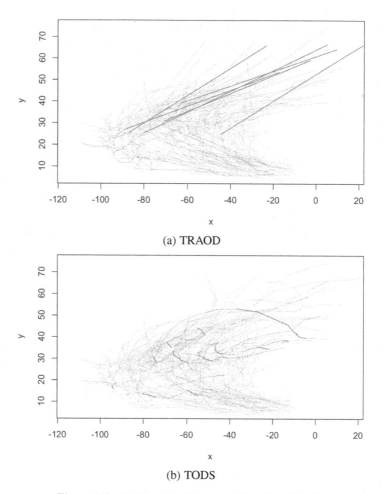

(a) TRAOD

(b) TODS

Figure 3.7. Outlier detection result for *Best* Tr*ack*.

As shown in Figure 3.7(a), a total of six trajectory outliers with outlying *t*-partitions are detected by TRAOD. We can observe that most of the outlying *t*-partitions and trajectory outliers are quite long and do not behave that differently from their neighboring trajectories. As discussed earlier, the main reason is that the close trajectories of a *t*-partition are determined by two issues [Lee *et al.*, 2008a]: one is that it is within the smallest distance and the other is that the length of the close trajectory must be larger than that of the tested *t*-partition. If a t-partition, L_i, does not have sufficient close trajectories with length greater than that of L_i, it is regarded as an outlying t-partition.

In addition, the trajectory outliers are identified according to the ratio of the sum of its outlying t-partitions' lengths to its total length. We observe that long t-partitions in the upper right region are identified as outlying t-partitions because they are distant from most of the other trajectories and few close t-partitions have a larger length than theirs. Correspondingly, since the sum of lengths of these t-partitions possesses a definite proportion relative to the trajectories that they belong to, such trajectories are identified as trajectory outliers even when the remainder portions of them are similar with their surrounding trajectories.

Whereas TODS instead focuses on detecting TF-*outlier* and MO-*outlier* that are significantly distinct from their neighborhood according to DF. As illustrated in Figure 3.7(b), there are 12 MO-*outliers* (their portions including TF-*outliers*) detected by the TODS algorithm. Compared with trajectory outliers detected by TRAOD, MO-*outliers* are not always long trajectories. But we can see that the directions of MO-*outliers* are significantly different from those in their local neighborhood. Thus, the outlier detection result of TODS is more reasonable than that of TRAOD.

Results for *Taxi Shanghai15*. We apply the OTODS algorithm on *Taxi Shanghai*15 to detect traffic abnormal incidents in the urban road network of Shanghai during the interval [8:00–8:30] on 14 and 15 April 2015, respectively. Longitude and latitude are chosen as SF and speed is regarded as DF. We regard the real-time average speed of each AF as the velocity of the corresponding road segment. We choose a test area (the road area surrounding the Middle Ring Road) to visualize the outlier detection result of the OTODS algorithm. As shown in Figure 3.8, light line marked without alphabetical notation represent the road segments where the normal motion traces of taxis are located on, bright line marked with lowercase alphabetical annotation represent TF-*outliers* (the lanes in a certain road segments) within the interval [8:29–8:30] and dark line marked with uppercase alphabetical annotation represent MO-*outliers* (the lanes in a certain roads) within the interval [8:00–8:30]. We observe that the speeds of most outliers (TF-*outliers* and MO-*outliers*) are significantly higher than that of their vicinities. High speed always implies traffic fluency on the road. During peak hours, the information about the roads where there is high speed is extremely useful and can be delivered to the public for optimal route planning in real time.

Furthermore, as can be seen from Figure 3.8(a) and (b), although there is no obvious difference between the traffic situations in the same time period on 14 and 15 April, significant variations have emerged in the results of trajectory outlier detection, including the number of TF-*outliers* and MO-*outliers* and the positions where outliers occur. In comparison with the traffic situation on 14 April (see Figure 3.8(a)), the speeds on most of the roads (including the roads that the outliers are located on and general roads) on 15 April (see Figure 3.8(b)) are obviously higher, especially for the roads near Middle Ring Road.

This case may coincide with the execution of a known traffic administration rule by the Shanghai Public Security Bureau, who have extended the prohibited driving time on some of the elevated highways (e.g., Middle Ring Road) by an hour from 15 April 2015 that includes the morning rush hour [7:00–10:00] and evening rush hour [16:00–19:00]. This means that many vehicles are not allowed on elevated highways for a longer period of time. Therefore, owing to the reduction of vehicles, the velocities of two-way lanes in Middle Ring Road and a small number of neighboring road segments are accelerated within the interval [8:00–8:30], as illustrated in Figure 3.8(b). This tallies with the new traffic control policy. It demonstrates that the OTODS method can be effectively used to identify abnormal traffic situations in real time.

Results for ***Taxi Shanghai13.*** For effectiveness validation purpose, we also conduct the TODS and OTODS algorithms on *Taxi Shanghai*13. We aim to continuously identify TF-*outliers* and MO-*outliers* on *Taxi Shanghai*13 according to the velocity feature. Similarly, we choose the longitude and latitude coordinates as SF and regard velocity as DF. Taking the TF-*outliers* detected by TODS as an example: the portions of the test area and the outlier detection results (within [8:00–10:00] a.m. on 8 October) are visualized in Figure 3.9. Figure 3.9(a) shows the movement distribution of taxis traces (highlighted in light lines). The average speed on most roads is not beyond 20 km/h. The TF-*outliers* (highlighted in black lines) detected by TODS is

(a) 2015.4.14

Figure 3.8. Outlier detection result for *TaxiShanghai*15.

(b) 2015.4.15   *(Continued)*

Figure 3.8.

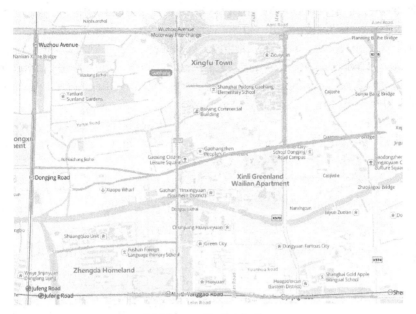

(a) Movement distribution

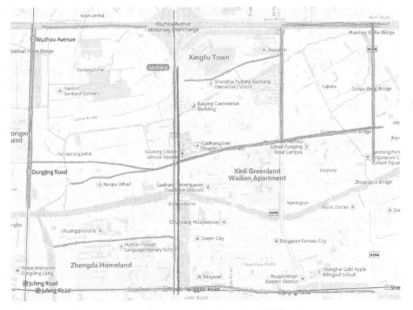

(b) TF-*outliers* detected by TODS

Figure 3.9.   Outlier detection result for *Taxi Shanghai* 13.

illustrated in Figure 3.9(b). Black thin lines indicate that only a few abnormal trajectories (with exceptional speed of 50–60 km/h) occur on parts of the roads. The TF-*outliers* represented by black thick lines indicate a road segment where taxis travel with significantly different speeds than on neighboring road segments. This outlier detection result coincides with the ground truth outliers.

Metrics. In order to conduct a comparative analysis of the effectiveness for both algorithms, we use Precision, Recall and F-measure as the criteria measurement. They are defined as

$$\text{Precision} = \frac{|R \cap D|}{|D|},$$

$$\text{Recall} = \frac{|R \cap D|}{|R|}$$

and

$$F\text{-measure} = \frac{2 \times \text{Precision} \times \text{Recall}}{\text{Precision} + \text{Recall}},$$

where R denotes the manually labeled outlier set and D denotes the detected outlier set by our proposal. Precision indicates how accurately the algorithm detects outliers and Recall measures how completely outliers are detected. To deeply understand how the parameters impact outlier detection, we compare the results of both algorithms via Precision, Recall and F-measure by utilizing different thresholds (d, d_a, ρ and ι), as illustrated in Figures 3.10–3.12. Note that d (or d_a) uses the variation of latitude and longitude; the distance of 0.0001 corresponds to about 11 meters.

First, we investigate the precision of both algorithms, with the results under the different distance threshold (d or d_a) and anomaly threshold (ρ or ι) plotted in Figure 3.10. From Figure 3.10(a) and (c), the TODS and OTODS algorithms have high precision when $\rho \geq 2$ for a TF-*outlier*, because the local anomaly factors of most TF-*outliers* reach about 2. While OTODS uses a smaller d_a ($d_a = 0.0032$) to attain the same Precision as TODS with a larger d ($d = 0.0256$), this is so because a smaller d_a enables all the trajectory fragments in one AF to be closer to one another. Accordingly, the LAF of such an AF represents the

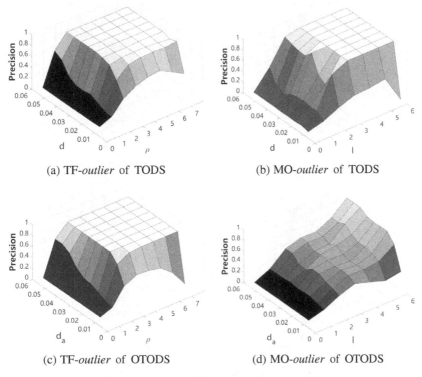

Figure 3.10. Precision (*Taxi Shanghai* 13).

outlierness of trajectory fragments in it more precisely. In addition, comparing the MO-*outlier* detected by TODS (see Figure 3.10(b)) with that by OTODS (see Figure 3.10(d)), the TODS has a higher precision than OTODS, and OTODS obtains nearly the same precision as TODS when $\iota = 6$. This is in line with our intuition that the anomaly evaluation of trajectory fragments is transformed into that of AFs, and the average outlierness of AFs guarantees approximately the same high precision as the trajectory fragments originally.

Second, we report the recall rate of both algorithms under a different distance threshold (d or d_a) and different anomaly threshold (ρ or ι), as shown in Figure 3.11. It is observed that the TODS and OTODS algorithms have almost the same recall rate. Meanwhile, the recall rate of both algorithms gradually drops as the anomaly threshold (ρ or ι)

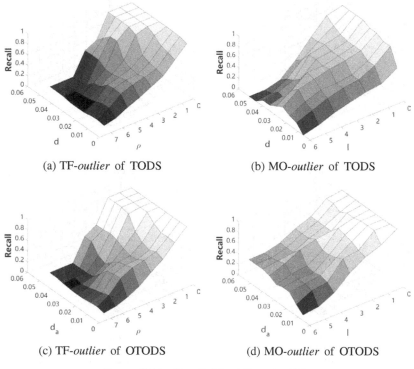

(a) TF-*outlier* of TODS   (b) MO-*outlier* of TODS

(c) TF-*outlier* of OTODS   (d) MO-*outlier* of OTODS

Figure 3.11.   Recall (*Taxi Shanghai* 13).

increases. Further increasing the value of d or d_a does not help any more. The reason is that almost all the outliers (TF-*outlier* or MO-*outlier*) can be found when ρ (or ι) = 1 or 2. It is worth mentioning that OTODS identifies the outlierness of trajectory fragments by using AFs, but the validity of the AF and LC structures ensures that OTODS detects almost all the outliers, and thus achieves a high recall rate.

Third, we examine F-measure of the TODS and OTODS algorithms under different thresholds, as shown in Figure 3.12. We observe that both algorithms obtain the best F-measure for TF-*outlier* detection when $\rho = 2$ and d (or d_a) ≥ 0.0032, and for MO-*outlier* detection when $\iota = 2$ and d (or d_a) $= 0.0032$. This is due to the average pairwise distance of trajectory fragments being about 0.0032 on *Taxi Shanghai* 13, and at the same time the LAFs of most TF-*outliers* and EAFs of MO-*outliers* reach about 2. From the above results, we conclude that our proposal can tolerate noisy

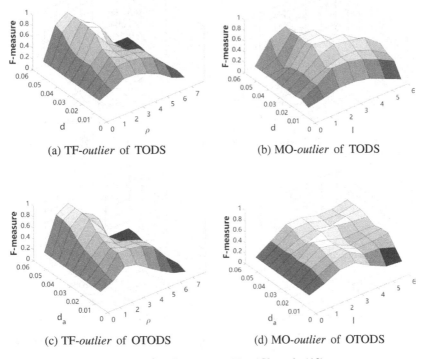

(a) TF-*outlier* of TODS   (b) MO-*outlier* of TODS

(c) TF-*outlier* of OTODS   (d) MO-*outlier* of OTODS

Figure 3.12. F-measure $(Taxi\,Shanghai\,13)$.

disturbance and has a lower false alarm rate on account of the evolutionary anomaly assessment. Furthermore, OTODS can attain almost the same effectiveness as TODS, as long as the thresholds are set appropriately.

3.4.3 *Efficiency evaluation*

In this section we conduct a study to assess the efficiency of our proposal by comparing TODS with OTODS when dealing with streaming trajectories. The number of trajectories gradually grows from $40k$ to $280k$. Figure 3.13(a) shows the execution time comparison (expressed as seconds) between TODS and OTODS upon $Taxi\,Shanghai\,13$. The execution time of both algorithms scale linearly with data size, and OTODS is superior to the one processed by TODS with the progression of a trajectory stream.

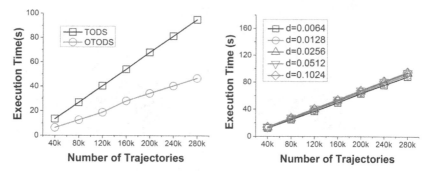

(a) Execution time comparison between (b) Execution time of TODS versus d
TODS and OTODS

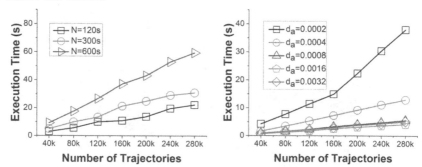

(c) Execution time of OTODS versus N (d) Execution time of OTODS versus d_a

Figure 3.13.   Execution time comparison over *Taxi Shanghai* 13.

The faster processing rate of OTODS is contributed by the structures of AFs and LCs. That is, we estimate the local anomaly factor of each AF in each LC instead of evaluating the local anomaly factor for each trajectory fragment. More importantly, for the OTODS algorithm, along with the time window moving forward, only a small amount of AFs in certain LCs are influenced, whether new fragments are inserted or obsolete fragments are deleted. Therefore, the OTODS algorithm significantly outperforms the TODS algorithm. This also demonstrates the time-quality trade-off by comparing F-measure and execution time of both algorithms. The OTODS algorithm is capable of detecting the outliers upon streaming trajectories with promising efficiency.

Moreover, in order to further test the robustness of the TODS and OTODS algorithms, we study the sensitivity of both algorithms under different parameter settings. We run the comparative experiments by varying the values of d, N and d_a, respectively.

(1) **Varying d:** Because d is the distance threshold for determining the neighborhood of trajectory fragment, it is important to investigate its effect on the performance of the TODS algorithm. Figure 3.13(b) shows the processing time comparison of TODS when varying d from 0.0064 to 0.1024. There is little difference in the comparison results of TODS with different values, and TODS attains the best efficiency when $d = 0.0064$. TODS is almost insensitive to the value of d. The slight increase of execution time when the value of d increases is because more neighbors can be found within a larger d, and the computing costs of ldd and LAF increase accordingly.

(2) **Varying N:** Figure 3.13(c) shows the processing time comparison of OTODS when varying N ($N = 120$ s, 300 s and 600 s respectively), the *timebin* is set as 30 s, 60 s and 120 s, respectively. We observe that the processing time of the OTODS algorithm increases as the trajectory data continues to flow in, and it is modestly influenced by a larger window size. It is based on the fact that a larger window size leads to more incoming trajectories needing to be simplified into fragments and then detected for existing outliers. Even so, the processing time of the OTODS algorithm is only 59 s when $N = 600$ s.

(3) **Varying d_a:** Figure 3.13(d) shows the processing time comparison of OTODS when varying d_a from 0.0002 to 0.0032. With the increase of trajectory data, the execution time increases accordingly, and OTODS attains the best efficiency when $d_a = 0.0016$. This is due to the fact that a smaller d_a leads to substantial AFs, which increases the cost of searching the nearest AF for each incoming trajectory fragment and the computation overhead of ldd and LAF. From the above experimental results, we conclude that the TODS and OTODS algorithms can effectively identify outliers upon the trajectory stream, while OTODS is more efficient than TODS.

3.5 Related Work

Trajectory outlier detection is one of the most valuable analysis tasks. In different scenarios, the trajectory outlier has been characterized in diverse notions, such as abnormal sub-trajectory [Lee *et al.*, 2008a], abnormal trajectory [Knorr and Ng, 1998, 1999; Knorr *et al.*, 2000], abnormal moving objects [Yu *et al.*, 2014], abnormal road segments [Li *et al.*, 2009; Liu *et al.*, 2011; Chawla *et al.*, 2012; Pan *et al.*, 2013], abnormal events [Pan *et al.*, 2013], etc. Existing detection techniques [Mao *et al.*, 2017a] involve the classification-based approach [Li *et al.*, 2007; Yang *et al.*, 2013], historical similarity-based approach [Lei, 2016; Ge *et al.*, 2011; Liu *et al.*, 2014; Li *et al.*, 2009; Liu *et al.*, 2011; Chawla *et al.*, 2012; Pan *et al.*, 2013], distance-based approach [Knorr and Ng, 1998, 1999; Knorr *et al.*, 2000; Ramaswamy *et al.*, 2000; Lee *et al.*, 2008a; Bu *et al.*, 2009; Yu *et al.*, 2014], direction- and density-based approach [Ge *et al.*, 2010], isolation-based approach [Zhang *et al.*, 2011; Chen *et al.*, 2011, 2013], etc.

Anomaly detection in static trajectory data set. The most intuitive trajectory outlier detection technique is to build a classification model based on a labeled data set to differentiate an outlier from normal data [Li *et al.*, 2007; Yang *et al.*, 2013]. Nevertheless, it is difficult to obtain a good training data set for training and validating the anomaly detection model. Since the classification-based approach requires high computational stages to train and rebuild the classifier periodically, such an approach is not tailored to detect outliers upon streaming trajectories. The historical similarity-based approach attempts to construct a global feature model to detect outliers by mining frequent patterns on historical trajectories. Such a global feature model can attain higher detection precision by ignoring the evolutionary property in the streaming context [Ge *et al.*, 2010; Lei, 2016; Ge *et al.*, 2011; Liu *et al.*, 2014; Li *et al.*, 2009; Liu *et al.*, 2011; Chawla *et al.*, 2012; Pan *et al.*, 2013].

Nevertheless, the detection models built upon historical trajectories are still unable to identify new abnormal behaviors in trajectory streams. With no need of any prior distributional assumptions, the distance-based outlier detection approaches define outliers as trajectories that are far from most of the other trajectories. Knorr *et al.* (1998) regarded an object's whole trajectory as the basic unit and attempted to find an abnormal trajectory that stood it apart from the majority of the other trajectories.

In order to detect the abnormal sub-trajectory, Lee *et al.* (2008a) proposed a partition-and-detect framework (TRAOD method) that integrates the distance-based and density-based approaches. Before detecting a trajectory outlier, they partitioned the trajectories into line segments using an approximation method based on the minimum description length (MDL) principle. Due to an $O(n)$ time complexity of this approximate method, we adapt it to simplify the trajectory stream data, as illustrated in Section 3.3.1. But the TRAOD algorithm still focuses on discovering a few objects that are distant from most of the other objects. Additionally, the execution overhead of the distance-based approach is at least quadratic with respect to the number of trajectories, so it is unsuitable for streaming trajectories.

Anomaly detection in trajectory stream. The aforementioned approaches scan the data set multiple times, whereas the streaming outlier detection algorithms tend to run in a one-pass manner. Due to the huge volume, rapid updating, sparsity and skewed distribution of streaming trajectories, relatively few researches on outlier detection upon trajectory streams exist [Chen *et al.*, 2013; Bu *et al.*, 2009; Yu *et al.*, 2014].

By comparing the difference between historical trajectories and an ongoing trajectory, Chen *et al.* (2013) presented an *iBOAT* algorithm to detect anomalous sub-trajectories in real time. Bu *et al.* (2009) proposed a local clustering-based approach for identifying an outlying trajectory segment of single moving objects. To reduce the computation and memory costs in outlier detection, Bu *et al.* (2009) utilized a local cluster, a piecewise VP-tree based index structure and a minimum heap as a pruning mechanism. However, this approach is not well suited for the trajectory stream, which is populated with voluminous objects as the moving patterns get more complex and dynamic.

Aiming at discovering the abnormal moving objects over high-volume trajectory streams, Yu *et al.* (2014) presented neighbor-based trajectory outlier definitions (point neighbor-based outlier and trajectory neighbor-based outlier), which consider the spatial similarity among objects and the duration of spatial similarity over time. Then they proposed a MEX framework equipped with three fundamental optimization principles (minimal support examination, time-aware examination and lifetime-triggered detection) to detect both kinds of outliers.

Nevertheless, the above approaches determine the outlierness based solely on spatial proximity among trajectories. They fail to consider the difference of the moving behavior property among trajectories with respect to their neighbors. While such behavior difference indicates a semantic spatial relationship, this can be more valuable than spatial proximity in determining the cause of the outlierness.

Moreover, the aforementioned methods scarcely consider the evolutionary nature of a trajectory outlier. Therefore, they cannot be directly applied to solve our proposed outlier detection problem. In order to detect local outliers and evolving outliers with respect to their neighbors without the influence of noise disturbance, a feature grouping-based outlier detection technique is required to capture the behavior difference (or outlierness) among each trajectory and its local neighbors in real-time, and obtain the evolving outlierness of each trajectory by accumulating its historical outlierness and instant outlierness.

3.6 Conclusions

Existing outlier detection techniques on a trajectory stream determine the outlierness of trajectories based upon a spatial proximity relationship. However, cannot discover the outliers that have numerous close neighbors, while behaving differently from their neighbors. In this chapter, we first divided the features of the trajectory into two groups (*Similarity Feature* and *Difference Feature*), and addressed the issue of identifying local and evolutionary trajectory outliers online. On this basis we proposed a framework to identify outliers upon streaming trajectories. It consists of two components — the trajectory simplification phase and the outlier detection phase. We presented a basic algorithm (TODS) and an optimized algorithm (OTODS) that incorporates a new data structure (*Ally Fragment*) to detect both types of outliers. We validated our proposal for effectiveness and efficiency by conducting extensive experiments on three real data sets, and show that our proposed algorithms are efficient in continuously detecting both types of outliers upon trajectory streams.

Chapter 4

Online Analyzing upon Distributed
Trajectory Streams

4.1 Background

The proliferating deployments of positioning devices and surveillance equipments have expedited exponential growth of position stream data arriving from disparate sources. For instance, the surveillance inspection spots deployed in city traffic crossroads record the information of passing vehicles and their moving behavior characteristics (e.g., speed) in real time. These are then transmitted through leased lines to the servers of the traffic control centers in their respective regions.

The sequences of positions received continuously by the servers in various regions form distributed trajectory streams. This necessitates efficient streaming analysis to extract timely insights to meet the needs of real-time applications. Centralizing the massively distributed trajectory streams to the central server and then analyzing them afterwards raises the issue of computing and storage capacities. Thus, the whole analyzing process should be distributed throughout the entire network of nodes (servers). With the advent of open-source distributed frameworks like Spark and Storm, exploiting the distributed solution for trajectory analysis becomes possible. In this chapter, we are primarily concerned with designing highly scalable decentralized clustering and outlier detection methods over distributed trajectory streams.

In a bid to cluster or identify the outliers upon streaming trajectories, we present a framework to cluster evolving streaming trajectories using the sliding-window model in Chapter 2. We will then propose a *feature-grouping based* outlier detection framework to estimate the moving behavioral outlierness of trajectories with regard to their neighbors in Chapter 3. Nevertheless, these techniques cannot be directly applied to distributed streaming cases owing to the following challenges. First, the trajectory data distribution is highly skewed and changes over time. Accordingly, clusters and outliers may behave differently across various regions and evolve gradually. To address this issue, the clusters and outliers shall be initially tracked on the remote site. In addition, the global clusters and evolving abnormal entities are discovered by the coordinator site, which has been continuously gathering results from the remote sites. Another noticeable problem is that clustering and outlier detection needs to be executed in a timely manner to ensure preventive actions can be taken as early as possible. This involves two key issues, one is to exploit efficient parallel processing processes of the remote sites and the other is to reduce the amount of data to be transferred among the sites during the whole execution procedure.

To tackle the above mentioned issues, we will propose a distributed clustering framework and a distributed outlier detection framework upon trajectory streams in this chapter. Both these frameworks consist of the parallel processing component on the remote sites and the global processing component on a single coordinator site.

First, in order to keep track of the evolving clusters in distributed trajectory data streams, we present a distributed synopsis structure to extract the clustering characteristic of the trajectory cluster. On the basis of that, with the aim of reducing the transferring overheads and improving the clustering performance upon the distributed trajectory streams, we develop an incremental algorithm for online clustering upon the distributed trajectory streams (called OCluDTS). The OCluDTS algorithm leverages the sliding-window model and consists of two phases. At the first phase (the local clustering phase), the most recently arrived sets of trajectories at each time instant in the current time window for all the remote sites are conducted clustering in parallel to obtain the local clustering results. At the second phase (the local clustering results merging phase), the local clustering results of all the remote sites are transferred to the coordinator to participate in the re-clustering process to derive the global clustering results.

Second, we propose the first distributed *feature-grouping based* outlier detection framework to identify outliers upon trajectory streams. It consists of parallel outlier detection on the remote sites and evolving anomaly object detection on a single coordinator. For the remote sites, the trajectory fragments derived by trajectory simplification are grouped into clusters, and then detection is implemented to output the trajectory fragment (or fragment cluster) outlier based on the behavior dissimilarity in relation to their respective neighborhoods. For the coordinator, upon receiving the trajectory fragment outliers detected by the remote sites, the outlierness duration of the corresponding object is updated and checked to see whether it exceeds the given anomaly timebin count threshold to pinpoint the evolutionary anomaly object.

The remainder of this chapter is structured as follows. In Sections 4.2 and 4.3, we outline the preliminary concepts as well as the schemes, and elaborate on the details of two methods. In Section 4.4, a series of performance evaluations on various data sets are given. Section 4.5 reviews the related work in literature. Finally, in Section 4.6, we succinctly conclude this chapter.

4.2 Online Clustering Over Distributed Trajectory Streams

4.2.1 *Problem definition*

In this chapter, we consider a distributed-computing environment with a single coordinator and M remote sites. Let S denote a set of local trajectory streams received by M remote sites, i.e., $S = \cup_{k=1}^{M} S_k$. The local stream, S_k, located at the kth remote site is defined here as follows.

Definition 4.1 (Local Trajectory Stream). The local trajectory stream, $S_k = \{p_1^1, p_1^2, p_1^3, \ldots, p_2^1, \ldots\}$, refers to the infinite sequence of position points of multiple moving objects that are received by the kth remote site, and p_i^j is the location (latitude and longitude) of one object, o^j, at timestamp, t_i, in 2D space, i.e., $p_i^j = (x_i^j, y_i^j)$.

In order to assess the data distribution of the trajectory in real time, incoming data needs to be clustered online in recent time intervals. The infinite trajectory data stream can be split into multiple finite sub-trajectory streams using the sliding-window model. It ensures that the clustering analysis will only handle the latest trajectory data in the current time window. Therefore, the trajectory data that arrives at each remote site can be transformed into the finite data set in a fixed time interval using the time-based sliding-window model. This enables us to extract and incrementally maintain the clustering characteristic of most recently arrived trajectories, and further reduce the influence of concept drifting on clustering accuracy.

Definition 4.2 (Local Stream of Time-based Sliding Window). Given a local trajectory stream, S_k, a window size, W and a starting timestamp, t_s, a local trajectory stream using a time-based sliding window (denoted as S_k^W) is a finite set of stream elements with $S_k^W = \{p_s^1, p_s^2, \ldots, p_{s+W-1}^1, p_{s+W-1}^j \cdots\}$.

The sliding-window model enables clustering to be implemented on the most recent arrived trajectories at any time, while the trajectory data before the current time window is viewed as inactive. Each two consecutive location points (p_i, p_{i+1}) are connected into one trajectory line segment, L_i, accordingly. The trajectories of the moving objects are regarded as the sets of line segments, i.e., $\{L_1, L_2, \ldots, \}$. Clustering for the trajectory line segments in the current time window needs to measure the similarity among line segments. According to Definition 2.7, the similarity between any two trajectory line segments is depicted as the linear sum of the spatial proximity and temporal closeness between line segments.

To guarantee real-time clustering on trajectory data, it is imperative to reduce the transferring overheads between the remote sites and the coordinator (i.e., data transfer volume) as much as possible. In our work, it manifests as the size of the local clustering result that was transferred from the remote sites to the coordinator. Toward this end, a two-layer compact synopsis data structure, called *Exponential Histogram of Distributed Temporal Trajectory Cluster Feature* (or DF for short), is defined. Each bucket of a DF that is divided according to the arrival time is a *Distributed Temporal Trajectory Cluster Feature* (or TF^D for short), which attempts to summarize the features of the latest arrived trajectory line segments in a local stream at each time instant. Also, we use the *Minimum Bounding Rectangle* (or MBR for short) to represent the spatial range of all the line segments incorporated in a TF^D.

Definition 4.3 (Distributed Temporal Trajectory Cluster Feature (or TF^D for short)). Given a set of consecutive trajectory line segments, $C = \{L_1, L_2, \ldots, L_n\}$, received by any remote site at current time, TF^D, is of the form $(\text{LS}_{\text{cen}}, \text{LS}_p, \text{LS}_{\text{len}}, BL, \text{TR}, n, t)$.

- LS_{cen}: The linear sum of the line segments' center points;
- LS_P: Linear sum of the product of the line segments' angle and length;
- LS_{len}: Linear sum of the line segments' length;
- BL: The bottom left corner of the MBR;
- TR: The top right corner of the MBR;
- n: The number of line segments;
- t: The timestamp of the most recent line segment.

Similar to Chapter 2, we can draw a line segment to represent the moving pattern of TF^D in terms of the central point (cen $= \text{LS}_{\text{cen}}/n$) and the angle ($\theta = \text{LS}_P/\text{LS}_{\text{len}}$). The two intersection points are treated as the starting and ending points of the representative trajectory line segment, denoted as TF^D.rp$_s$ and TF^D.rp$_e$.

To ensure that the obsolete clustering characteristics can be eliminated effectively, on the basis of the *Exponential Histogram*, we exploit a synopsis structure here as follows.

Definition 4.4 (Exponential Histogram of Distributed Temporal Trajectory Cluster Feature (or DF for short)). Given an error threshold, ϵ, DF is a collection of multilevel TF^{D}s on the subsets $(C_1, C_i, C_j, \ldots (1 \leq i < j))$ of a trajectory cluster that arrived at a remote site with the following constraints:

1. $|C_1| = 1$;
2. $\forall i \geq 2$, $|C_i| = |C_{i-1}|$ or $|C_i| = 2 \cdot |C_{i-1}|$;

3. When $|C_i| = 2^l$, the level of C_i is named as l, and the number of TF^Ds in l-level is at most $\lceil\frac{1}{\epsilon}\rceil + 1$.

Similar to Chapter 2, we obtain a representative line segment for a *DF* in terms of the central point (cen $= (\sum_i \mathrm{TF}^D_i.\mathrm{cen} \times \mathrm{TF}^D_i.n)/(\sum_i \mathrm{TF}^D_i.n))$ and the angle ($\theta = (\sum_i \mathrm{TF}^D_i.\theta \times \mathrm{TF}^D_i.n)/(\sum_i \mathrm{TF}^D_i.n))$. The two-layer ($\mathrm{TF}^D$ and DF) synopsis structure enables us to extract the clustering characteristics of the trajectory data at different intervals. This satisfies the compact requirement of distributed trajectory stream data processing as well as local clustering result transferring, and further reduces the amount of data transferred. In addition, the DF synopsis can promptly remove the influence of obsolete trajectories when clustering, and hence avoids concept drifting.

Finally, we summarize the problem definition here as follows.

Given a union of local trajectory streams within a sliding window of size, W, that is distributed in M remote sites, our goal is to group the data of all the local trajectory streams that flow into the current time window, into different clusters according to the spatio-temporal similarity.

4.2.2 Overview

Consider a distributed-computing environment with a single coordinator and M remote sites. As illustrated in Figure 4.1, the local trajectory stream arrives at each remote site continuously, and the task of the coordinator is to receive the clustering request and return the global clustering result. Transferring the local trajectory stream data from all the remote sites to the coordinator and then conducting clustering would lead to a great amount of computation and communication overheads. Instead of that, a more feasible solution is to implement clustering for the respective local stream on each remote site in parallel and finally merge the local clustering results, which can improve the efficiency of online clustering upon distributed trajectory streams.

In this chapter, we first propose an online algorithm to cluster distributed trajectory streams using the sliding-window model, called OCluDTS. It is composed of two basic executive processes, i.e., clustering upon the local trajectory stream that is received at each remote site in

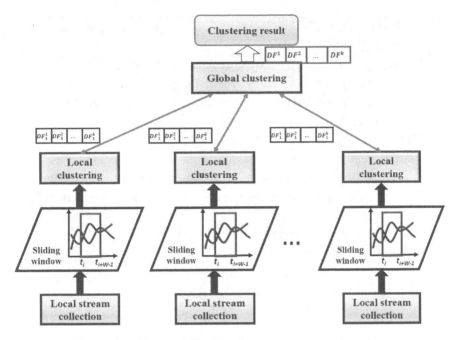

Figure 4.1. Frame of distributed trajectory stream clustering.

parallel, and global clustering of the coordinator upon all the received local clustering results. In a bid to reduce the communication overhead, the local clustering result is represented by the compact synopsis data structure (Definition 4.4), which is leveraged by the remote sites and the coordinator. At every time instant in the current time window, the coordinator only conducts clustering by merging the local clustering results transferred from the remote sites. This guarantees better clustering accuracy while saving a large amount of communication overheads and computation overheads. The detailed description of the OCluDTS algorithm is presented in Algorithm 10.

First, the local trajectory stream data that arrived at each remote site is split into a set of trajectory data within limited time horizons using the sliding-window model, and implemented using the local clustering analysis. Subsequently, every remote site sends its respective clustering result (represented as k' DFs, here $k' < k$) in real time to the coordinator, and the coordinator would recluster all the local

---

Algorithm 10: OCluDTS (Online Clustering over Distributed Trajectory Streams)

Input: $\{S_1, S_2, \ldots S_M\}$: A set of local trajectory streams; W: sliding window size; ϵ: error threshold; k: maximum number of DFs on the coordinator, and t_c: current time instant;

Output: Z: Set of all generated DFs at t_c;

1 **foreach** *remote site* **do**

2 | /*Upon arrival of new trajectory data at t_c, Cluster them and send the clustering result (i.e., k' DFs) to the coordinator*/;

3 | $Z_i \leftarrow \emptyset$;

4 | /*Let Z_i denote the set of DFs on the ith remote site*/;

5 | Initialize Z_i;

6 | **foreach** *line segment L_q in S_i* **do**

7 | | find the most similar DF (denoted as h);

8 | | **if** $\text{Diff}(h.rp, L_q) < d_{\min}$ **then**

9 | | | Absorb(L_q, h);

10 | | **else**

11 | | | **if** $|Z_i| < k'$ **then**

12 | | | | create a DF (denoted as h_{new}) that absorbed a $\text{TF}_0^D(L_q)$;

13 | | | | $Z_i \leftarrow Z_i \cup h_{\text{new}}$;

14 | | | **else**

15 | | | | **if** $\exists h_o \in Z_i, (|t_c - h_o.t| \geq W)$ **then**

16 | | | | | $Z_i \leftarrow Z_i \setminus \{h_o\}$;

17 | | | | **else**

18 | | | | | find the most similar DF pair to merge;

19 | Send Z_i to the coordinator;

Algorithm 10: (*Continued*)

---

20 **for** *the coordinator* **do**

21 | /*Receive the local clustering results from M remote sites, i.e., $M \cdot k'$ DFs, and re-cluster them to output the global clustering result (denoted as Z, i.e., k DFs)*/;

22 | **while** *receive Z_j from the jth remote site* **do**

23 | | $Z \leftarrow Z \cup Z_j$;

24 | | $j \leftarrow j + 1$;

25 | | **if** $|Z| > k$ **then**

26 | | | find the most similar DFs pair to merge;

27 | | **if** $j = M$ **then**

28 | | | break;

29 | $j \leftarrow 0$;

30 | **return** Z;

---

clustering results (represented as $M \cdot k'$ DFs) from M remote sites, and then output the global clustering result (represented as k DFs). This two-phase strategy of clustering on local trajectory stream data and then merging the local clustering results afterwards can ensure the same high accuracy as centralized clustering upon the trajectory stream. Moreover, rather than centralizing the massively distributed trajectory streams to the coordinator and then clustering them, the OCluDTS approach simply considers transferring the local clustering results from the remote sites to the coordinator. This sharply reduces the communication cost among the nodes and further improves the executive efficacy of the distributed algorithm.

4.2.2.1 *Parallel clustering of the remote sites*

The remote site conducts clustering by organizing incoming trajectory streams within each time window into micro-batches. The sliding-window model ensures that the remote site processes the trajectory data in real time, which involves clustering the newly arrived data while eliminating the influence of obsolete data. Subsequently, the remote site sends its local clustering result to the coordinator (lines 1–9 in Algorithm 10). If Z_i denotes the set of DFs on the ith remote site, then the size of Z_i is at most k'. It means that no more than k' DFs is maintained in the memory on the remote site at any time.

Similar to Chapter 2, when a line segment, L_q, arrives, we attempt to find its most similar DF (denote as h) from the existing DFs, and absorb it into h. If none of the most similar DF is found, a new DF that absorbs TF($\{L_q\}$) would be created on the condition that the number of DFs is less than k'. Once the number of DFs exceeds k', we eliminate the obsolete DFs and then merge the most similar DFs. The detailed procedures for absorbing L_q into h and merging the most similar DFs are similar to Algorithms 3 and 4.

In the actual applications, the trajectory data that arrived at each remote site is skewed. In extreme cases, a few remote sites would not receive any new trajectories due to no moving objects passing by. It is imperative to design an effective mechanism to regularly check whether any outdated trajectory data exists on all remote sites, in addition to the moving objects that visit frequently. Toward this end, we check all the nodes to find and eliminate the least recent updated DFs, to lessen the influence of outdated trajectory data on clustering quality.

4.2.2.2 *Global clustering of the coordinator*

As the remote sites only conduct clustering on their respective arrived local trajectory stream data, the cluster that resides on the boundary of the cross-regions may be split into several sub-clusters on different remote sites. To solve this issue, the local clustering results of all the remote sites shall, at each time instant, be re-clustered to derive the final global clustering result, i.e., k DFs (lines 20–30 in Algorithm 10). Specifically, upon receiving the local clustering results from any remote sites, the coordinator conducts pairwise similarity comparisons between DFs to find the most similar clusters pair according to the given distance threshold. If found, the clusters pair would be merged into one cluster. At most k clusters would be kept on the coordinator, and the value of k is determined by the maximum memory processing capability of the coordinator. Since the clusters are represented by their respective representative trajectory line segments, clustering on the local clustering results (at most $M \cdot k'$ DFs) is actually to implement clustering on $M \cdot k'$ representative line segments. Note that the clustering technique can be any weighted clustering analysis method, including the partition-based, hierarchical merging, or density-based method.

4.2.2.3 *Time complexity analysis*

As compared to clustering through centralizing the distributed trajectory stream data, the distributed clustering mechanism that divides the whole computation load into multiple remote sites to conduct clustering in parallel obviously reduces the total execution overhead of clustering. The execution overhead of the OCluDTS algorithm is composed of two parts: (i) the operational overheads of parallel clustering on the remote sites (denoted as $Cp_i(1 \leq i \leq M)$) and global clustering on the coordinator (denoted as Cp_c), and (ii) the time to transfer local clustering results from the remote sites to the coordinator (denoted as $Cm_i(1 \leq i \leq M)$).

Let n denote the amount of the incoming trajectory data for all the remote sites at the current time instant, and n_{max} ($n_{max} > n/M$) and n_{min} ($0 \leq n_{min} \leq n/M$) denote the maximum number and minimum number of the incoming data on the individual remote site, respectively. Then the cost of local clustering involves that of searching for the most similar DF for L_q $O(n_{max} \cdot k)$, merging the most similar DFs pair $O(k'^2)$, and eliminating the obsolete DFs pair $O(k')$. Thus, the value of Cp_i at most reaches $O(n_{max} \cdot k + k'^2 + k')$. When the amount of trajectory data received by the remote site at a certain time instant is quite large, we have $n_{max} \gg k'$, and Cp_i approximately takes $O(n_{max} \cdot k')$. For the coordinator, Cp_c is mainly used to conduct pairwise similarity comparisons between DFs to merge the most similar DFs pair, which at most takes $O(M^2 \cdot k'^2)$.

Due to the uneven distribution of trajectory stream data and different processing capability of the remote sites, the total overhead of transferring the local clustering results from the remote sites to the coordinator is less than the sum of serial transmission costs of all the remote sites. Cm_i can be calculated by the gap between the starting time instant of the first transmission remote site and the ending time instant of the last transmission remote site. Let $|DF|$ denote the size of

DF, then the maximum transmission cost of the remote site takes $O(n_{max} - n_{min} + |DF|) \cdot k')$.

4.2.2.4 *Optimization strategy*

To improve the performance of the OCluDTS algorithm, we take into account the reduction of the computation cost and communication overhead. Firstly, during the process of re-clustering on the local clustering results, the number of pairwise similarity comparisons between DFs takes $O(M^2 \cdot k'^2)$, which requires extremely high computation overhead as the number of remote sites increases. The times where comparison is carried out shall be reduced substantially to lower the computation overhead. In the actual applications, the distributed trajectory data stream is obtained by the independent gathering of central servers deployed in various regions. At any time, a trajectory and those from the distant regions cannot be absorbed into the same cluster. In view of this, when the coordinator conducts pairwise similarity comparisons, each local clustering result (k' DFs) only needs to be compared with those from its adjacent regions. That is, pairwise similarity comparisons simply require to be implemented between any remote site and its neighbor sites, which helps to lessen the calculation cost of re-clustering. Let M' ($M' < M/2$) denote the maximum number of neighboring sites of any remote site, then the global clustering on the coordinator, Cp_c, is at most $O(M \cdot M' \cdot k'^2)$.

Secondly, since the clustering algorithm upon distributed trajectory streams is limited by the network bandwidth, the communication overhead inevitably becomes the bottleneck of the algorithm. As compared to directly transferring the local trajectory stream data, the OCluDTS algorithm only needs to transfer the local clustering results (represented by the synopsis data structure, i.e., DFs) between the remote sites and the coordinator, which significantly reduces the communication overhead. However, with the increase of the number of remote sites, it still requires much transmission costs. To further boost the capability of the distributed algorithm, it is imperative to shorten the time of transferring the local clustering results as soon as possible.

In addition, the skew distribution property of a trajectory in road network scenarios may manifest itself where some roads have a small number of trajectories during a long time period, while other few roads have a myriad of trajectories in short time periods. As the trajectories of most regions keep data locality for a short time, i.e., without significant clustering distribution changes, the remote site that has no clustering distribution changes at the current time instant is not required to transfer the clustering result to the coordinator.

In particular, each remote site needs to calculate the gap between the average SSQ value (denoted as $AverageSSQ_c$) of the clustering results obtained at the current time instant and that (denoted as $AverageSSQ_p$) obtained at the previous time instant. Given a threshold, δ, the remote site is regarded as unchanged iff $|AverageSSQ_c - AverageSSQ_p| < \delta(\delta \le 0.0001)$, and it does not need to transfer its clustering result to the coordinator. When processing the big data, the above optimization strategy will reduce the transferring data amount and keep the computation cost of re-clustering of the coordinator down. Based on the pruning mechanism of the similarity calculation as well as the optimization strategy of the "test first and transfer later", the OCluDTS algorithm could achieve the significant performance gains.

4.3 Outlier Detection Over Distributed Trajectory Streams

4.3.1 *Problem definition*

To guarantee that various moving objects of different sampling rates report their locations at least once in a time interval, the term "timebin" is used to describe a basic time interval (represented by m timestamps, here $m \ge 1$). As new position points arrive continuously, the local trajectory stream is typically processed in a *sliding window*. Here, the *time-based sliding window* model is leveraged. Let N represent the window size and T_c denote the current timebin; only the most recent stream elements p_{T_i} ($T_c - N + 1 \le T_i \le T_c$) are implemented outlier detection. Whenever the window slides forward, it moves forward by 1 timebin.

It is space-efficient to summarize each trajectory by reserving a small number of sample points. Similar to Chapter 3, each trajectory is simplified into a set of characteristic points via trajectory simplification, and every two consecutive characteristic points are connected into a trajectory fragment, denoted as tf. A trajectory thus becomes an ordered sequence of fragments. Let $F = f_1, \ldots, f_L$ denote L features extracted from the attributes of trajectories, and the features are divided into two groups: *Similarity Feature* $(f_1, \ldots, f_b)$, or SF for short, e.g., latitude and longitude coordinates, which are used to find the spatial neighbors for each trajectory fragment, and *Difference Feature* $(f_{b+1}, \ldots, f_L)$, or DF for short, e.g., speed, direction, etc., which are used to identify the trajectory fragment whose motion behavior is obviously distinct from its vicinity.

Let $w_1, \ldots, w_L$ denote the weight of L features separately, and $\text{dis}_l(\text{tf}_i, \text{tf}_j)$ denote the distance between tf_i and tf_j by the feature, f_l. Here, $\text{dis}_l(\text{tf}_i, \text{tf}_j)$ can be any typical distance metric (e.g., Euclidean, LCSS and DTW, etc.). Furthermore, Diff_1 (or Diff_2) denotes the distance between tf_i and tf_j by SF (or DF), i.e., $\text{Diff}_1(\text{tf}_i, \text{tf}_j) = \sum_{l=1}^{b} w_l \cdot \text{dis}_l(\text{tf}_i, \text{tf}_j)$ and $\text{Diff}_2(\text{tf}_i, \text{tf}_j) = \sum_{l=b+1}^{L} w_l \cdot \text{dis}_l(\text{tf}_i, \text{tf}_j)$.

Given a proximity threshold d $(d > 0)$, trajectory fragments can be grouped into clusters (denoted as FC) in terms of the distance (Diff_1) between the fragments by SF, and the fragments inside a cluster are neighbors to each other. The aggregated summarization of FC can be maintained using the synopsis data structure, called the Fragment Cluster Feature (CF).

Definition 4.5 (Fragment Cluster Feature, CF). CF of a fragment cluster, $\text{FC}_i = \{\text{tf}_1, \text{tf}_2, \ldots, \text{tf}_n\}$, is of the form $(\text{ls}_{\text{cen}}, \text{ls}_p, \text{ls}_{\text{len}}, \text{ls}_{\text{df}}, \text{cor}_{\text{bl}}, \text{cor}_{\text{tr}}, n)$.

- ls_{cen}: The linear sum of the fragments' center points;
- ls_p: The linear sum of the product of the fragments' angle and length;
- ls_{len}: The linear sum of the fragments' length;
- ls_{df}: The linear sum of the fragments' weighted sum of DF;
- cor_{bl}: The bottom left corner of MBR;
- cor_{tr}: The top right corner of MBR;
- n: The number of fragments.

The Minimum Bounding Rectangle (MBR, for short) is leveraged to represent the spatial region of each cluster. The representative fragment, rp_i, of a fragment cluster FC_i can be derived using the method in Chapter 2. We first obtain the central point and the angle with $\frac{\text{ls}_{\text{cen}}}{n}$ and $\frac{\text{ls}_p}{\text{ls}_{\text{len}}}$, respectively. Then a line is plotted across the central point, along the angle, and extended to reach the borders of the MBR. The intersection points are regarded as the starting and ending points of rp_i.

Hereafter, in order to identify an anomaly fragment cluster, one needs to detect an anomaly representative fragment. Whether it is an anomaly trajectory fragment or anomaly representative fragment detection at T_c, the key step is to estimate the anomaly degree of a trajectory fragment, tf_i (or representative fragment rp_i), with regard to its neighborhood (denoted as $N_{T_c}(tf_i)$ or $N_{T_c}(rp_i)$). $N_{T_c}(tf_i)$ includes the other fragments within the cluster that tf_i belongs to. $N_{T_c}(rp_i)$ includes the representative fragments of FC_i's neighboring clusters in terms of a given proximity threshold, d_c $(d_c > d)$ by SF.

Here, we employ the concepts of *local difference density* (ldd) and *local anomaly factor* (LAF) in Chapter 3. ldd is defined as the inverse of the average difference of each fragment to its neighbors by DF, i.e., $ldd_{T_c}(tf_i) = \frac{|N_{T_c}(tf_i)|}{\sum_{tf_j \in N_{T_c}(tf_i)} \text{Diff}_2(tf_i, tf_j)}$. The LAF is used to measure the probability of the fragment being an outlier based on ldd, i.e., $LAF_{T_c}(tf_i) = \frac{\sum_{tf_j \in N_{T_c}(tf_i)} \frac{ldd_{T_c}(tf_j)}{ldd_{T_c}(tf_i)}}{|N_{T_c}(tf_i)|}$. In general, a higher value of LAF indicates that a trajectory fragment (or fragment cluster) is more likely to be an outlier.

Definition 4.6 (Anomaly Trajectory Fragment). Given a local outlier threshold ρ $(\rho > 1)$, trajectory fragment, tf_i, at timebin, T_c, is called a fragment outlier (or *F-outlier*, for short), iff $LAF_{T_c}(tf_i) > \rho$.

Definition 4.7 (Anomaly Fragment Cluster). Given a local cluster outlier threshold, ρ_c $(\rho_c \geq \rho)$, a fragment cluster, FC_i, and its representative fragment, rp_i, FC_i at timebin, T_c, is identified as a fragment cluster outlier (or FC-*outlier*, for short), iff $LAF_{T_c}(rp_i) > \rho_c$.

Considering the evolving nature of streaming trajectories, the object with abnormal fragments in several timebins (maybe inconsecutive) is intrinsically an abnormal moving object. To verify the abnormal moving property of the object, we shall continuously observe the objects that have anomaly trajectory fragments in the current time window. As the objects usually move across various regions, the trajectories of the objects would arrive at several remote sites.

To identify the evolutionary anomaly object, the anomaly trajectory fragments detected by the remote sites need to be transferred to the coordinator at per timebin. The coordinator sets a list (denoted as list_{O_i}) of anomaly timebins for the object, O_i, that has an anomaly fragment, and conducts an object outlier detection by judging whether the size of list_{O_i} (denoted as $|\text{list}_{O_i}|$) reaches the given threshold, thr_a.

Definition 4.8 (Evolutionary Anomaly Object). Given an anomaly timebin count threshold, thr_a ($\frac{N}{3} \leq \text{thr}_a < N$), an object, O_i, at timebin, T_c, is an evolutionary object outlier (or EO-*outlier*, for short), iff $|\text{list}_{O_i}| \geq \text{thr}_a$.

Problem statement. Given a local outlier threshold, ρ and ρ_c, anomaly timebin count threshold, thr_a, and a union of local trajectory streams within a sliding window of size N that is distributed in multiple remote sites, our goal is to continuously detect F-*outlier*, FC-*outlier* and EO-*outlier* over distributed trajectory streams.

4.3.2 *Overview*

In this section, we propose a distributed framework, called ODDTS, to continuously identify trajectory outliers over distributed streams. Our distributed solution is inherently parallel and can perform on any modern distributed infrastructure. In subsequent experiments, we use Spark to perform an analysis by organizing incoming trajectory streams within each time window into micro-batches, which need to be as small as possible to guarantee low latency. ODDTS consists of remote site processing and coordinator processing; the detailed description is outlined in Algorithm 11.

At each timebin, the workflow is summarized as: (i) Remote site processing (lines 1–3), including (a) trajectory simplifying and clustering: incoming trajectory data is simplified into fragments and then grouped into clusters, and (b) F-*outlier* and FC-*outlier* detection: F-*outlier* and FC-*outlier* are identified according to behavior dissimilarities among trajectory fragments (or representative fragments) and their respective neighborhoods, and (ii) coordinator processing, EO-*outlier* detection: on the basis of F-*outlier*s transferred by the remote sites, the timebin for

---

Algorithm 11: ODDTS (Outlier Detection over Distributed Trajectory Streams)

Input: S: A trajectory stream which consists of M subsets in current time window;

Output: (1) A_F: A set of *F-outliers*;

(2) A_{FC}: A set of FC-*outliers*;

(3) A_O: A set of EO-*outliers*;

1 **foreach** *remote site* **do**

2   Upon arrival of new trajectory data, detect *F-outliers*, (A_F), and FC-*outliers*, (A_{FC}), by implementing FCD algorithm;

3   Send A_F to the coordinator;

4 **for** *the coordinator* **do**

5   Upon receiving A_F from any remote site, detect EO-*outliers*, (A_O), by implementing EOD algorithm;

6 **return** A_F, A_{FC} *and* A_O;

---

identifying *F-outlier* is inserted into the anomaly timebin list of the object that *F-outlier* belongs to. Then the size of the anomaly timebin list of the influenced object is updated and compared with the given threshold, thr_a, to identify the EO-*outlier* (lines 4–5).

In our distributed environment, the remote sites only communicate with the coordinator, whose function is to implement efficient outlier detection in parallel while minimizing the communication cost between the coordinator and the remote sites during the detection process.

4.3.2.1 *Remote site processing*

The main tasks of the remote sites are to implement outlier detection on respective incoming trajectory data in parallel and return detection results to the coordinator in a timely manner. The detailed description of the parallel outlier detection algorithm (or FCD, for short) is presented in Algorithm 12. Initially, incoming trajectories are split into a set of consecutive trajectory fragments with the least information loss. Through trajectory simplifying (denoted by TraSimp), a small number of characteristic points are derived from raw trajectories using the method

---

Algorithm 12: FCD (*F*-outlier and *FC*-outlier Detection)

Input: S_k: A local trajectory stream at T_c and ρ, ρ_c: the local outlier thresholds;

Output: (1) A_F: A set of *F*-outliers;

       (2) A_{FC}: A set of FC-*outliers*;

1 **foreach** *trajectory,* Tr, *in* S_k **do**

2    $\text{Tr}_{\text{simp}} \leftarrow \text{TraSimp}(Tr)$;

3    $\text{Tr}_{\text{all}} \leftarrow \text{Tr}_{\text{all}} \cup \text{Tr}_{\text{simp}}$;

4 Generate a set of trajectory fragments, TF_c, from Tr_{all};

5 Group the trajectory fragments of, TF_c, into FCs according to d;

6 **foreach** *trajectory fragment,* tf_i, *in each* FC **do**

7    $\text{LAF}_{T_c}(\text{tf}_i) \leftarrow \dfrac{\sum_{\text{tf}_j \in N_{T_c}(\text{tf}_i)} \frac{\text{ldd}_{T_c}(\text{tf}_j)}{\text{ldd}_{T_c}(\text{tf}_i)}}{|N_{T_c}(\text{tf}_i)|}$;

8   **if** $\text{LAF}_{T_c}(\text{tf}_i) > \rho$ **then**

9       $A_F \leftarrow A_F \cup \{\text{tf}_i\}$;

10 **foreach** *fragment cluster,* FC_i, **do**

11   Derive its representative fragment, rp_i ;

12 **foreach** *representative fragment,* rp_i, **do**

13   Find its spatial neighbors, $N_{T_c}(\text{rp}_i)$, according to d_c;

14    $\text{LAF}_{T_c}(\text{rp}_i) \leftarrow \dfrac{\sum_{\text{rp}_j \in N_{T_c}(\text{rp}_i)} \frac{\text{ldd}_{T_c}(\text{rp}_j)}{\text{ldd}_{T_c}(\text{rp}_i)}}{|N_{T_c}(\text{rp}_i)|}$;

15   **if** $\text{LAF}_{T_c}(\text{rp}_i) > \rho_c$ **then**

16       $A_{FC} \leftarrow A_{FC} \cup \{\text{FC}_i\}$;

17 **return** A_F *and* A_{FC};

---

in Mao *et al.* (2017b), and every two consecutive characteristic points are connected into a trajectory fragment (lines 1–4). To identify the outlier with respect to its spatial neighborhood, the trajectory fragments are grouped into clusters (FCs) via hierarchical clustering according to the proximity threshold, d (line 5). Here, a STR-*tree* index technique is leveraged to accelerate clustering.

For *F-outlier* detection, each trajectory fragment shall be measured by the abnormality degree of its motion behavior relative to the others in the same cluster, which involves the calculations of ldd and LAF (lines 6–7). Through comparing the values of ldd between each trajectory fragment and its vicinity by DF, we derive the value of LAF for each fragment at T_c. The trajectory fragments with LAF's values exceeding ρ are reported as *F-outlier*s (lines 8–9). Then, the object that *F-outlier* belongs to is treated as an EO-*outlier* candidate and is transferred to the coordinator. For FC-*outlier* detection, to identify an anomaly fragment cluster is to essentially detect anomaly representative fragments as relative to its neighboring representative fragments. Specifically, for each fragment cluster, we obtain its representative fragment (lines 10–11) and search for its neighboring representative fragments that are within distance, d_c (lines 12–13) by SF from it. Then the value of ldd of each representative fragment is derived by comparing the distance between itself and its neighboring representative fragments by DF. The LAF's value of each representative fragment is also derived and used to detect FC-*outlier* in terms of the local anomaly threshold, ρ_c (lines 14–16).

Pruning step. The most time consuming part of this phase is the ldd calculation, which involves pairwise difference calculations among trajectory fragments within a cluster and that among neighboring representative fragments. Costs of ldd calculations would become comparatively expensive, especially when massive amount of trajectories arrive at one timebin. To speed up *F-outlier* and FC-*outlier* detection, unnecessary ldd calculations need to be pruned.

After clustering trajectory fragments, the mean of the fragments' weighted sum of a DF within a cluster is derived by $\frac{\text{ls}_{df}}{n}$, denoted as AVG_{DF}. During *F-outlier* detection, only the trajectory fragment whose weighted sum of DF higher (or lower) than μ times of AVG_{DF} ($\mu > 1$) shall compute the values of ldd and LAF. Also, the mean of the representative fragments' weighted sum of DF within a similar neighborhood can be derived, and on the basis of which the representative fragments with weighted sum of DF higher (or lower) than μ times of that mean, needs a ldd and LAF calculation. When such a pruning step can quickly eliminate the need of examining a large number of fragments, the operational overhead of the ldd calculation is sharply reduced and the parallel outlier detection process achieves significant performance gain.

4.3.2.2 *Coordinator processing*

With the evolution of trajectories, a moving object which has anomaly trajectory fragments in several timebins (maybe inconsecutive) is intrinsically an object outlier, e.g., a speeding car. It is desirable to exploit a procedure to track the evolving abnormal behaviors of objects from the starting timebin to the recent timebin in the current time window. At each timebin, upon receiving the detected results (i.e., EO-*outlier* candidates) from the remote sites, the coordinator would implement an EO-*outlier* detection called EOD, whose detailed description is given in Algorithm 13. In the current time window, the timebin for identifying the object O_i's fragment as a *F-outlier* is viewed as an

---

Algorithm 13: EOD (<u>E</u>volutionary Moving <u>O</u>bject <u>D</u>etection)

    Input: A_F: A set of *F-outlier*, and thr_a: the anomaly timebin
          count threshold;

    Output: A_O: A set of EO-*outliers*;

1 **foreach** *F-outlier* in A_F **do**

2   Obtain the object ID (denoted as O_i) that *F-outlier* belongs to;

3   **if** list_{O_i} *not exists* **then**

4   Create list_{O_i};

5          $\text{list}_{O_i} \leftarrow \emptyset$;

6   **else**

7   /* T_o denotes the oldest timebin of list_{O_i} */

8   **while** $T_o < T_c - N + 1$ **do**

9              $\text{list}_{O_i} \leftarrow \text{list}_{O_i} - T_o$;

10          $\text{list}_{O_i} \leftarrow \text{list}_{O_i} \cup T_c$;

11   **if** $|\text{list}_{O_i}| \geq \text{thr}_a$ **then**

12              $A_O \leftarrow A_O \cup \{O_i\}$;

13 **return** A_O;

---

anomaly timebin and inserted into list_{O_i} (lines 1–10). list_{O_i} would be maintained with the sliding time window, i.e., the obsolete anomaly timebins shall be eliminated as a new one is inserted into list_{O_i} (lines 8–10). Once the size of list_{O_i} grows beyond the anomaly timebin count threshold, thr_a, the object, O_i, would be reported as an EO-*outlier* (lines 11–12).

4.3.2.3 *Time complexity analysis*

For each timebin, given the maximum number of incoming trajectories, n, and the window size, N, the execution overhead of the ODDTS algorithm is composed of two parts: (i) the operational overheads of parallel outlier detection on the remote sites and the EO-*outlier* detection on the coordinator, and (ii) the time to transfer detection results from the remote sites to the coordinator. Let n_p ($n_p < n$) denote the maximum number of incoming trajectory data on the individual remote site at a certain timebin which results in *F-outlier* and FC-*outlier* detection incurring a complexity of $O(n_p \log n_p)$ using the STR-*tree* index. Let n_O denote the maximum number of moving objects in the current time window. When all the objects have *F-outliers* at a certain timebin, the worst computational cost of the coordinator is $O(n_O)$, which scarcely happens.

Let Com_k denote the cost of transmitting EO-*outlier* candidates from one remote site to the coordinator; the whole transferring overhead Com is $\sum_{k=1}^{M} \text{Com}_k$. Let n_{EO} denote the maximum number of EO-*outlier* candidates at some timebin, where Com at most requires $O(M(n_{EO}))$ and the worst-case cost is $O(n_O)$. Communications can even be avoided when none of the *F-outliers* is detected by any remote site. Since $n_p \gg n_O$, the ODDTS algorithm approximately takes $O(n_p \log n_p)$, and even an ideal complexity of $O(\frac{n}{M} \log \frac{n}{M})$. That the execution overhead is in the linear order of M indicates that ODDTS is scalable with regard to the number of remote sites. As compared to the computational cost of the centralized version (i.e., $M = 1$, $O(n \log n)$), the execution overhead of ODDTS is significantly reduced owing to parallel outlier detections of the remote sites with minimal communication cost.

4.4 Empirical Evaluation

4.4.1 *Experimental setup*

In this section, all the experiments are conducted on a cluster of five nodes running *Spark-2.1.0-bin-hadoop 2.7* on *centos 7.2*. Each node consists of 20 physical cores *Intel 2.2GHz* processors, and the nodes are interconnected with a 10 Gbps Ethernet.

First, we conduct the comprehensive experiments on the taxi trajectory data sets to validate the effectiveness and scalability of the OCluDTS algorithm by comparing the OCluDTS and TSCluWin algorithms. It is worth noting that none of the existing solutions is tailored to clustering over distributed trajectory streams, and thus none are suitable to compare with OCluDTS.

Since taxis drive frequently, most of them reduce the sampling frequency to save energy and get reasonable response time. Different vehicles collect the position information with different intervals. In this section, the time interval within each time window is set to 1 minute to guarantee that various moving objects of different sampling rates report their locations at least once. During the experiments, we simulate the distributed trajectory streams by sending data from the disk files to different nodes in a compute cluster with a specified transfer rate. Unless mentioned, the parameters are: $\epsilon = 1/3$, $M = 16$, $k = 300$, and $W = 5$ minutes.

Then, we conduct extensive experiments on two real data sets to assess the effectiveness and efficiency of the ODDTS method over distributed streams. It is worth noting that none of the existing solutions is tailored to trajectory outlier detection over distributed streams. Thus, they are not suitable to compare with ODDTS. The values of parameters are set for each data set based on our experimental tuning. Unless mentioned otherwise, the window size, W, is set to 30 minutes and the *timebin* is set to 2 minutes.

Data sets. We evaluate our proposed method on two real data sets: taxi trajectory data set of 2013 (or *Taxi*13, for short) and the taxi operational data set of 2015 (or *Taxi*15, for short). During the experiments, we simulate the trajectory stream by sending data from the disk files to the compute cluster with a specified transfer rate. The transfer rate can be adjusted by changing the number of streaming elements at each timebin.

Taxi13 contains more than 400 GB of trajectory data generated by taxis in Shanghai and Beijing in the fourth quarter of 2013. It includes four attributes of timestamp, velocity, longitude, and latitude coordinates. To evaluate the robustness of ODDTS for trajectory data in different scale of regions, we further derive two data sets of Shanghai from *Taxi*13: *Taxi13-1* with 1.89 million records, and *Taxi13-2* with 3.69 million records.

Taxi15 contains more than 200 GB of trajectory data derived by 13,600 taxis in Shanghai in April 2015. It has about 114 million points per day with six attributes of vehicle ID, time, longitude, and latitude, speed, taxi status (free/occupied), etc. We select a test area consisting of about 315 road segments, and each road segment has at least one lane in each direction. The ground truth outlier set is manually verified through the comparative velocity analysis for each trajectory fragment (or road segment) and its neighbors at each timebin by the volunteers. Labeling of the outliers is determined by the majority of the volunteer.

4.4.2 *Effectiveness evaluation of* **OCluDTS**

To verify the capability of the evolutionary clustering analysis of our proposal, we first implement the OCluDTS algorithm on *Taxi*13. Specifically, we choose the taxi trajectory data during the period (from 8:46 to 9:05 a.m.) on 9 October 2013 to cluster and derive the clustering results within four time intervals. The visual clustering results are shown in Figure 4.2. We observe that the OCluDTS algorithm can conduct an evolutionary clustering analysis on the real trajectory data in real time. Additionally, the clustering results (the representative trajectories highlighted in black) within four time intervals can indicate real-time traffic flow and reflect the sustainability of road networks.

In a bid to verify the effectiveness of the OCluDTS algorithm, we compare the clustering result of the OCluDTS algorithm (adopting optimization strategy) and the micro-clustering result of the TSCluWin algorithm by calculating the value of AverageSSQ under different window

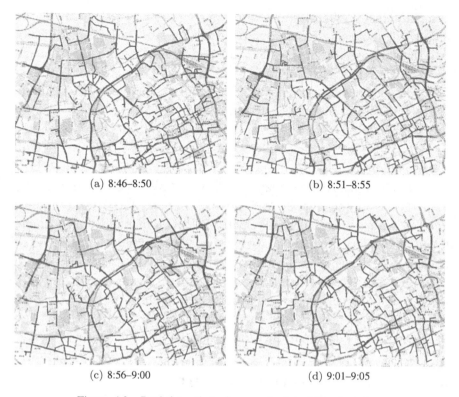

(a) 8:46–8:50   (b) 8:51–8:55

(c) 8:56–9:00   (d) 9:01–9:05

Figure 4.2. Real-time clustering result of taxis' trajectories.

sizes. Figure 4.3 shows the value of AverageSSQ obtained by two approaches (OCluDTS and TSCluWin) over time when the window size is set to 5 and 10 minutes, respectively. We observe that in all cases, OCluDTS behaves better (with a smaller AverageSSQ value) than TSCluWin.

There are two reasons: (i) the synopsis structure (i.e., DF) of OCluDTS is more reasonable than that (i.e., EF_o) of TSCluWin due to the former considering the influence of a longer trajectory line segment, and hence the representative trajectory line segment of OCluDTS can better represent the data distribution characteristics than that of TSCluWin, and (ii) to meet the amount threshold of clusters (i.e., k), TSCluWin may merge the micro-cluster and its distant neighbors into one micro-cluster, which easily derives a larger AverageSSQ value and reduces the overall

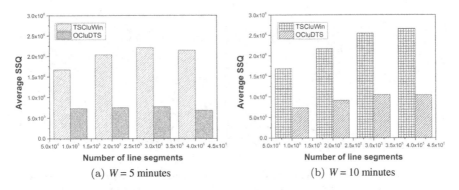

Figure 4.3. Quality comparison.

performance. In comparison to TSCluWin, for the OCluDTS algorithm, each remote site only conducts clustering on its respective data stream, the result of which is relatively compact. Even the coordinator needs to re-cluster to meet the specified number of clusters, so that it can avoid merging the clusters that are a greater distance apart.

4.4.3 *Efficiency evaluation of OCluDTS*

In this section, we assess the efficiency and scalability of OCluDTS when dealing with streaming trajectories. We evaluate the execution overhead of OCluDTS through varying the amount of data, the number of remote sites, and the value of k.

First, we compare the execution overhead between OCluDTS and TSCluWin. The whole execution overhead of the OCluDTS algorithm is broken down into time spent on key phases: the operational overheads of parallel clustering on the remote sites, global clustering on the coordinator and the time to transfer local clustering results from the remote sites to the coordinator. Since the re-clustering cost of the coordinator is a tiny proportion of the overall execution cost, we mainly estimate the parallel clustering cost and the communication overhead among the nodes. As shown in Figure 4.4(a), we can see that the execution overheads of the OCluDTS and TSCluWin algorithms increase as the trajectory data continue to flow in (the number of trajectories increases from 50,000 to 400,000), and OCluDTS keeps superior to that processed by TSCluWin. Do note that when the parallel clustering phase finishes, i.e., after every

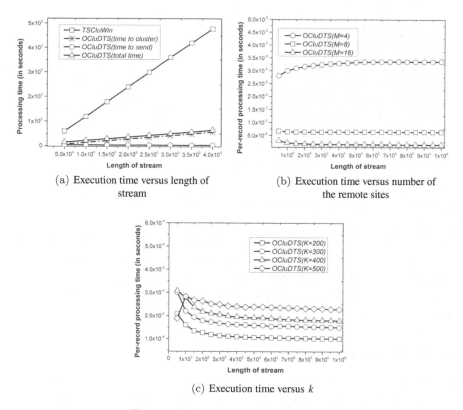

(a) Execution time versus length of
stream

(b) Execution time versus number of
the remote sites

(c) Execution time versus k

Figure 4.4.   Execution time comparison.

remote site has completed its processing, the maximal parallel clustering cost is chosen as the evaluation criterion.

Figure 4.4(a) reports the maximal parallel clustering cost (denoted as *time to cluster*) and the total execution time (denoted as *total time*). We can see that the parallel clustering overhead of OCluDTS increases as the trajectory data continues to flow in, and the overall execution cost is mainly determined by the time spent to implement local clustering in parallel for all the remote sites. As far as the communication overhead is concerned, we observe from Figure 4.4(a) that the communication overhead (denoted as *time to send*) has no obvious change as the amount of data increases (on an average of 3.8 seconds). As the distributed algorithm only involves transferring the local clustering results (k'DFs) from the remote sites to the coordinator, the data amount is far less than that of transferring the trajectory data. Therefore, the performance of OCluDTS is obviously improved as compared to TSCluWin. It verifies the scalability of OCluDTS with respect to data scale.

Then, we studied the scalability of OCluDTS with reference to the number of remote sites. As shown in Figure 4.4(b), the per-record processing time of OCluDTS using a different number of remote sites ($M = 4, 8, 16$, respectively) is reported. As the trajectory data continues to flow in (from $50k$ to $1,000k$), the costs of all the approaches grow slightly with data size, e.g., 0.00326 seconds for $M = 4$, 0.0006 seconds for $M = 8$ and 0.00017 seconds for $M = 16$. As discussed earlier, a little more time is required to transfer the local clustering result when using more remote sites, but in the meantime, the total execution overhead is sharply reduced due to the vast time savings of the parallel clustering procedure. Accordingly, as more remote sites are used, the total time consumption of OCluDTS is reduced. Therefore, OCluDTS provides significant scalability advantages when more remote sites are available, and OCluDTS shows the best performance when $M = 16$, as illustrated in Figure 4.4(b).

Furthermore, to test the robustness of OCluDTS in the presence of uncertainty, we study the sensitivity of OCluDTS to parameter k. Figure 4.4(c) shows the per-record processing time of OCluDTS ($M = 16$) when the number of clusters is varied ($k = 200, 300, 400$, and 500, respectively). We can see that when the data scale increases from $50k$

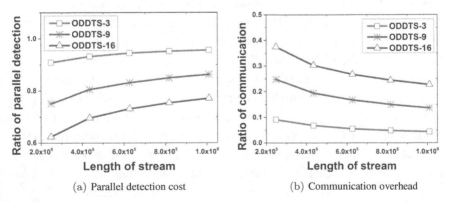

(a) Parallel detection cost   (b) Communication overhead

Figure 4.5.   Ratio of detection and communication overhead to total execution overhead.

to $1,000k$, the execution overhead of OCluDTS is slightly changed using a different number of clusters (for example, between 0.0001 and 0.0003 seconds). As the value of k increases, the execution overhead of OCluDTS goes up slightly (a minimum of 0.000115 seconds when $k = 200$ and a maximum of 0.00024 seconds). So, owing to the lower communication overhead, OCluDTS is less affected by the parameter k as more remote sites participate in the parallel clustering procedure. The above effectiveness and performance experiments establish that OCluDTS can cluster for distributed trajectory streams in a promising efficiency, while attaining better accuracy than the centralized solution.

4.4.4 *Effectiveness evaluation of ODDTS*

For an effectiveness validation purpose, we conduct ODDTS (setting with 16 remote sites) on *Taxi*15. We aim to identify *F-outliers*, FC-*outliers*, and EO-*outliers* according to the velocity feature. We choose the longitude and latitude coordinates as SF and regard velocity as DF. Local outlier thresholds are empirically set as follows: $\rho = 2.5$ and $\rho_c = 3.5$. The portions of the test area and outlier detection results are visualized in Figure 4.6. Figure 4.6(a) shows the movement distribution of taxis' traces (marked with light gray strap) within [8:00, 8:30] a.m. on 15 April. The average speed of most roads is not beyond 30 km/h. Outliers at timebin ([8:29–8:30]) a.m. detected by ODDTS are illustrated in Figure 4.6(b). *F-outliers* highlighted in long thin black lines indicate that only a few abnormal trajectories (with speeds of 83 km/h) occur on parts of the roads. The EO-*outlier* (highlighted in short black line) represents a speeding car (with mean velocity of 155 km/h during multiple timebins). FC-*outliers* (highlighted in thick black lines) show that the roads where a majority of taxis travel on have significantly different speeds (68 km/h) from their neighbors (with mean speed of 25 km/h). The outlier detection result coincides with the ground truth outliers. During peak hours, such information like the roads with high speed will help drivers plan optimal routes in real time.

Metrics. In a bid to further verify the effectiveness of ODDTS, we use F-measure as the criteria measurement. It is defined as F-measure $= \frac{2 \times \text{Precision} \times \text{Recall}}{\text{Precision} + \text{Recall}}$, where Precision $= \frac{|R \cap D|}{|D|}$ and Recall $= \frac{|R \cap D|}{|R|}$. R denotes the manually labeled trajectory outlier set, and D denotes the

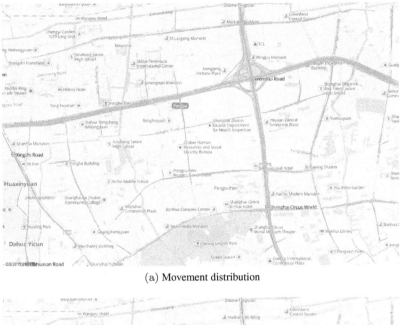

(a) Movement distribution

(b) Outlier detection result

Figure 4.6. Outlier detection on *Taxi15*.

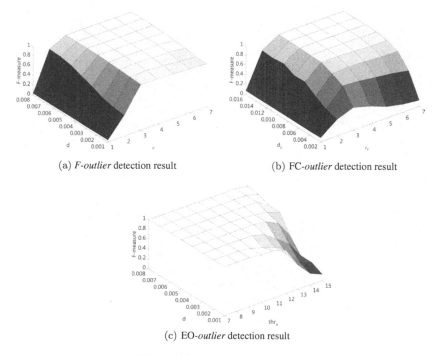

(a) *F-outlier* detection result   (b) FC-*outlier* detection result

(c) EO-*outlier* detection result

Figure 4.7. *F*-measure (*Taxi*15).

detected outlier set by our proposal. F-measure reaches a high value only when both Precision and Recall are high. To understand how the parameters impact outlier detection, we implement ODDTS with different threshold (including d, d_c, ρ, ρ_c and thr_a) settings to evaluate the value of F-measure, as illustrated in Figure 4.7. Note that d uses the variation of latitude and longitude; the distance of 0.0001 corresponds to about 11 meters.

We observe that ODDTS obtains almost the high F-measure for F-outlier detection when $\rho \geq 3$ and $d \geq 0.003$, for FC-*outlier* detection when $\rho_c \geq 3.5$ and $d_c \geq 0.008$, and for EO-*outlier* detection when $d > 0.004$ and $\text{thr}_a \geq 7$. It can be concluded that ODDTS attains better detecting validity as long as the thresholds are set appropriately.

4.4.5 *Efficiency evaluation of* OCluDTS

We proceed to assess the efficiency of ODDTS. The whole execution overhead is broken down into time spent on key phases: the parallel detection cost of the remote sites, the detection cost of the coordinator, and the communication overhead for transferring outlier detection results. Since the detection cost of the coordinator is a tiny proportion of the overall execution cost, we mainly estimate the parallel detection cost and the communication overhead by implementing ODDTS on *Taxi13-2*. The number of trajectories gradually grows from 250k to 1010k.

Note that after the parallel outlier detection phase finishes after every remote site has completed its detection, the maximal parallel detection cost is chosen as the evaluation criterion. Figure 4.5(a) reports the ratio of the maximal parallel detection cost to the total execution time. We can see that the parallel detection overheads of ODDTS with three different numbers of the remote sites (abbreviated as ODDTS-3, ODDTS-9, and ODDTS-16, respectively) increase as the trajectory data continues to flow in, while ODDTS-16 guarantees the greatest time savings. It can be concluded that the overall execution cost is mainly determined by the time spent to implement the outlier detection in parallel for all the remote sites. Owing to the high efficiency of the parallel detection phase, less detection cost would be spent as more remote sites participate in the parallel detection procedure.

As far as the communication overhead is concerned, Figure 4.5(b) shows the ratio of the communication time to the total execution time. We observe that the ratio reduces with data size, and the communication overhead grows slightly with the increase of number of remote sites. Fortunately, even though the amount of trajectory data reaches 1010k, the communication cost of ODDTS-16 is at most the ratio of 22% of the total execution overhead. As more remote sites execute outlier detection in parallel, a little more time is spent to transfer the outlier detection results from the remote sites to the coordinator site during the detection process. However, instead of transferring all the data to the coordinator for detecting, ODDTS simply needs to transmit the detection results on the local streams. The communication cost of ODDTS is far less than the time savings that parallel detections bring about, and hence is always a small portion of the whole execution overhead.

To verify the effectiveness of the pruning process, we compare the running time of ODDTS with that of its unpruned version (denoted as ODDTS$_{no}$) by implementing them on *Taxi15*. As shown in Figure 4.8(a),

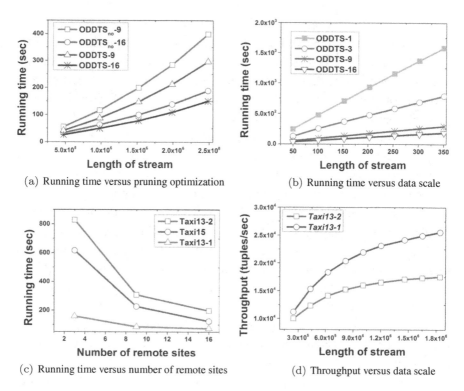

(a) Running time versus pruning optimization

(b) Running time versus data scale

(c) Running time versus number of remote sites

(d) Throughput versus data scale

Figure 4.8.   Execution overhead.

the execution overheads of ODDTS-9 and ODDTS-16 are significantly improved, relative to the solutions (ODDTS$_{no}$-9 and ODDTS$_{no}$-16) without the pruning process. In addition, ODDTS-16 saves more time for parallel detection. This is due to a large number of unnecessary ldd calculations being pruned and thus the cost of the parallel detection procedure is greatly reduced.

Then, we evaluate the impact of data scale on the execution overhead of ODDTS by comparing it with its centralized version (abbreviated as ODDTS-1). We implement ODDTS on *Taxi13-2* using a different number of remote sites ($M = 1$, 3, 9, and 16, respectively). As illustrated in Figure 4.8(b), when the trajectory data continues to flow in (from 490k to 3500k), the costs of all the approaches scale linearly with data size. But the distributed versions perform much better than the centralized version, with ODDTS-16 especially showing the best performance.

As discussed earlier, a little more time is required to transfer the outlier detection result when using more remote sites, but in the meantime, the total execution overhead is sharply reduced owing to vast time savings of the parallel detection procedure. Therefore, the performance of the distributed solution is obviously improved as compared to the centralized version.

Also, we studied the scalability of ODDTS with respect to the number of remote sites. We conduct ODDTS on *Taxi13-1*, *Taxi13-2*, and *Taxi15* separately. As shown in Figure 4.8(c), as more remote sites are used, the total time consumption of ODDTS on the three data sets are reduced. It also demonstrates the advantage of ODDTS contributed by the efficient parallel detection phase with minimal communication cost. The transmission overhead is much smaller than the time savings of parallel detections and is also less sensitive to the variation of the number of remote sites. Therefore, ODDTS provides significant scalability advantages when a large number of remote sites is available.

Furthermore, to verify the performance gain of ODDTS, we conduct a comparative analysis on the throughput of ODDTS-16 on *Taxi13-1* and *Taxi13-2*. Throughput is defined as the average number of tuples processed each second. As can be observed in Figure 4.8(d), as compared to the larger scale data set (*Taxi13-2*), the smaller one (*Taxi13-1*) provides higher throughput owing to less data processed in every timebin. Moreover, both the throughputs of ODDTS on the two data sets scale linearly with the increase of data. This also confirms the scalability of ODDTS with respect to the increasing amount of data. Such significant performance gains benefit from the parallel detection procedure. The above experiments establish that ODDTS can handle distributed trajectory streams with promising efficiency.

4.5 Related Work

The centralized solutions are not tailored to distributed trajectory streams. Even scalable techniques of them still require excessive execution overheads for handling continuously increased distributed stream data when compared to the stringent response time requirements of actual applications. Additionally, distributed distance-based's [Cao *et al.*, 2017] and distributed local outlier's [Yan *et al.*, 2017] detection methods cannot be directly applied to identify trajectory outliers.

Recently, in the aspect of the distributed trajectory analysis, a surge of researches have been devoted to trajectory querying in a distributed data set [Ma *et al.*, 2009; Zeinalipour-Yazti *et al.*, 2013]. Ma *et al.* (2009) presented a MapReduce-based framework for query processing over trajectory data. Zeinalipour *et al.* (2006) proposed two distributed spatio-temporal similarity searching methods using locally computed lower and upper bounds on the trajectory similarity function. It targets the scenario where each trajectory is divided into a few subsequences that are stored in different remote sites. Its goal is to solve the top-*k* query quickly, though the communication cost is not considered. Zeinalipour *et al.* (2013) presented a crowdsourced trace similarity search framework for implementing distributed queries on trajectories that are stored *in situ* on smartphones. Zhang *et al.* (2017) proposed a communication cost-saving approach to process distributed top-*k* similarity queries over trajectory streams by utilizing the multi-resolution property of the *Haar wavelet*. However, the distributed trajectory query solutions are not well suited for clustering and the outlier detection problem.

4.6   Conclusion

In this chapter, on the basis of the distributed computing platform, we first proposed a two-phase online clustering algorithm upon distributed trajectory streams, called OCluDTS, to solve the issue of efficient clustering on the trajectory streams derived by multiple disperse nodes. It attempts to boost the clustering efficiency on distributed trajectory streams by reducing the communication overhead among the nodes (i.e., the remote sites and the coordinator). For each remote site, the incoming trajectory data within per time window is clustered and maintained using the defined synopsis structure (denoted as DF). Then, the local clustering results derived by parallel clustering on all the remote sites would be transferred to the coordinator and participate in re-clustering. This two-phase clustering mechanism can guarantee that the distributed solution achieves the same clustering accuracy as the centralized one. Furthermore, the pruning mechanism of the similarity calculation as well as the optimization strategy of "test first and transfer later" enables the OCluDTS algorithm to improve efficiency. A theoretical analysis and comprehensive experimental results on the real-world data set demonstrate that the OCluDTS algorithm is of high quality and high scalability on distributed trajectory streams.

Second, we propose a two-phase distributed *feature-grouping based* outlier detection method, termed as ODDTS, to identify three types of trajectory outliers (*F-outlier*, FC-*outlier* and EO-*outlier*) over distributed streams. Our proposal can achieve obvious performance gains through a parallel outlier detection mechanism with minimal transmission overhead among the nodes. The evaluative experiments on real-world data proved that ODDTS could obtain high detection precision and scale well for evergrowing data volumes and an increasing number of remote sites. Moreover, our distributed solution is generic and can be applied in most parallel and distributed trajectory processing scenarios.

Chapter 5

Cloned Vehicle Detection

5.1 Background

In recent decades, increasing numbers of cloned vehicle offenses have emerged throughout the world. Lawbreakers can clone the vehicle identification number (or VIN for short) of the legitimately-owned vehicle and install it on stolen or illegally modified vehicles. As a result, cloned vehicle crime not only undermines traffic order and society safety, but also does great harm to legal vehicle owners or even the national economy. Take the United States as an example, the Federal Bureau of Investigation (FBI) reported that more than 1,000 cloned vehicles in Tampa were sold to buyers (witting and unwitting) in 20 American states and other countries in the world, with estimated losses of more than 25 million dollars. The pernicious effects of cloned vehicle crime have increased broad social concerns. It necessitates a high-efficiency detection mechanism to pinpoint cloned vehicles.

In earlier researches, cloned vehicle identification generally employs the RFID-based technique, optical implicit code-based technique, automotive-style-recognition-based technique, etc. However, it is difficult to apply the above methods in production for different reasons. Specifically, the deployment costs for the two former kinds of techniques are too high to popularize, and the last one is susceptible to the influence of the outside environment. With the widespread use of video surveillance technology, the inspection spots are deployed in city traffic crossroads, which gather information (e.g., the license plate and the time appeared) of passing vehicles through equipped cameras. Accordingly, the positional sequences of inspection spots that vehicles pass by have formed into the passing vehicles' trajectories. This provides us opportunities to discern the cloned VIN by analyzing the moving traces of passing vehicles.

Since one vehicle cannot show up in two or more places at the same time, this is called the phenomenon of *spatial–temporal contradiction*. According to the report, the Shanghai police in 2016 detected two Maseratis with the same VIN appearing in different areas at the same time. It was this trail that led the police to discover that the owner of one of these "cars" had stolen the VIN of the legal one. Based on this report, if more than two vehicles with the same VIN are detected by different inspection spots located far apart in a short space of time, they are identified as cloned vehicles. The detection method [Li and Liu, 2015] based on the *spatial–temporal contradiction* using ANPR (Automatic Number Plate Recognition) data usually needs to set an appropriate speed threshold. It identifies a vehicle as being cloned by judging whether its speed is beyond the given threshold.

Traffic conditions behave differently across regions and change over time, therefore, the spatial–temporal contradiction-based method easily attains lower precision because a fixed threshold cannot cope well with the changing traffic situation. Given this, we first propose a cloned vehicle detection framework (called CVDH) based on the spatial–temporal contradiction, which derives the speed threshold of each road by modeling the speed distribution of a road. In addition, since it is hard to extract a correct speed threshold for the road with a small number of historical trajectories, the speed changes caused by sudden traffic accidents cannot be seen by the historical trajectory data. Inspired by the trajectory outlier detection mechanism in Chapter 3, the abnormality analysis of moving behavior within the local neighborhood can be introduced into cloned vehicle detection.

Furthermore, to help the authorities to pinpoint the cloned vehicles, we need to discern the different behavioral patterns of cloned vehicles and even figure out the motives behind them. This makes more sense when solving cloned vehicle crimes. For instance, members from the same family may own various vehicles using the same VIN. Thus, they may have regular behavior patterns, such as appearing in a fixed position during a regular time period every day. In another example, in some cities in China, taxi drivers use the same VIN so that they can pay less rent to the taxi company. Their movement behaviors may manifest as the phenomenon of "wandering" throughout the city.

Besides the above mentioned patterns, more offenders use cloned VINs to commit traffic violations such as speeding, drink driving, illegal overtaking, etc. For example, in the Jiangsu province of China, a Jaguar was caught frequently speeding. It turned out that it had a fake VIN. Thus, modeling the temporal behavior patterns of cloned vehicles and then investigating the motives behind these cases are more conducive to traffic safety management and crime prevention.

Based on the above analysis, to detect cloned vehicles and differentiate their distinct behaviors, the following challenges shall be addressed: (i) For roads with enough historical trajectories, the extracted speed thresholds based on historical data enables us to identify the cloned vehicle correctly; (ii) for roads with sparse historical trajectories or those that incur sudden traffic jams, the extracted speed thresholds based on historical data are insufficient to accurately identify cloned vehicles; (iii) traces of vehicles using the same plate number have generally blurred into one another, which increases the difficulty to discern the behavior patterns of different vehicles with the same VIN; and (iv) the difficulty of extracting distinct spatial–temporal behavior patterns of different types of cloned vehicle crime by using the traditional time-series pattern mining algorithm.

To tackle the aforementioned challenges, we propose a Cloned Vehicle Detection Framework (CVDF). It comprises two parts: (i) detecting the cloned vehicle, which is implemented according to the speed threshold extraction upon historical trajectory (denoted as CVDH), or incorporating speed threshold extraction upon historical data with a behavior abnormality analysis within the local neighborhood (denoted as CVDN); and (ii) differentiating the traces of various vehicles with the same VIN and discerning their spatial–temporal behavior patterns.

Specifically, we make the following contributions: (1) addressing the issue of cloned vehicle detection, and then bringing forward a two-phase detection framework, called CVDF, to detect the cloned vehicles and ascertain their distinct behavior patterns; (2) presenting a detection method based on the extracted speed thresholds from historical data, and a hybrid detection method that combines speed threshold extraction upon historical trajectory with a behavior abnormality analysis within the local neighborhood; and (3) presenting a *matching degree-based* clustering method to discern the trajectories of various objects and then designing a mining mechanism to differentiate the behavior patterns; and (4) evaluating our proposals by conducting numerous comparative experiments on the large-scale real-world trajectory data. Experimental results manifest the effectiveness of our proposal.

The remainder of this chapter is organized as follows. In Section 5.2, the problem is formally defined. In Section 5.3, we outline the CVDF scheme and analytically study two detection methods. In Section 5.4, a series of contrast experiments are conducted on a real data set to evaluate our proposal. In Section 5.5, we review the latest works related to our research. Finally, we conclude this chapter in Section 5.6.

5.2 Preliminaries

In this section, some necessary preliminary notions are provided and the problem of detection as well as pattern extraction of the cloned vehicle is formalized. Table 5.1 summarizes major notations used in the rest of this chapter.

Inspection spots equipped with cameras are deployed in city traffic crossroads. These collect the information of passing vehicles (e.g., the passing time and VIN).

Definition 5.1 (Location of Inspection Spot). An inspection spot is denoted as I_i(ID, lon, lat). Here, lon and lat represent the longitude and latitude of I_i, respectively.

Each positional point in a vehicle's trajectory that is collected by the inspection spot, I_i, at timestamp, t_j, is denoted as $p_j = (I_i, t_j)$.

Definition 5.2 (Trajectory of Vehicle). The positional sequence of inspection spots that a vehicle, v, traverses is viewed as its trajectory, denoted as $\text{Traj}^v = \langle p_0, p_1, \ldots p_n \rangle$.

Table 5.1. List of notations.

Notation	Definition
I_i	The location of the inspection spot, i
$p = (I_i, t_j)$	The location of a vehicle at timestamp, t_j
Traj^v	The trajectory of vehicle whose VIN is v
$\text{tf} = \{p_j, p_{j+1}\}$	The trajectory fragment connected by p_j and p_{j+1}
$r = \langle I_s, I_e \rangle$	The road between I_s and I_e
g	A time period
D_g	The speed distribution of a road in the time period, g
k	The abnormal behavior frequency threshold
ρ	The local anomaly factor
tp_v	The behavior pattern of the vehicle, v
δ_p	The minimum support for a residence place
δ_f	The minimum support for a moving pattern
SDS	The speed distribution set
SDL	The speed distribution list
$N_{tf}(\text{tf}_i)$	The local neighborhood of tf_i
tr_v	The fixed residence place of vehicle, v

Two consecutive positional points are connected into a trajectory fragment, tf, denoted as $\text{tf} = \{p_j, p_{j+1}\}$, and the road, r, between two adjacent inspection spots is denoted as $r = \langle I_s, I_e \rangle$. To identify the cloned vehicles, it is necessary to derive the appropriate speed threshold of each road within each time period. Note that the traffic situation may vary significantly with the change of road and time. Even for the same time period, the speeds of vehicles on a road are still different. Thus, the average speed cannot symbolize the actual traffic situation of a road, and the speed distribution is more suitable for describing the traffic condition of a road.

Figure 5.1 depicts the speed distribution of a road, $r = \langle I_s, I_e \rangle$, from 11:00 a.m. to 12:00 a.m. We can see that the speed distribution is characterized by middle concentration and scattered sides. Here, the *Gaussian Distribution* is used to model the speed distribution of a road, r, within the period, g. Based on historical traces of vehicles, the **speed distribution** of a road can be calculated by the speeds of vehicles that pass by the road within various time periods.

$$\text{pr}_{(r,g)}(\text{sp}) = \frac{1}{\sqrt{2\pi}\sigma} e^{-\frac{(sp-\mu)^2}{2\sigma^2}}, \tag{5.1}$$

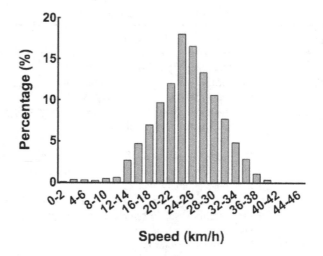

Figure 5.1. An example of a road's speed distribution.

where sp represents the speed of a vehicle passing the road, $r = \langle I_s, I_e \rangle$, within the time period, g. The speed distribution of each road is derived by computing the parameters of the Gaussian Distribution, i.e., mean μ and variance σ^2. Here, *the maximum likelihood estimation* is used to estimate the parameters of the Gaussian Distribution.

$$\hat{\mu} = \frac{1}{n} \sum_{i=1}^{n} \text{sp}_i,$$
(5.2a)

$$\widehat{\sigma^2} = \frac{1}{n} \sum_{i=1}^{n} \text{sp}_i^2 - \hat{\mu}^2.$$
(5.2b)

Here, n and sp_i denote the number of samples and the sampled speed, respectively. The parameters of the Gaussian Distribution are estimated based on the historical trajectory data. Specifically, three statistic values, i.e., $x = \sum_{i=1}^{n} \text{sp}_i$, $y = \sum_{i=1}^{n} \text{sp}_i^2$, and n can be computed directly, and if the estimated values, $\hat{\mu}$ and $\widehat{\sigma^2}$, can be derived based on x, y, and n, then the speed distribution is established.

Subsequently, the speed threshold of each road within each time period can be derived according to the estimated speed distribution.

For each Gaussian Distribution, equation

$$\text{pr}_{(\langle I_s, I_e \rangle, g)}[\mu - 3\sigma \leq sp \leq \mu + 3\sigma] = 99.7\%$$

is held. It means that when the vehicle passes the road, r, in a specified time period, g, the probability of its travel speed between $(\mu - 3\sigma, \mu + 3\sigma)$ achieves 99.7%.

The speed threshold of a given road and time period can be expressed as follows:

$$sp_{th} = \hat{\mu} + 3\hat{\sigma}. \tag{5.3}$$

Here $\hat{\mu}$ and $\hat{\sigma}$ denote the estimated parameters of each speed distribution and sp_{th} denotes the normal speed threshold of a road. Once the speed of any trajectory fragment, tf_i, exceeds the speed threshold $(\hat{\mu} + 3\hat{\sigma})$ of the corresponding road, tf_i is considered to be abnormal.

Although the speeds of some vehicles are less than $(\hat{\mu} - 3\hat{\sigma})$ due to movements such as parking or traffic jams, they cannot be judged as abnormal behavior. Therefore, to detect the abnormal behavior of the cloned vehicle, we will only consider the situation where the speed of a trajectory fragment is greater than the speed threshold $(\hat{\mu} + 3\hat{\sigma})$.

The speed distribution set, SDS, of each inspection spot pair is described as follows:

$$\text{SDS} = \{\langle I_{s_1}, I_{e_1}, \text{SDL}_1 \rangle, \ldots, \langle I_{s_n}, I_{e_n}, \text{SDL}_n \rangle\}. \tag{5.4}$$

Here, I_{s_i} and I_{e_i} denote the starting and ending spot of a road segment, and SDL_i represents the speed distribution list of $\langle I_{s_i}, I_{e_i} \rangle$. The list SDL_i contains the speed distribution of each time period and SDL_i can be described as follows:

$$\text{SDL}_i = \{D_1, D_2, \ldots, D_{\mathscr{G}}\}.$$

Considering that the traffic conditions of the roads change with time, the day is divided into $\mathscr{G}$-periods. The speed distribution of each time period is expressed as $D_j = \langle g_j, x_j, y_j, n_j \rangle (1 \leq j \leq \mathscr{G})$. Here, g_j denotes the time period of this distribution, while x_j, y_j, and n_j are three statistics of D_j.

As mentioned in Section 5.1, the sparsity characteristic of the trajectory itself and the sudden traffic accidents would result in a specific deviation between the speed distribution extracted from historical data and actual traffic conditions. Inspired by the trajectory outlier detection method presented in Chapter 3, the speed abnormality analysis within the local neighborhood is introduced into the cloned vehicle detecting procedure.

Similar to Chapter 3, we use the LAF measure to assess the probability of trajectory fragment, $\text{tf} = \{p_i, p_j\}$, for being an outlier with regard to its local neighbors, i.e., $\text{LAF}(\text{tf}_i) = \frac{\sum_{\text{tf}_j \in N_{\text{tf}}(\text{tf}_i)} \frac{\text{ldd}_{\text{tf}}(\text{tf}_j)}{\text{ldd}_{\text{tf}}(\text{tf}_i)}}{|N_{\text{tf}}(\text{tf}_i)|}$, where $N_{\text{tf}}(\text{tf}_i)$ represents the local neighbor trajectory fragments of tf_i, and ldd is defined as the inverse of the average difference of tf_i to its local neighbors, i.e., $\text{ldd}_{\text{tf}}(\text{tf}_i) = \frac{|N_{\text{tf}}(\text{tf}_i)|}{\sum_{\text{tf}_j \in N_{\text{tf}}(\text{tf}_i)} \text{Diff}(\text{tf}_i, \text{tf}_j)}$. Here, $\text{Diff}(\text{tf}_i, \text{tf}_j)$ denotes the difference between any two trajectory fragments. In general, a higher value of LAF indicates that a trajectory fragment is more likely to be abnormal.

After detecting the cloned vehicle, we attempt to discern the trajectories of different vehicles sharing the same VIN. First, the points in the mixed trajectories need to be grouped into different classes that belong to various vehicles. One critical step is to compute the possibility of the next inspection spot visited by the vehicles, which can be accomplished by calculating the *transition probability* based on the historical trajectories between two inspection spots.

Definition 5.3 (Transition Probability). Given a pair of inspection spots and a time period, g, transition probability, $\text{TPr}_{I_i, I_j}^{(g)}$, indicates the probability of the vehicle passes I_i to I_j in g.

$$\text{TPr}_{I_i, I_j}^{(g)} = n_{I_i, I_j}^{(g)} / \sum_k n_{I_i, I_k}^{(g)},$$

where $n_{I_i, I_j}^{(g)}$ denotes the number of vehicles passing from I_i to I_j and $\sum_k n_{I_i, I_k}^{(g)}$ denotes the number of vehicle passing by I_i.

For any two consecutive points in a normal trajectory, they shall have high spatial–temporal proximity. While in the trajectories of the cloned vehicles, there should be a significant difference between two consecutive points. It is because they are generated by different vehicles. Hence, by combining the transition probability with the spatial-temporal proximity factor, we provide the likelihood estimation that the two points are generated by the same object as follows:

Definition 5.4 (Matching Degree).

$$\varphi_{p_i,p_j} = \left(\lambda \times S \left(\frac{1}{\Delta T_{p_i,p_j}} \right) + (1 - \lambda) \times S \left(\frac{1}{\Delta D_{p_i,p_j}} \right) \right) \times \mathrm{TPr}_{I_i,I_j}^{(g)},$$

where $\Delta T_{p_i,p_j}$ and $\Delta D_{p_i,p_j}$ denote the time gap and road network distance between p_i and p_j, respectively. $\lambda (0 < \lambda < 1)$ denotes the user-specified weight of time and $S(x)$ represents the *Sigmoid* function [tim()]. I_i, I_j are the inspection spots that record p_i, p_j (https://en.wikipedia.org/wiki/Sigmoid_function).

Since several vehicles with the same VIN may travel on the roads within the same time period, their traces would mix. Based on the *matching degree* measurement, the points in the mixed traces could be matched into multiple spatial–temporal series that belong to various vehicles. After that, the behavior pattern of each vehicle can be extracted. Some vehicles have regular behavior patterns, which means that they pass the same places during a similar period every day. This behavior pattern can be represented as: $tp_{v_i} = I_0 \xrightarrow{\alpha_1} I_1 \xrightarrow{\alpha_2} \dots \xrightarrow{\alpha_k} I_k$, where $\langle I_0, I_1, \dots, I_k \rangle$ is a positional sequence of inspection spots that the vehicle visits, and $\langle \alpha_1, \dots, \alpha_k \rangle$ is a sequence of temporal annotations. Besides that, there are other vehicles that have a fixed place of residence, but with a random spatial range of daily activities, this kind of behavior pattern can be represented as $tr_{v_i} = I_i \rightarrow I_j \rightarrow \dots \rightarrow I_k \rightarrow I_l$, where I_i and I_j denote the locations where the driver lives.

Problem Definition: Given the trajectory data collected by the inspection spots, our task is to detect the cloned VIN based on the speed thresholds extracted from the historical trajectory data and moving behavior abnormality analysis within the local neighbor trajectories. We then mine the spatial–temporal behavior patterns of the cloned vehicles.

5.3 Overview

In this chapter, we propose a Cloned Vehicle Detection Framework (CVDF). As illustrated in Algorithm 14, CVDF comprises two parts:

Algorithm 14: CVDF($\mathscr{I}, \mathscr{S}, w, k, \delta_p, \delta_f, \mathscr{G}$)

Input: $\mathscr{I}$: Historical trajectory data set; $\mathscr{S}$: the trajectory stream;
w: the sliding window size; k: the abnormal behavior;
frequentness threshold; δ_p, δ_f: the minimum support for
residence place and frequent pattern; $\mathscr{G}$: the number of the
time period; and ρ: the abnormality threshold;

Output: $\mathscr{CV}$: Cloned VIN set; $\mathscr{R}$: the residence places; and
$\mathscr{F}$: frequent pattern;

1 /*Cloned Vehicle Detection*/
2 Speed distribution set: SDS $\leftarrow$ *construct*_SDS($\mathscr{I}$) Cloned
vehicle candidate set: $E \leftarrow \emptyset$ **foreach** *Trajectory stream $\mathscr{S}'$ in
current time window* **do**
3 $\quad$ | $\mathscr{CV} \leftarrow$ CVDH($\mathscr{S}, E,$ SDS, w) (or
$\quad$ | CVDN($\mathscr{S}, E,$ SDS, w, k, ρ))
4 /*Moving Behavior Pattern Extraction*/
5 **foreach** VIN v in $\mathscr{CV}$ **do**
6 $\quad$ | $\text{Traj}_{set} \leftarrow \text{Traj}_{set} \bigcup object\_identification(\text{Traj}^v)$
7 $\mathscr{R}, \mathscr{F} \leftarrow pattern\_mining(\text{Traj}_{set}, \delta_p, \delta_f, \mathscr{G})$ **return** $\mathscr{CV}$, $\mathscr{R}$
and $\mathscr{F}$;

(i) detecting the cloned vehicles according to the speed threshold extracted
from the historical trajectory data, or the moving behavior abnormality analysis within local neighborhoods (lines 1–5) and (ii) mining
the moving behavior patterns of the objects using the same cloned VIN
(lines 6–9).

In the first stage, we establish the speed distribution for each road
(represented as an inspection spot pair) in a different time period using the
historical trajectory data. On the basis of that, we derive the normal speed
threshold of that road and present the pseudocode of the speed distribution
modeling in Algorithm 15. Then, based on the sliding-window model,
we continuously observe the behavior of a trajectory and construct the
candidate cloned VIN set E (line 3). For each trajectory in the current
time window, we can derive the abnormal behavior frequentness of all the
trajectories by comparing the speed of the trajectory fragment with the
extracted speed threshold, or estimating the moving behavior abnormality

---

Algorithm 15: *construct_SDS($\mathscr{I}$)*

Input: $\mathscr{I}$: Historical trajectory data set;
Output: SDS: Speed distribution set;

1 SDS $\leftarrow \emptyset$ **foreach** $i-th$ *trajectory* Traj^v *in* $\mathscr{I}$ **do**

2   **foreach** p_j, p_{j+1} *in* Traj^v **do**

3   **if** *validate*(p_j, p_{j+1}) = **false then**

4   *continue*

5          $//sp$: the average speed between p_j and p_{j+1} $//g$: the time period at which p_j is located $//I_s, I_e$: the inspection spots collect p_j, p_{j+1} **if** SDS *does not contain* SDL$_{I_s,I_e}$ **then**

6   SDL$_{I_s,I_e}$.*initialize*() SDS.*add*(SDL$_{I_s,I_e}$)

7          $D \leftarrow$ SDL$_{I_s,I_e}$.*get*(g)
        $D.x \leftarrow D.x + sp; D.y \leftarrow D.y + sp^2; D.n \leftarrow D.n + 1$
        SDS.*update*(SDL$_{I_s,I_e}$)

8 **return** SDS*;*

---

within local neighborhoods of trajectories. Once the frequentness of a vehicle exceeds the predefined threshold, k, it is identified as a cloned vehicle (line 4). Algorithms 16 and 17 illustrate the detection process in detail.

In the second stage, we first distinguish the trajectories of various vehicles sharing the same cloned VIN (lines 7–8). A similarity metric is introduced to measure with confidence any two points in the mixed trajectories generated by a single object. After that, the trajectory points generated by the same object are clustered into one class, which is used to reconstruct that object's trajectory. Then, we analyze the trajectories of each object and mine its respective moving behavior pattern, which helps to pinpoint the vehicle with cloned VIN (line 9).

5.3.1 *Cloned vehicle detection*

In this subsection, we present two cloned vehicle detection methods by only considering the extracted speed thresholds from historical data, and then incorporating speed threshold extraction upon historical trajectory data with a moving behavior abnormality analysis within local neighboring

---

Algorithm 16: CVDN($\mathscr{S}$, E, SDS, w, k, ρ)

Input: $\mathscr{S}$: Trajectory set within the current period; E: cloned VIN candidate set; SDS: speed distribution set; w: sliding window size; k: anomaly frequency threshold; and ρ: abnormality threshold;

Output: $\mathscr{CV}$: Cloned VIN set; E: cloned VIN candidate set; and SDS: speed distribution set;

1 **foreach** $\langle v_i, CList_i \rangle$ *in* E **do**
2   **if** $CList_i.length() = w$ **then**
3        $CList_i.delete(0)$
4     $CList_i.add(0)$

5 **foreach** $\text{Traj}^{v_i} \in \mathscr{S}$ **do**
6     $num \leftarrow outlier\_num(\text{Traj}^{v_i}, \text{SDS}, \rho)$ $update(\text{Traj}^{v_i}, \text{SDS})$ **if** $num \neq 0$ **then**
7   **if** E *not contains* v_i **then**
8           $CList_i \leftarrow \emptyset$ $CList_i.add(0)$ $E.add(\langle v_i, CList_i \rangle)$
9        $CList_i.set(CList_i.length() - 1, num)$ $E.update(\langle v_i, CList_i \rangle)$ **if** $CList_i.get\_amount() > k$ **then**
10           $\mathscr{CV} \leftarrow \mathscr{CV} \bigcup \{v_i\}$

11 **foreach** $\langle v_i, CList_i \rangle \in E$ **do**
12   **if** $CList_i.get\_amount() = 0$ **then**
13        $E.remove(\langle v_i, CList_i \rangle)$

14 **return** $\mathscr{CV}$;

---

trajectories. First, the speed distribution of each road is established upon historical trajectory data, on which the normal speed threshold of each road can be derived. Then, the sliding-window model is used to help to constantly monitor the movement behaviors of the vehicles. In each time window, we attempt to find abnormal trajectory fragments and accumulate the outlier frequentness of each suspicious vehicle. Finally, the vehicle whose abnormal behavior frequentness exceeds the given threshold is identified as a cloned vehicle.

Algorithm 17: *outlier_num*(Traj$_i$, SDS, ρ)

Input: Traj^{v_i}: Trajectory; SDS: speed distribution set; and
  ρ: abnormality threshold;
Output: *num*: Number of abnormal behavior;

1 *num* $\leftarrow$ 0 **foreach** p_j, p_{j+1} *in* Traj^{v_i} **do**

2   $//I_s, I_e$: the inspection spot of p_j, p_{j+1} **if** $|\langle I_s, I_e \rangle| \geq \eta$ **then**

3   sp$_{\text{th}}$ $\leftarrow$ SDL$_{I_s,I_e}$.*get_speed_threshold*() **if** $v_{p_j,p_{j+1}}$ > sp$_{\text{th}}$
    then

4   *num* $\leftarrow$ *num* + 1

5   **else**

6   tf^* $v_j \rightarrow v_{j+1}$ find the neighbors $N_{\text{tf}}(\text{tf}^*)$ of tf*

7   LAF(tf*) $\leftarrow$ $\dfrac{\sum_{\text{tf}_j \in N_{\text{tf}}(\text{tf}^*)}\left\{\frac{\text{LDD}_{\text{tf}}(\text{tf}_j)}{\text{LDD}_{\text{tf}}(\text{tf}^*)}\right\}}{|N_{\text{tf}}(\text{tf}^*)|}$ **if** LAF(tf*) > ρ **then**

8   *num* $\leftarrow$ *num* + 1

9 **return** *num;*

5.3.1.1 *Speed distribution establishment*

Supposing during 5 minutes into traveling, a vehicle is recorded by two inspection spots that are 10 km apart. However, in reality the vehicle cannot pass through two distant inspection spots in such a short time. This phenomenon is called a *spatial–temporal contradiction*. Based on this observation, we can detect the cloned vehicle in terms of speed abnormality relative to historical speeds. Considering that traffic situations vary with time, a fixed speed threshold will result in low accuracy of cloned vehicles detection.

Tremendous amounts of historical trajectory data provide us opportunities to extract appropriate speed thresholds of different roads within various time periods. We attempt to model the speed distribution based upon historical data to explore the traffic condition of the road, $r = \langle I_i, I_j \rangle$. Note that the speed distributions of $\langle I_i, I_j \rangle$ and $\langle I_j, I_i \rangle$ are different due to different directions of traffic flows. According to the speed distribution, we can derive the normal speed threshold for $\langle I_i, I_j \rangle$ and detect cloned VINs based on it.

Algorithm 15 details the process of establishing the speed distribution set, SDS, based on historical trajectory data. Given the historical trajectory data set, $\mathscr{I}$, for each trajectory, $Traj^v$, in $\mathscr{I}$, we traverse all the points to update the speed distribution set. First, the rationality for every two consecutive points, p_j, p_{j+1}, in $Traj^v$ is validated by the function, *validate*() (line 4). If the traveling time interval between two points is too long or the average speed is extremely high, it means that the vehicle may be stationary during this time period, or it is a cloned vehicle. In this case, the speed between these two points cannot be used to construct speed distribution. After the validating process, if the matched speed distribution list for the inspection spot pair $\langle I_s, I_e \rangle$ (line 9) does not tally, the corresponding speed distribution list SDL_{I_s, I_e} of the I_s, I_e is initialized, and three statistic values x, y, and n of each distribution D in SDL_{I_s, I_e} are set to *zero* (line 10). After that, the speed distribution list, SDL, is inserted into the SDS (line 11). At last, the speed between points, p_j, p_{j+1}, is used to update the statistics of the distribution in the corresponding time period (lines 12–14).

5.3.1.2 *Cloned vehicle detection*

Initially, we put forward a naive detection method based on the speed thresholds that were extracted from historical trajectory data, called CVDH. The average speed between consecutive points in a trajectory is calculated directly and is used to detect a vehicle's abnormal behavior. Once the average speed of a trajectory fragment, $tf(p_i, p_j)$, exceeds the corresponding speed threshold, $tf(p_i, p_j)$ is identified as an abnormal trajectory fragment.

However, as the speed threshold is derived from the historical data, the cloned vehicle detection method based on the speed threshold is unfit for all the cases due to the following reasons:

- If the size n of the sampled data that was used to build the speed distribution is too small, the established speed distribution makes no sense statistically. As shown in Figure 5.2, the teardrop-shaped, geometry represents an inspection spot, and the dashed arrow indicates the direction of traffic flow between the inspection spot pair. The speed distributions among the inspection spot pairs in Figure 5.2 are

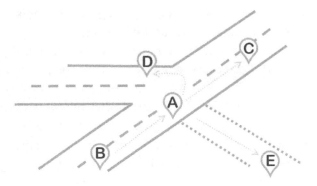

Figure 5.2. A deployment case of inspection spots.

built on the historical trajectory data during 20 days. Specifically, the sample size n of speed distribution, D, for $\langle I_A, I_E \rangle$ is smaller than 20, indicating that on average, no more than one vehicle passes by $\langle I_A, I_E \rangle$ each day. Since the result of the maximum-likelihood estimation is not accurate with a small sample size, the distribution D of $\langle I_A, I_E \rangle$ is unavailable.

- The speed distributions extracted from historical data cannot reflect any sudden traffic accidents or road changes. For example, a traffic accident such as a rear–front collision would influence the speeds of nearby vehicles. This kind of effect is unseen from historical data. Not only this, from Figure 5.2, I_D is a newly deployed inspection spot and I_E is located on a newly built road. However, there is still no historical trajectory data associated with I_D, and when the vehicle passes by two newly built inspection spots, there will not be any corresponding historical data that can tell us whether any unusual behavior has occurred (or not).

Therefore, the speed distribution is valid when a large amount of sample data is available, and the inspection spot pair satisfying the valid speed distributions can be regarded as a neighboring inspection spot pair (NIS-Pair). In Figure 5.2, $\langle I_B, I_A \rangle$, $\langle I_A, I_C \rangle$, and $\langle I_A, I_D \rangle$, are NIS-Pair. For NIS-Pair, the speed threshold derived based on speed distribution can be adopted to detect abnormal behaviors directly. For the non-neighboring inspection spot pair (NNIS-Pair), e.g., $\langle I_A, I_E \rangle$, a mechanism is needed to design abnormal behavior detection of the vehicles.

Moreover, the traffic conditions of the roads are dynamically changing and context-related. It is observed that if a road is congested, its adjacent roads are likely to be affected as well. Therefore, for a trajectory fragment, tf_i, which is connected by the NNIS-Pair, the behavior difference between tf_i and its local neighbors can be used to assess its abnormality. The behavior differences between the trajectories mainly manifest as speed, direction, etc. For example, the speed of a vehicle, v_i, passing the road, r, is 90 km/h. However, the speed of other vehicles passing the road, r, at the same time period is around 30 km/h, thus v_i is identified as an outlier for its speeding behavior. Besides, supposing the road, r, lies between inspection spots, I_s and I_e, and v_i is detected by I_e and I_s sequentially. However, the nearby trajectory fragments are all passing from I_s to I_e, therefore v_i is identified as an outlier due to its converse driving.

For the case in Figure 5.2, since the sample size of historical data between $\langle I_A, I_E \rangle$ is too small, the inspection spot, I_E, is not the neighbor of I_A. Contrarily, I_C and I_D are the neighbors of I_A as there are many vehicles passing them. Given the asymmetry of the inspection spot pair, I_B is not the neighbor of I_A but I_A is the neighbor of I_B. For the trajectory fragment, tf_i, passing by $\langle I_A, I_E \rangle$ at the time period, g, the other trajectory fragments passing by $\langle I_A, I_C \rangle$ or $\langle I_A, I_D \rangle$ in g are regarded as local neighbors of tf_i, denoted as $N_{\mathrm{tf}}(\mathrm{tf}_i)$.

We adopt the concepts of *local difference density* (LDD) and *local anomaly factor* (LAF) in Chapter 3 to calculate the *abnormality* of a trajectory fragment relative to its local neighboring trajectories.

Abnormality is described as the difference between a trajectory fragment and its neighboring fragments. A detailed description of LAF and LDD is given in Chapter 3. In our study, the behavior difference between trajectory fragments mainly takes speed into account. Specially, for a trajectory fragment, tf_i, $\mathrm{Diff}^{\mathrm{sp}}(\mathrm{tf}_i, \mathrm{tf}_j)$ equals to the speed difference between tf_i and tf_j, iff the speed of tf_i is larger than the speed of tf_j, otherwise, $\mathrm{Diff}^{\mathrm{sp}}(\mathrm{tf}_i, \mathrm{tf}_j)$ equals to *zero*. In general, a higher $\mathrm{LAF}(\mathrm{tf}_i)$ indicates that the trajectory fragment, tf_i, is more likely to be abnormal. For the trajectory fragment, tf_i, passing by a NNIS-Pair, tf_i is considered to be abnormal only if $LAF(tf_i)$ is larger than the abnormality threshold, ρ.

At this point, cloned vehicle detection is implemented by a combination of **speed-based** checking with moving behavioral abnormality identification. At this point, based on the CVDH method, we propose a <u>C</u>loned <u>V</u>ehicle <u>D</u>etection method that incorporates the behavior abnormality analysis within the local <u>N</u>eighborhood, called CVDN.

Once a license plate is cloned, two or more vehicles using the same VIN may drive on the road at the same time. As a result, the abnormal frequentness of the cloned VIN is larger than the normal one within a time period. We observe the behavior of the two VIN's trajectory within recent w time periods, continuously based on the sliding-window model, and identify a VIN as cloned iff its abnormal behavior frequentness exceeds the threshold, k. After a trajectory fragment is identified as abnormal, the corresponding VIN is marked as a candidate cloned VIN and put into the candidate cloned VIN set E. The structure of E is shown as follows:

$$E = \{\langle v_1, CList_1 \rangle, \langle v_2, CList_2 \rangle, \ldots, \langle v_n, CList_n \rangle\}. \tag{5.5}$$

Here, $CList_i (1 \leq i \leq n)$ is a list whose length is within w, and each element in the list records the frequentness of abnormal behavior of the VIN v_i in each time period.

For any candidate cloned vehicle, we constantly update its abnormal frequentness during w time periods. Whenever the window slides forward, the outdated data will be deleted and the incoming data is inserted.

Figure 5.3 shows an example of the abnormal behavior frequentness variation of a trajectory during multiple time periods. Here the window

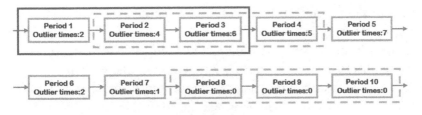

Figure 5.3. An example of a sliding window.

size, w, is set to 3, and the anomaly behavior frequentness threshold, k, is set to 14, which means that the VIN is considered to be cloned iff the frequentness sum of its abnormal behaviors exceeds 14 in three consecutive time periods.

As new data arrives, the window keeps sliding and the data in E is accordingly updated. As shown in Figure 5.3, when the window slides to the time period 1, 2, and 3 sequentially, the frequentness of abnormal behavior from v_i within these time periods is recorded in $CList_i$, respectively. When the window slides to the dashed box (including the time periods 2, 3, and 4), the expired data (arrived in time period 1) is removed from $CList_i$, and the newly arrived data (in time period 4) is inserted into the $CList_i$. At this time, the sum of the abnormal behavior frequentness becomes 15, and VIN v_i is regarded as a cloned VIN due to its abnormal behavior frequentness that exceeds the threshold k. Accordingly, when the window slides to the time period 8, 9, and 10 sequentially, there is no abnormal behavior recorded in $CList_i$, therefore v_i is removed from E.

Algorithm 16 illustrates the process of CVDN. Given the trajectory set within the current time period, $\mathscr{S}$, with the cloned VIN candidate set E, the speed distribution set, SDS, the sliding window size, w, the threshold, ρ, and anomaly behavior frequentness threshold, k, for each $CList_i$ in E. If the length of the $CList_i$ equals w, the expired data in $CList_i$ needs to be removed (lines 1–3) and the anomaly behavior frequentness in the current time period of $CList$ is initialized to *zero* (line 4). Then we traverse all the trajectories in this period, for each trajectory $Traj^{v_i}$ in $\mathscr{S}$, the anomaly behavior frequentness at this period is calculated (line 6), as illustrated in Algorithm 17.

In Algorithm 17, the abnormality of each trajectory point pair needs to be estimated. For example, for the points pair, p_j, p_{j+1}, we first check the sample size of the corresponding speed distribution (line 4). If the sample size is larger than the threshold, η, the speed threshold that is derived from the speed distribution is used to detect the abnormality of the points pair directly (lines 5–7). Otherwise, the abnormality of the trajectory fragment, tf*:p_j, p_{j+1}, is derived by calculating the LAF(tf*) between tf* and its local neighboring trajectory fragments, N_{tf}(tf*) (lines 9–11). If the LAF(tf*) is larger than the threshold, ρ, it indicates that tf* is likely to be an anomaly fragment relative to its neighbors $N_{tf}(tf^*)$ (lines 12–13).

After traversing all the points pairs in a trajectory, Algorithm 17 returns the anomaly behavior frequentness of that trajectory.

As illustrated in Algorithm 16, after calculating the abnormal behavior frequentness, the trajectory data is used to update the statistics of the corresponding speed distribution (line 7). If the abnormal behavior frequentness, *num*, of trajectory $Traj^{v_i}$ is larger than *zero* and the cloned VIN candidate set E does not contain v_i, v_i is inserted into E (lines 9–12) and needs to be continuously observed during subsequent time periods.

Then, the frequentness of abnormal behavior within the current time period in *CList* (lines 13–14) is updated, and the total number of abnormal behavior in *CList* is obtained. VIN v_i is identified as a cloned VIN and put into the cloned VIN set, $\mathscr{CV}$, iff its abnormal behavior frequentness exceeds k (lines 15–16).

After finished the detection, if the abnormal behavior frequentness of v_i during w time periods is *zero*, the corresponding VIN is removed from the candidate set E (lines 17–19). Finally, the algorithm returns the cloned VIN set, $\mathscr{CV}$. With the window sliding forward, Algorithm 16 is implemented to detect the cloned vehicle in the new time period by continuously updating E and SDS.

5.3.2 *Cloned vehicle behavior pattern mining*

After cloned vehicle detection, it is imperative to discern the trajectories of different objects that use the same VIN, and then extract the moving behavior patterns of various objects. In this section, we first propose a trajectory identification method to discern the traces of different objects with the same VIN, then mine their distinct moving behavior patterns from these traces.

5.3.2.1 *Trajectory identification of individual object*

A cloned VIN can be used by multiple vehicles. When they drive on the roads at the same time, their respective position data will mix. To differentiate the trajectories of different objects, it is necessary to group the mixed trajectories into the classes that belong to various objects.

Dai (2016) designed a trajectory identification algorithm T PA based on a maximum unreachable speed between two points. If the speed between any two points is smaller than the maximum unreachable speed, the two points are considered to be generated by the same object. Given a cloned VIN's trajectory, $Traj^v = \{p_1,\ p_2,\ p_3\}$, if the speed between $\langle p_1, p_3 \rangle$ and $\langle p_2, p_3 \rangle$ is smaller than the maximum unreachable speed, $\langle p_1, p_2 \rangle$ is larger than the maximum unreachable speed. According to T PA, p_1 and p_2 cannot be generated by the same object. But T PA does not give a specific solution to determine which vehicle generates p_3. Besides this, as we mentioned before, the fixed maximum unreachable speed cannot describe the traffic situation of a road accurately. Thus, T PA cannot solve this identification problem effectively.

The key step is to match each point into the classes that belong to different objects. First of all, any two points need to be rationally verified based on the shortest travel time. For example, if the inspection spot, I_j, detects a vehicle with the VIN $'8805'$ at 20:13:25, and another inspection spot, I_k, detects a vehicle with the same VIN at 20:13:40. But the actual distance between I_j and I_k is 5 km, therefore, I_j to I_k cannot be traveled in such a short time. If the two points are unreachable in a certain time period, then they cannot be generated by the same object.

In light of the above, we use the shortest travel time to judge the rationality between any two points. First, the maximum speed between any two neighboring inspection spot is obtained from the speed distribution.

The shortest travel time of these neighbor inspection spots can be calculated by the ratio between the distance of them and the corresponding maximum speed derived from the speed distribution. To this end, we build a directed weighted graph $G(\mathcal{V}, \mathcal{E})$ of all the inspection spots, where $\mathcal{V}$ denotes a set of inspection spots and $\mathcal{E}$ denotes a set of edges whose weight is the shortest travel time between the inspection spots. In the beginning, the inspection spots have an edge whose weight is the shortest travel time if and only if they are adjacent. Then our schema uses the *Dijkstra* algorithm to calculate the shortest travel time among all the inspection spot pair. Similar to the speed distribution, the shortest travel time varies across time. If the time gap between any two points is shorter than the corresponding shortest travel time, they are viewed as unreachable in such a short time slot and cannot be generated by the

---

Algorithm 18: *object_identification*(Traj^v)

Input: Traj^v: Mixed trajectory;

Output: *TrajSet*: Trajectory set;

1 *TrajSet* ← ∅;

2 Traj$_0^v$ ← {p_0};

3 *TrajSet* ← *TrajSet* ∪ {Traj$_0^v$};

4 **for** p_i **from** p_1 **to** $p_{\text{Traj}^v.size()-1}$ **do**

5   Traj$_{match}^v$ ← *find_best_match*(p_i, *TrajSet*);

6   **if** Traj$_{match}^v$ = *NULL* **then**

7   *num* ← *TrajSet.size*();

8   Traj$_{num}^v$ ← {p_i};

9   *TrajSet* ← *TrajSet* ∪ {Traj$_{num}^v$};

10   **else**

11   *append*(Traj$_{match}^v$, p_i);

12 **return** *TrajSet*;

---

same object. After the *shortest travel time*-based rationality verification, the *matching degree*-based clustering method is leveraged to discern the trajectories of different objects. The matching degree and the shortest travel time enable us to judge whether these points are generated by the same vehicle.

Algorithm 18 illustrates the detailed process of identifying the trajectory of each object. Figure 5.4 shows an example of the cloned vehicle trajectory, points, p_0, p_1, . . . , p_5, are collected by inspection spots at consecutive timestamps. The dotted lines represent the chronological order of these points. We combine this with the example in Figure 5.4 to explain this process. Suppose the first point, p_0, in the cloned vehicle trajectory, Traj^v, is generated by the vehicle, v_0, and p_0 is put into Traj$_0$ (lines 2–3).

Then, we need to judge whether p_1 is generated by v_0 or not, after which we attempt to compare the time interval between p_0 and p_1 with the corresponding shortest travel time. Suppose the time interval between them is less than the shortest travel time, we will not be able to find the existing trajectory for p_1 (line 6). p_1 is supposed to be generated

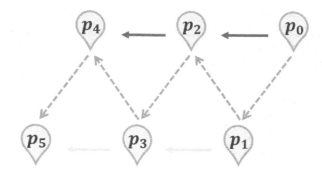

Figure 5.4.   An example of identifying the objects' trajectories.

by the other vehicle, v_1. Thus, we put p_1 into Traj_1^v (lines 6–9). So far, there are two trajectories that are generated by v_0 and v_1, respectively. Then we need to judge the rationality and calculate the matching degree of (p_0, p_2) and (p_1, p_2), respectively (line 5). If the rationality of both point pairs is false, p_2 is supposed to be generated by another vehicle, v_2. Otherwise, p_2 is absorbed into the existing vehicle's trajectory with the highest matching degree (line 11).

In the same way, the rest points in the cloned vehicle trajectory are processed successively and hence two trajectories are derived. As shown in Figure 5.4, one trajectory is denoted as $\text{Traj}_0^v = \{p_0, p_2, p_4\}$ and the other is represented as $\text{Traj}_1^v = \{p_1, p_3, p_5\}$.

5.3.2.2 *Moving behavior pattern extraction*

The behavior pattern of the cloned vehicle can be depicted as the time-related inspection spots sequence that a driver passes frequently. Extracting the daily moving behavior pattern of the cloned vehicle enables traffic agencies to make sense of its moving trend, e.g., predict the future location of cloned vehicles based on its current position and even figure out the different motives behind the cloned vehicle cases.

Through observing the inspection spots data for a month, the moving behavior pattern of cloned vehicles with regular behavior can be roughly divided into two categories. In the first case, vehicles have a fixed place of residence but with a random spatial range of daily activities, which may indicate the daily movement of taxis. This kind of behavior pattern can be represented as follows:

$$tr = I_i \rightarrow I_j \rightarrow ... \rightarrow I_k \rightarrow I_l,$$

where I_i, I_j and I_k, I_l stand for the inspection spots near the residence place, respectively.

In the second case, the vehicles pass by the same places with a similar travel time, and they behave regularly every day. For example, on a weekday, a white collar worker usually leaves his home residence at about 8:00 a.m., then arrives at his company at 9:00 a.m. and leaves at 5:00 p.m. It takes one hour for him to return to his residence. The example of this pattern can be represented as follows:

$$tp = I_i \xrightarrow{\text{1 hour}} I_j \xrightarrow{\text{8 hour}} I_k \xrightarrow{\text{1 hour}} I_l,$$

where I_i, I_l denote the inspection spots near his residence, and I_j, I_k denote the inspection spots near his company.

Algorithm 19 summarizes the details of mining the frequent moving behavior pattern, which consists of two steps. In the first step (lines 2–6), the algorithm discovers the driver's home residence. The points where the trajectory begins and ends may be adjacent to the area of his residence. Due to the fact that many people drive across the whole day, it is not appropriate to take the first and last k points from the trajectory during a day to determine his place of residence. Therefore, according to the time gap between two consecutive points, the original trajectory during many days, Traj_set, is partitioned into a set of trajectory segments, S (line 3). The time range of each trajectory segment, s_i, is determined by the vehicle's driving time. For example, a vehicle runs from 10:00 a.m. to 3:00 a.m. the next day. So the time range of a trajectory segment, s_i, of this vehicle is started at 10:00 a.m. and lasts for 17 hours. Then, we put the first and last k points of each trajectory segment, s_i, in S into the set KP (lines 4–5). The area mined from the points in KP whose quantity satisfies the minimum support, δ_p (line 6), is regarded as the residence place of the vehicle's owner.

In the second step (lines 8–12), the moving behavior pattern of the object is mined. The vehicle may behave differently during different time periods; the moving behavior patterns in $\mathscr{G}$ periods are derived,

---

Algorithm 19: *pattern_mining*(Traj_*set*, δ_p, δ_f, $\mathscr{G}$)

Input: *TrajSet*, δ_p, δ_f, $\mathscr{G}$: A set of trajectories during consecutive days;

Output: $\mathscr{R}$: Residence places set; and $\mathscr{F}$: Frequent pattern set;

1 $\mathscr{R} \leftarrow \emptyset$, $\mathscr{F} \leftarrow \emptyset$, $KP \leftarrow \emptyset$;

2 /*STEP 1*/ ;

3 $S \leftarrow segment(TrajSet)$;

4 **for** s_i **in** S **do**

5     $KP \leftarrow KP \bigcup first\_last\_point(s_i, k)$;

6 $\mathscr{R} \leftarrow find\_residence\_place(KP, \delta_p)$;

7 /*STEP 2*/ ;

8 **for** g **from** 1 **to** $\mathscr{G}$ **do**

9     $SubTrajSet^g \leftarrow get\_sub\_traj(TrajSet, g)$;

10    $H \leftarrow Dynamic\_I\_Pattern(SubTrajSet^g, \delta_f)$;

11   p : the longest pattern in H;

12    $\mathscr{F} \leftarrow \mathscr{F} \bigcup \{p\}$;

13 **return** *pattern* $\mathscr{R}$ *and* $\mathscr{F}$;

---

respectively. First, each trajectory in *TrajSet* is divided into different sub-trajectories according to the time periods, and the sub-trajectory set, *SubTrajSet^g*, contains all the sub-trajectories in the time period, g (line 9). We apply the trajectory pattern mining algorithm in Giannotti *et al.* (2007) to extract the frequent behavior pattern H from each *SubTrajSet^g* (line 10). Giannotti *et al.* (2007) add new items continuously to the existing frequent sequences and derived the longer frequentness sequence that satisfies the requirements.

Initially, a projection database is generated according to the corresponding frequent sequence, $\mathscr{S}$, the frequent items whose support degree are greater than the minimum support threshold, δ_f, that would have been mined from the projection database. If the time gap between the items satisfies the annotation constraint, the item would be added into the sequence, $\mathscr{S}$. Given *minimum support* and the sequence length threshold, the longest frequent sequence, p, which satisfies the condition is regarded as the typical pattern of the vehicle in this period (lines 11–12).

The daily moving behavior pattern and the residence place of the vehicles can be used to predict the future movements of cloned vehicles and improve the accuracy for hunting them down. For a vehicle, v_i, with regular behavior, according to the pattern, $\text{tp}_{v_i} = I_i \xrightarrow{\alpha_1} I_j \xrightarrow{\alpha_2} \ldots \xrightarrow{\alpha_k} I_k$, we can predict that v_i may appear in one or more inspection spots of the sequence. If v_i is detected at the inspection spot, I_i, we can infer that the next inspection spots where v_i could pass through are likely to be in the sequence after I_i.

Besides these two cases, some vehicles use cloned VINs to avoid punishment for illegal driving. The trajectories of these vehicles are always accompanied with high-frequency abnormal behaviors relative to their local neighborhoods. These abnormal behaviors may manifest themselves in the forms of considerable differences in speed and direction within their local neighborhood, such as speeding, driving in reverse, illegal turnings, etc. Hence, similar with the cloned vehicle detection phase, for each trajectory segment, we continuously capture its behavioral outlier and accumulate the frequency of abnormal behavior displayed by the object. We finally extract its behavior pattern that consists of all kinds of traffic violation events.

5.4 Empirical Evaluation

5.4.1 *Experimental setup*

All the codes of our framework are written in Java and all our experiments are run at a computer with dual-core 3.4 GHz CPU and 8 GB of main memory. We use real-world ITS surveillance data sets generated by 535 inspection spots in Nanjing. Each record contains 16 attributes, such as the VIN of the passing vehicle, lane number, timestamp, direction, etc. After analyzing the data recorded by these inspection spots, we found that eight inspection spots malfunctioned, hence the data collected by these inspection spots are excluded. So, based upon the data recorded by the remaining 527 inspection spots, we derived more than 80,000,000 trajectories of 2.8 million VINs.

5.4.2 *Experimental result*

We first explain the rationality of speed distribution and then conduct evaluations of cloned vehicle detection. In this subsection, the speed distributions of each inspection spot pair are modeled upon the trajectory data from 1 to 20 September, and the speed thresholds of any road within different time periods are derived. In our experiments, 160,000 inspection spot pairs are recorded, and about 960,000 speed distributions are established. It is observed that the average speed of the road varies greatly between peak and off-peak periods. Therefore, based on the observation of typical traffic fluctuation patterns, we divide a day into six periods and ensure each period is of a similar traffic condition. Six periods include 00:00–05:59, 06:00–06:59, 07:00–10:59, 11:00–13:59, 14:00–17:59, and 18:00–23:59.

We use the trajectories from 1 to 10 September to establish the speed distributions and derive the speed thresholds between all the inspection spot pairs. Then the trajectories between 11 and 20 September are used to detect the cloned vehicles. Fifty cloned VINs and 1101 legal VINs are labeled manually by the volunteers. To ensure the reliability of the experimental data set, we also use the synthetic trajectories to validate the effectiveness of our framework. To construct the synthetic trajectory data, we first select a trajectory of 21 legal vehicles, whose trajectories are recorded more than 50 times per day. The travel time of these vehicles are also similar. We constantly select two trajectory points from the trajectories of 21 legal vehicles, and mix them into one synthetic cloned trajectory in chronological order, and finally obtain 210 synthetic cloned trajectories.

5.4.2.1 *Rationality evaluation*

For each inspection spot pair, we not only derive the corresponding speed threshold based on speed distribution but also calculate the average speed of all the vehicles passing by it. The distribution of the road segments' average speed is shown in Figure 5.5(a). The horizontal axis represents the speed range and the vertical axis represents the ratio of the average speed in the corresponding time interval. As shown in Figure 5.5(a), the speed distributions whose average speed is between 10 and 20 km/h

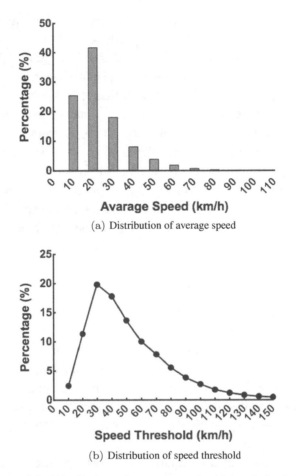

(a) Distribution of average speed

(b) Distribution of speed threshold

Figure 5.5. Distribution of average speed and speed threshold.

account for 41.7% of all the distributions. More than 98% of the speed distributions' average speed is less than 60 km/h, and the average speed of all the distributions is less than 80 km/h.

Figure 5.5(b) shows the distribution of the speed threshold of all the roads and the vertical axis represents the ratio of the speed threshold to the corresponding interval. It can be found that the speed thresholds among the inspection spot pairs mainly concentrate in a range from 20 to 60 km/h, and more than 90% of the distributions' speed thresholds are less than 80 km/h. Furthermore, there are very few inspection spot pairs with a speed threshold exceeding 100 km/h.

The traditional method uses the fixed threshold (e.g., 120 km/h) to detect the cloned vehicle. But the average speeds of the roads are different and generally the average speed is less than 120 km/h. Therefore, the traditional method cannot effectively detect the cloned vehicle in an actual road network. Through comparing two diagrams in Figure 5.5, we find that the speed threshold calculated by the speed distribution is significantly greater than the average speed but far less than the fixed speed threshold (e.g., 120 km/h) applied in the traditional detection method. We use the Gaussian Distribution to model the speed distribution of the road and thus derive a more reasonable speed threshold based on it.

5.4.2.2 *Effectiveness evaluation*

We evaluate the influence of the parameters on our proposed cloned vehicle method CVDN, and then compare it with CVDH to assess the effectiveness of our proposal. As mentioned before, CVDH uses the speed thresholds derived from the historical trajectory data to detect abnormal behavior. We conduct the effectiveness evaluation on two data sets, including a real-world data set (containing 1101 legal VINs and 50 cloned VINs, and a synthetic data set containing 1101 legal VINs and 210 cloned the VINs).

In order to conduct a comparative analysis of the effectiveness of both methods, we use Precision, Recall, and F-measure as the criteria measurements. They are defined as follows:

$$\text{Precision} = \frac{|R| \cap |D|}{|D|}, \tag{5.6a}$$

$$\text{Recall} = \frac{|R| \cap |D|}{|R|}, \tag{5.6b}$$

$$F\text{-measure} = \frac{2 \times \text{Precision} \times \text{Recall}}{\text{Precision} + \text{Recall}}. \tag{5.6c}$$

Here, R denotes the manually labeled or synthetic cloned VIN set and D represents the cloned VIN detected by our proposal. Precision

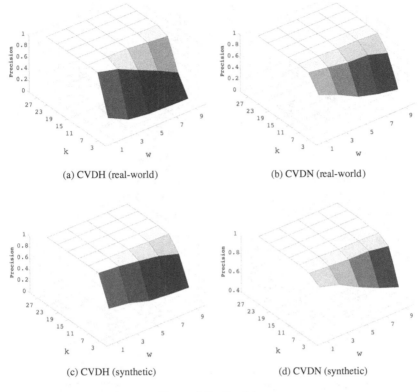

(a) CVDH (real-world) (b) CVDN (real-world)

(c) CVDH (synthetic) (d) CVDN (synthetic)

Figure 5.6. Precision.

reveals the detection accuracy of the cloned VIN and Recall measures the coverage of cloned VINs detected by our proposals. F-measure rises as the value of Precision or Recall increases. To understand the influence of the parameters on the accuracy of cloned VIN detection, we compare the results of both algorithms via Precision, Recall, and F-measure assessment under various parameters (i.e., w and k), as shown in Figures 5.6–5.8.

Precision. First, we investigate the precision of both algorithms under the different sliding window size, w, and abnormal behavior frequency threshold, k. As shown in Figure 5.6, for real-world and synthetic data sets, both the CVDH and CVDN methods could achieve their highest precision under $w \leq 3$ and $k \geq 7$. But as compared to CVDN, CVDH

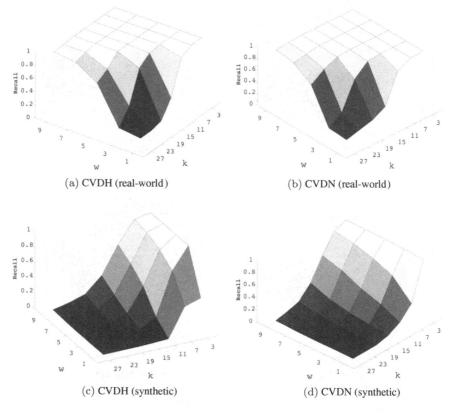

(a) CVDH (real-world) (b) CVDN (real-world)

(c) CVDH (synthetic) (d) CVDN (synthetic)

Figure 5.7. Recall.

requires a higher k to attain the same high precision. This is because CVDH does not take the traffic situation into account. When the value of k is small, CVDH easily mistakes the legal vehicle as the cloned VIN. Note that this precision would reach 1 when k is larger than 11, because normal vehicles cannot incur such a great number of abnormal behaviors in a short time period.

Recall. Second, we report the recall rate of both algorithms under a different w and k. As shown in Figure 5.7, it can be found that there are significant differences between the recall rates of both algorithms on two data sets. For the real-world data set with 50 marked cloned VINs, the recall achieves higher value with the increment of w or the decrement of k. A similar tendency is also found on the synthetic data

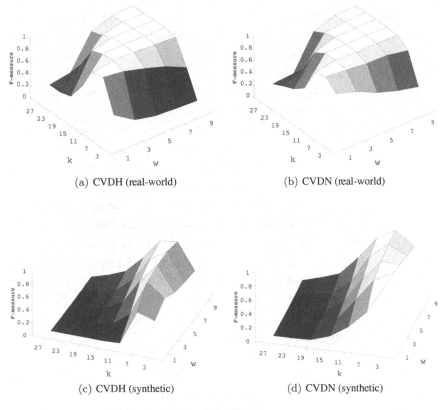

(a) CVDH (real-world) (b) CVDN (real-world)

(c) CVDH (synthetic) (d) CVDN (synthetic)

Figure 5.8. *F*-measure.

set. However, the recall value on the synthetic data set is relatively low, especially when $k > 11$. The reason is that the manually labeled cloned VINs often have significant abnormal behaviors. In the real-world data set, sometimes more than two vehicles use the same cloned VIN at the same time, hence the density of the corresponding trajectory data is higher. Instead, the synthetic clone trajectory data set is generated by mixing two legitimate vehicle traces, which have relatively low density. It leads to the number of abnormal trajectories being unable to attain the high value. With the increment of the window size, w, the cloned vehicles almost have abnormal behaviors within each time period, and the VINs of these vehicles can be verified. Specifically when $k \leq 7$ and $w \geq 3$, both algorithms reach the highest recall value.

F-measure. Third, we examine F-measure of the CVDH and CVDN under different parameters. As shown in Figure 5.8, CVDH obtains its best F-measure when $w \geq 5$ and $k \geq 7$ on both data sets, and CVDN achieves its best F-measure when $k \geq 3$ and $w \geq 1$. It can be found that, as relative to CVDH, CVDN detects the cloned VIN more accurately under a smaller threshold, k, within a shorter time window, because the CVDN method adopts a more stringent definition of anomaly behavior, which reduces the misjudgments of normal vehicles. From the above results, we can conclude that both algorithms can detect the cloned VIN effectively. Furthermore, CVDN achieves the same effectiveness under the setting of a smaller sliding window size.

Next, we compare our proposals with TP-*Finder*. Through continuous observation for the trajectories of vehicles, TP-*Finder* identifies the *VIN* whose speed exceeds the predefined speed threshold as the cloned vehicle. Figures 5.9 and 5.10 depict the Precision, Recall, and F-measure of three methods on different data sets. The x-axis of these diagrams represents the observation time. From our experimental evaluations, TP-*Finder* obtains the best result when the speed threshold is set to 150 km/h.

In the Precision assessment experiment, CVDH and CVDN achieve higher value than TP-*Finder* on both data sets. Especially with the increment of the observation time, TP-*Finder* becomes less precise because it misjudges some of the normal vehicles by using the fixed speed threshold. In terms of Recall measurement, TP-*Finder* performs the best owing to its LAX criteria. CVDN performs best on both data sets when F-measure is estimating results. This means that it can detect the cloned VIN effectively.

5.4.2.3 *Efficiency evaluation*

We proceed to study the efficiency of CVDN by comparing it with CVDH. Figures 5.11 and 5.12 show the execution time of CVDH and CVDN. When the number of trajectories varies from $2k$ to $10k$, we assess the parameter sensitivity of both algorithms on two data sets. Figures 5.11(a) and 5.12(a) show the execution time of both algorithms as the window size, w, varies ($w = 1$ and 10, respectively). It is observed that the processing time of both methods rises as the window size, w, grows.

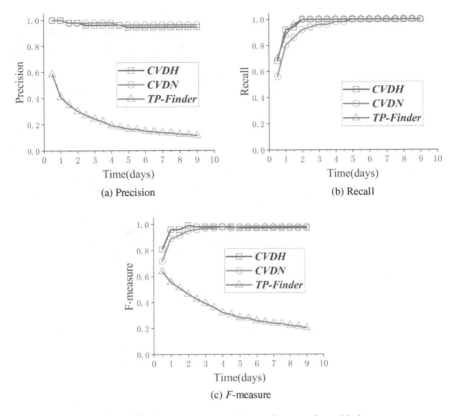

Figure 5.9. Effectiveness comparison under a real-world data set.

This is due to a larger window size that allows more incoming point pairs to be processed. Figures 5.11(b) and 5.12(b) show the execution time of CVDN and CVDH, as the number of anomaly threshold k varies ($k = 5$ and 15, respectively). The variation of k has little effect on the execution time of both algorithms, because the amount of data to be processed within a time window does not change under a different k value.

In total, no matter which data set is used, CVDN is slower than CVDH, because the latter determines the rationality of the trajectory point pair according to the average speed between the point pair. However, CVDN needs to first judge whether the corresponding historical distribution is available, and if not, the speed difference between adjacent trajectory segments would be calculated, which adds to the computation overhead.

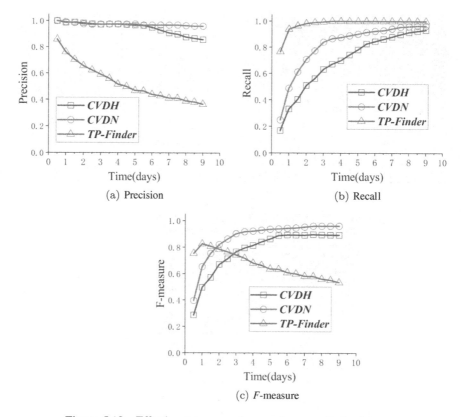

Figure 5.10. Effectiveness comparison under a synthetic data set.

Although the execution time of the algorithms changes under different parameters, the processing time of CVDN is no more than 250 ms when the number of trajectories is not beyond 1,000.

5.4.3 *Object identification and pattern extraction*

After detecting the cloned vehicles, 50 fake VINs are identified. According to the length of each trajectory, we choose the top 30 trajectories and require volunteers to match each point of the trajectory with a real vehicle. Similar to the task of the detection phase, we deploy the experiments of object identification on two data sets. We empirically set the weight of time and distance for the matching degree to 0.3 and 0.7, respectively, and set the minimum support in pattern extraction to 0.6.

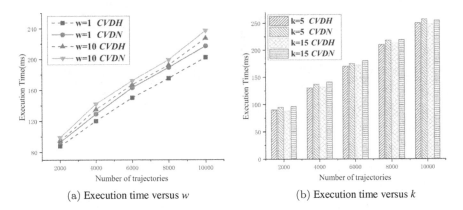

(a) Execution time versus w (b) Execution time versus k

Figure 5.11. Execution time comparison on a real-world data set.

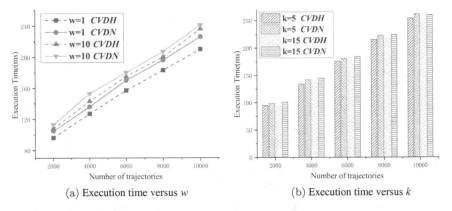

(a) Execution time versus w (b) Execution time versus k

Figure 5.12. Execution time comparison on a synthetic data set.

5.4.3.1 *Effectiveness evaluation*

Partial results of the trajectory identification and behavior pattern extraction are shown in Figure 5.13. Figure 5.13(a) shows the trajectories of VIN No. 8867 in a span of three days, which are marked with circle, square, and triangle, respectively. In the trajectory identification phase, we discern the trajectories of two vehicles with VIN No. 8867 (highlighted in solid and dotted lines, respectively), as illustrated in Figure 5.13(b). It can be observed that the vehicle represented by the dotted lines drives in a regular path, i.e., it visits fixed places in the same chronological order every day. Besides, the vehicle represented by the solid lines leaves and

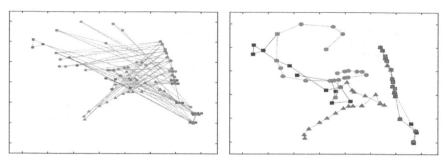

(a) Trajectories of cloned vehicle   (b) Object identification

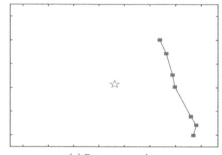

(c) Pattern extraction

Figure 5.13. Object identification and behavior pattern extraction.

returns to the same area, which is inferred to be where the vehicle's owner lives. The behavior patterns of the identified vehicles are presented in Figure 5.13(c). The star in Figure 5.13(c) represents the place where the vehicle is usually parked without regular moving behavior, and the black line on the right represents the pattern of a vehicle with regular behavior.

We use two data sets to evaluate the effectiveness of the proposed object identification algorithm. The synthetic data set is processed in the same way during the detection phase. The real-world data set contains 30 cloned VINs and 83 objects using the cloned VINs. The synthetic data set contains 210 cloned VINs used by 420 objects.

We compare the effectiveness of our object identification algorithm with TPA [Dai, 2016] on both data sets. TPA adopts the unified speed threshold (i.e., 120 km/h) to determine whether the consecutive points

Table 5.2. The precision (%) of two methods.

Data set	Real world	Synthetic
TPA	59.4	67.9
CVDF	84.5	92.3

Figure 5.14. Case study: the trajectory of a vehicle with a cloned VIN.

in the cloned vehicle trajectory are generated by the same vehicle, and groups the points of the same object into one class. Table 5.2 shows the precision of both algorithms on two data sets. Our object identification algorithm performs better than TPA. This is because TPA does not consider the influence of traffic conditions, and puts the points generated by different vehicles into one class. Note that the precision of algorithms on the synthetic data set is higher than that on the real-world data set. The reason is that each trajectory in the synthetic data set is the mixture of two objects' traces, but the real-world trajectory may be generated by more vehicles, which increases the complexity to discern the objects.

Furthermore, we also try to figure out the motives behind the cloned vehicles. Figure 5.14 shows a trajectory segment of a cloned vehicle. The vehicle ran with higher speed as relative to its neighboring vehicles. The results indicate that this driver probably use the cloned VIN for illegal driving.

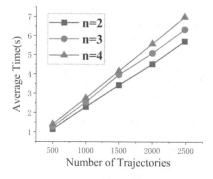

Figure 5.15. Execution overhead of object identification.

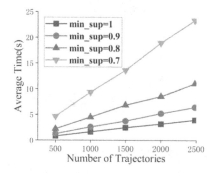

Figure 5.16. Execution overhead of pattern extraction.

5.4.3.2 *Efficiency evaluation*

Figure 5.15 shows the execution overhead of trajectory identification. It is observed that the execution time increases linearly with the number of trajectories, which means that the time complexity is proportional to the number of trajectories. The execution time increases with the number of vehicles (denoted as n) because it takes more time to compute the matching degree. Figure 5.16 shows the execution time of the behavior pattern extraction under various minimum support. It is found that the execution time decreases with the increment of the minimum support. As the value of the minimum support decreases, it takes more time to extract the behavior patterns. The above experiments establish that our proposals can differentiate the behavior patterns of the cloned vehicles with promising efficiency.

5.5 Related Work

Cloned vehicle detection has been extensively studied in recent years. In earlier researches, hardware-based solutions are generally adopted due to the absence of available data. Tang (2013) attempted to improve the anti-replication ability of the license plate by making a unique gap and thickening the border of each license plate. Deng *et al.* (2010) put forward a detection method based on RFID technology, which could store a vehicle's related information. When vehicles pass by the inspection spots at major crossings in the city, the installed microchip readers would match the plate number that has been pre-stored in the microchips, with the VINs recorded by the cameras to find the fake plate.

The hardware-based solutions can accurately detect cloned VINs to some extent, but traction is hard because the detection cost is so high and they need the buy-in of owners and governments. As image processing technology flourishes, the detection method based on vehicle-type identification has emerged [Iqbal *et al.*, 2010]. This technology extracts the vehicle type's features by processing the picture information recorded by the camera, and compares this information with the characteristics that are pre-stored in the database. However, such types of methods are susceptible to external factors like light. At the same time, it is hard to detect the cloned vehicles that are of the same type as the original vehicles.

With the popularization of the intelligent traffic system, the surveillance inspection spots deployed in city traffic crossroads continuously capture the movement information of passing vehicles, and the derived ANPR data provides us an opportunity to detect cloned vehicles. Li and Liu (2015) presented a cloned vehicle detection framework (called FP-*Detector*) using ANPR data. Based on the idea of *spatial–temporal contradiction observation*, the FP-*Detector* method attempted to detect the cloned vehicles in terms of a specified speed threshold. But traffic conditions behave differently across regions and change over time. Thus, the FP-*Detector* method easily attained lower precision and a high false alarm due to the use of the fixed speed threshold. *Speed distribution* modeling on historical trajectory data can help to derive the speed thresholds of different roads within different time slots. Detecting the cloned vehicles by using the derived various speed thresholds instead of a fixed threshold helps to improve the detection accuracy. Based on the speed distribution modeling using historical ANPR data, a detection method that uses the normal speed threshold extracted from historical data will work well.

However, since the distribution of trajectory data is skewed, few road regions incur a small number of trajectories most of the time. The derived speed thresholds based on sparse historical trajectory data is not effective enough to support cloned vehicle detection. Moreover, unexpected situations may affect the vehicles' speeds, such as traffic accidents or road repairs, which are unreflected in historical data. Inspired by the outlier detection technique proposed in Chapter 3, the moving behavior outlierness of each trajectory as relative to its local neighbors can be taken into account in the cloned vehicle detection process.

Furthermore, to gain insight into the motives behind cloned vehicle offenses, the cloned vehicles' moving patterns need to be discerned. To this end, we need to differentiate the trajectories of different vehicles using the same VIN first and then group the trajectories of the same vehicle into the same class. The critical point is to present a similarity metric that is used to assess the confidence of any two consecutive points generated by the same vehicle.

Most of the existing studies on trajectory similarity measurement focus on studying the distance metrics between the trajectory points or segments. Among them, the Euclidean distance (ED) [Faloutsos *et al.*, 1994] and the Closet–Pair Distance [Papadias *et al.*, 2003] consider the spatial factor, which is unfit for measuring the confidence of two points generated by the same vehicle. Spatial–temporal distance metrics include the Dynamic Time Warping (DTW) [Assent *et al.*, 2009], the Longest Common Sub Sequence (LCSS) [Vlachos *et al.*, 2006], the Edit Distance with Real Penalty (ERP) [Chen and Ng, 2004], and the Edit Distance on Real Sequence (EDR) [Chen *et al.*, 2005]. These methods are mainly applied for the trajectory segments, rather than for the single points. In addition, the above distance metrics cannot be suitable for addressing the issue of differentiating trajectories of various vehicles using the same plate number. Hence, we put forward the definition of *matching-degree* to measure the confidence of two adjacent points generated by the same vehicle.

In recent years, many researches on trajectory data mining have emerged [Tong *et al.*, 2018; Mao *et al.*, 2017b]. The frequent sequence pattern mining algorithm [Giannotti *et al.*, 2007; Agrawal and Srikant, 1995; Pei *et al.*, 2001; Zaki, 2001; Cao *et al.*, 2005; Giannotti *et al.*, 2006; Agrawal and Srikant, 1994] can be used to extract the behavior pattern of a cloned vehicle that has regular temporal behavior. The existing sequence patterns mining algorithms include *AprioriSome*, *AprioriAll* [Agrawal and Srikant, 1995], *PrefixSpan* [Pei *et al.*, 2001], and *SPADE* [Zaki, 2001]. Trajectory pattern can be represented as a set of trajectories sharing the property of visiting the same sequence of places.

5.6 Conclusion

In this chapter, we first propose a cloned vehicle detection framework called CVDF. It consists of two parts: detecting the cloned vehicle by incorporating speed threshold extraction upon historical data and the behavior abnormality analysis within the local neighborhood, and mining the moving behavior patterns of various objects with cloned VINs. Notably, we exploit a *matching degree-based* clustering method to reconstruct the trajectory of various vehicles with the same VIN. Then, we employ a hybrid spatial–temporal pattern extraction mechanism that incorporates the method developed by Giannotti *et al.*, 2007 and the frequent item mining algorithm [Agrawal and Srikant, 1994] to find the regular behavior pattern of the cloned vehicle. Moreover, we use the sliding-window model to continuously observe the behavior of the cloned vehicle and further pinpoint the vehicles with high-frequency illegal behavior. By conducting extensive experiments on real world and synthetic data sets, we compare our proposal with the state-of-the-art detection methods and object identification methods in term of effectiveness and efficiency. The experimental results demonstrate that our proposal can detect the cloned vehicle effectively, which provides a new way for solving cloned vehicle crime.

Chapter 6

Road Map Updating Using Trajectory Analysis

6.1 Background

With the widespread uses of various onboard navigators and the GPS navigation APP, digital maps have increasingly aroused universal concerns because of their accuracy. Today's commercially available digital maps have achieved an accuracy in the range of a few to ten meters, as well as coverage for the major highway road network and urban regions. However, the digital map may be incomplete or imprecise due to the rapid and continuous development of road construction and dynamically changing urban traffic conditions. For instance, after the map has been created, there may be new changes, such as existing roads being blocked for maintenance or becoming unavailable due to traffic congestion or road accidents, or new roads or intersections being built.

An inaccurate road map with disconnected and misaligned roads may cause experienced drivers to get lost or even cause traffic accidents. According to a report by TTG,[1] four British tourists in Florida were killed in a road accident because the GPS in the car instructed the driver to make a wrong U-turn at an intersection. Essentially, the accuracy and completeness of a digital map depend on whether road information is

---

[1] https://www.ttgmedia.com/news/news/four-british-tourists-killed-in-florida-car-crash-13731.

updated in a timely and effective manner. Therefore, a solution that will accurately update the road map needs to be found.

Nevertheless, such a task is difficult to achieve due to two factors: the rapid development of road construction and the ineffective map updating mechanism. Specifically, the rapid construction of roads has made it difficult to make digital map updates timely; the number of road changes all over the world change on a daily basis. At the same time, existing techniques do not precisely identify the changing of the road network topology and hence cannot guarantee the timeliness of map updating.

To ensure an effective updating of the road map, commercial map companies update digital maps by periodically conducting a geological survey of the entire road network, although this is expensive. To cut down on cost, the surveying period is long. Thus, the map updating rate lags behind the construction of new roads. An alternative mechanism is to adopt a crowdsourced map project to generate a customized map (e.g., *OpenStreetMap*), but this largely depends on the geographic data directly provided by the volunteers. As a result, the number of users and even their level of editing skills greatly influence the quality of the map updating. As mentioned above, it is desirable to devise a low-cost but highly reliable map updating mechanism.

The GPS trajectory data continuously generated by vehicles offers us an unprecedented opportunity to update digital road maps in a timely and cost-effective manner. Instead of incurring the expense of a complete road survey, huge amounts of trajectory data can be utilized to derive traffic statuses and traffic rules of different roads within various time periods. It could even be used to identify blocked roads and even generate entirely new sections of the road map. Recently, many research studies have been carried out on the updating or inference of road information using trajectory data, e.g., the missing roads inference [Wang *et al.*, 2013; Wu *et al.*, 2015; Shan *et al.*, 2015] and the road intersections detection [Fathi and Krumm, 2010; Wang *et al.*, 2015, 2017a; Tang *et al.*, 2017; Xie *et al.*, 2017; Xie and Philips, 2017; Li *et al.*, 2017]. Most of them mainly employ clustering on GPS trajectory data to infer or update the road map. In this chapter, we focus on the inference of several types of roads using trajectories, such as methods like the missing road inference, underground road identification, and road intersection detection.

6.1.1 *Missing road inference*

In the studies of missing road inference using trajectories, they can be grouped into two classes: *line-based* strategy (e.g., CrowdAtlas [Wang *et al.*, 2013]) and *point-based* strategy (e.g., Glue [Wu *et al.*, 2015], and COBWEB [Shan *et al.*, 2015]). To be specific, the former infers missing roads for a given map based on clustering considerable volume of unmatched trajectory segments, and the latter on massive unmatched trajectory points. These methods still face a series of problems, such as high computational overheads, low accuracy of inferred roads, and poor timeliness of map updating. Moreover, the *line-based* strategy has poor performance in processing low-sampling data (i.e., the sampling interval is longer than 30 seconds [Wu *et al.*, 2015]) because it may infer the roads with false directions when the line segments cross over several roads. Although *point-based* methods can overcome this issue, they easily infer some short road segments rather than long roads due to low coverage caused by *point-based* clustering.

As shown in Figure 6.1(a), two consecutive sampling points that are located on two roads are connected as a line segment, accordingly, an incorrect road $R_2\text{-}b$ is inferred by the *line-based* strategy. Though the *point-based* strategy solves the above deficiency, it infers two short road segments, $R_2\text{-}a$ and $R_2\text{-}b$, instead of a long road that covers them, as illustrated in Figure 6.1(b). Thus, the inferred roads in Figure 6.1(a) and (b) are incorrect. To improve the inferring accuracy and obtain the ideal result in Figure 6.1(c), a hybrid framework is needed to integrate the virtues of both the *line-based* and *point-based* strategies.

Furthermore, the aforementioned map updating mechanisms focus on inferring the missing roads on the trajectory data of dense areas. They usually define a threshold of the minimum clustering quantity standard and attempt to cluster unmatched trajectory line segments (or trajectory points) to infer the missing roads only when satisfying a specific threshold. Hence, for the top road region with sparse trajectory points in Figure 6.1(a) and (b), both the *line-based* and *point-based* strategies cannot infer the road, R_3, in Figure 6.1(c).

We can obtain two insights from the observation of trajectories. When the new roads first came into service, relatively few vehicles used them and thus the trajectory data for them were more sparse than that of normal

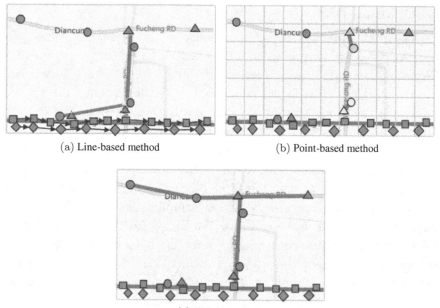

(a) Line-based method   (b) Point-based method

(c) Hybrid method

Figure 6.1.   An example of the line-based, point-based, and hybrid inferring method.

roads. Distinct from the noisy data, sparse trajectories may appear on such roads for many days, i.e., the amount of trajectories will not increase tremendously in a short time period. By simply lowering the threshold of the aforementioned methods, the noisy data may also be clustered and hence some incorrect roads can be inferred. As a result, both methods are not tailored to infer for missing roads in sparse trajectory areas. Given the two insights above, on the basis of the sliding-window model, we will first propose a two-phase road inferring framework, including candidate generation and missing roads inferring, called HyMU. In addition, we will employ a hybrid scheme to enhance the accuracy of map updating by integrating the *line-based* and *point-based* strategies.

6.1.2   *Underground road identification*

Underground roads provide a vital role in relieving urban traffic congestion. In general, there are two main types of underground roads: underpasses and tunnels. The underpass is an important kind of pedestrian crossing facility built near major urban roads that facilitate traffic flow and pedestrians' safety. The tunnel acts as a passage for vehicles and is usually built underground, through a hill, under the sea or underneath a railway or another road in metropolitan areas. In underground roads, the environment and how well it is lit have a great impact on the legibility of the traffic signs. A digital map with accurate underground road information can remind drivers to slow down and turn on their vehicles' headlights before entering tunnels, and it can also inform drivers which tunnel exit they should choose. However, some newly constructed underground roads are often not updated in a timely manner in the digital map. What's more, the road network of a city may not be easily gained. Hence, getting an accurate layout of where the underground roads are in a city remains a big challenge.

Fortunately, the difference of users' trajectories in and above underground provides us with a way to discover the underground roads in a city. Figure 6.2(a) shows the walking trajectory of a person going through an underpass (between points 5 and 6). Every dot represents a GPS point in the trajectory. Obviously, for points 1–5, and then from 6 to 14, the gap between each pair of consecutive points is similar and significantly shorter than the gap between points 5 and 6 comparably. The same situation is shown in Figure 6.2(b). The reason being is that GPS-enabled electronic devices cannot receive the signals when the user is going through the underground roads. As shown in Figure 6.2, the gaps between every pair of consecutive points before entering or exiting an underground road are similar, because the user is moving on the ground and GPS-enabled devices can receive the signals normally.

It is not difficult to discover underground roads when GPS devices work well and all the users move at nearly the same speed all the time. However, such a hypothesis cannot hold in real applications due to the following two reasons. First, the signals in urban canyons are weak and imprecise. Second, each user may change his or her speed very frequently. This results in the gaps between any two consecutive points varying a lot. In addition, without the road network, we cannot leverage a map-matching algorithm to handle the trajectories. Even then we cannot be certain whether a person is crossing a road (or not).

(a) Through the underpass

(b) Through the tunnel

Figure 6.2. Two trajectories through the underground roads.

Hence, discovering underground roads without a road network is indeed non-trivial.

The second aim in this chapter is to propose a three-step framework to deal with the issue of underground road detection. It includes an incremental clustering phase, where a number of line segments related to the aforementioned pattern are detected and incrementally maintained, a sub-trajectory detecting phase, where the number of the sub-trajectories passing a certain area is counted and stored, and a cluster filtering phase, where all the clusters are filtered and the underground roads' locations are obtained.

6.1.3 *Road intersection detection*

In road map inference, road intersection detection becomes of vital importance on account that the intersection has provided road information about geometric connectivity and allowable traveling directions. Traditional road intersection detection techniques depend on the geographic survey with mapping devices like telescopes and sextants, or image processing based on satellite images [Das *et al.*, 2011; Chen *et al.*, 2014], which are expensive and extremely time consuming. With the rapid development of GPS technology, commercial mapping companies have equipped specialized vehicles with GPS devices and deployed them on the roads to collect information about road intersections. Nevertheless, it is still a fairly labor-wasting effort to cover all the streets in urban areas, because very large amounts of updated information need to be recorded to keep the intersections up-to-date. The wide applications of GPS sensors in vehicles and smartphones have generated large collections of trajectories, which enable the timely and effective detection of intersections.

Several recent researches [Fathi and Krumm, 2010; Wang *et al.*, 2015, 2017a; Tang *et al.*, 2017; Xie *et al.*, 2017; Xie and Philips, 2017; Li *et al.*, 2017] utilize GPS trajectories to solve the issue of road intersection detection. They attempt to identify the road intersections according to the property that vehicles may turn at the intersections. Some of them strive for extracting a *turn point* at the intersections [Wang *et al.*, 2017a] directly, but the identification of a *turn point* is hard to implement in an actual road network due to the complexity of the road topology.

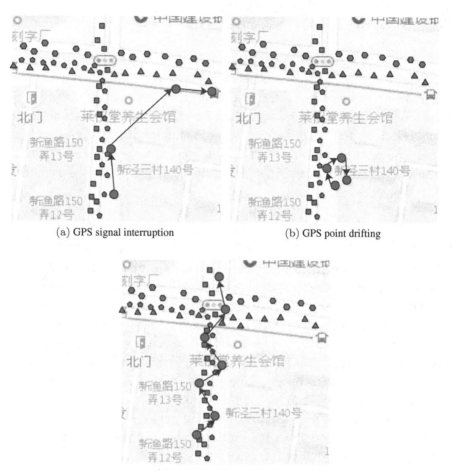

(a) GPS signal interruption

(b) GPS point drifting

(c) Behavior of lanes changing

Figure 6.3. Examples of the problems that intersection detection encountered.

In addition, the aforementioned approaches usually fail to work well in actual situations because of several challenges.

- *GPS signal interruption.* The reasons include artificial shutdown or device failure of GPS sensors embedded in the vehicles, which include these vehicles traveling in tunnels, under elevated roads and in city canyons. As shown in Figure 6.3(a), there are discontinuous big solid circle GPS points that are caused by GPS signal interruption. This leads to rather large variations in the direction and speed of the adjacent trajectory points at the road section, and thus makes intersection identification more difficult.

- *GPS point drifting.* A vehicle may temporarily stop on the road due to traffic jams, road accidents, etc. This would result in a lot of GPS points emerging from its traces with various directions in a short time due to non-trivial errors generated by GPS positioning devices. As exemplified in Figure 6.3(b), circled points (connected by arrows) show up as a "drifting" phenomenon. Specifically, there are points with great direction changes within a small spatial range, which increases the possibility of misjudgment of intersections.
- *Frequent heading changing on the road.* The headings of GPS trajectories may change frequently due to drivers changing lanes or overtaking, as shown in Figure 6.3(c). As one of the most important principles of extracting the intersections, the directional changes of trajectory points at the intersections are generally much more drastic than those on the road segments. Thus, it is indispensable to smoothen sharp headings of GPS points on the street.

To address the above challenges, the third aim in this chapter is to put forward a two-phase road intersection detection framework using GPS trajectories, called RIDF. It mainly includes improving the trajectory quality and intersection extracting. In the first phase, a data quality improving strategy that consists of splitting, resampling, and filtering is designed. It can solve the issues of GPS signal interruption and GPS point drifting. At the same time, it can eliminate some points with large heading changing on the road segment. In the second phase, an intersection detection mechanism includes cell candidate extraction and intersection location refinement. As shown in Figure 6.4, through the direction ratio statistic analysis incorporated with speed-based points screening, our detection mechanism could not only differentiate the intersections from the non-intersections, but also identify different-sized intersections.

The remainder of this chapter is organized as follows. In Sections 6.2–6.4, the preliminary concepts and schemes of inferring three types of roads are analytically studied. In Section 6.5, we review the latest work related to our research. Finally, in Section 6.6, we provide a conclusion and point out future directions.

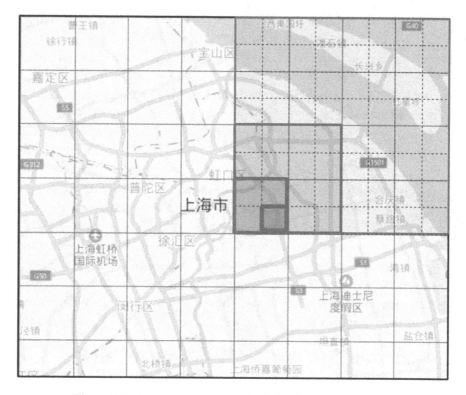

Figure 6.4. Splitting the map to the cells from top to bottom.

6.2 Missing Road Inferring

6.2.1 *Preliminaries*

A complete digital map contains road type, geometry, turn restriction, speed limit, etc. We aim to find the roads that have not been marked on the map, i.e., the missing roads. The road network, G, that corresponds to the map is defined as follows.

Definition 6.1 (Road Network). A road network is denoted by a graph, $G = (V, E)$, where V is a set of vertexes and E refers to a set of edges. Each edge, $e \in E$, represents a road segment.

To infer the missing roads, we need to cope with the continuously arrived trajectories. The trajectory of a moving object that consists of a series of GPS points is defined here as follows:

Definition 6.2 (Trajectory). The trajectory of a moving object, denoted as Tr, consists of a sequence of GPS points, (p_1, t_1), (p_2, t_2), $\cdots$, where p_i is the position at the timestamp, t_i. Such records arrive in chronological order, i.e., $\forall i < j$, $t_i < t_j$. Here, a trajectory segment is a line segment between two adjacent trajectory points, which is denoted as $Ts = (p_i, p_{i+1})$.

Trajectory data is collected in real time in a massive scale. In order to describe the portions of trajectories in different time periods, we employ the sliding-window model and a trajectory in a time window that is denoted as Tw. Given a window size, N, the window range at timestamp, t_0, is $(t_0, t_0 + N)$. Hereafter, we infer the missing road candidates based on the trajectories in each time window.

Due to different resolutions of various GPS-enabled equipments and a city canyon that is surrounded by high-rise buildings, the collected trajectory data is noisy. According to our observation, the noisy trajectories often behave abnormally in the direction or distance relative to their respective neighborhoods. The neighborhood of a trajectory segment, $Ts^{(x)}$, is defined as follows.

Definition 6.3 (Trajectory Segment Neighborhood). Given a trajectory segment, $Ts^{(x)}$, a distance threshold, th_{dis}, and a set of trajectory segments, TS, if we denote $dist(Ts^{(x)}, Ts^{(y)})$ as the shortest distance between any two points in two line segments, the neighborhood of $Ts^{(x)}$ is defined as follows:

$$Nd(Ts^{(x)}) = \{Ts^{(y)} \in TS | dist(Ts^{(x)}, Ts^{(y)}) \leq th_{dis}\}.$$

Here, the distance measurement employ *Difference Measurement* defined in Chapter 2. Correspondingly, the neighborhood of any trajectory point, p_i, is denoted as $Nd(p_i)$, which represents the set of points that their distances to p_i are within a distance threshold, th_{dis}. Subsequently, we define a noisy trajectory segment here as follows:

Definition 6.4 (Noisy Trajectory Segment). Given a trajectory segment, $Ts^{(x)}$, and the directions' distribution of its surrounding segments, $U(Ts^{(x)})$, $Ts^{(x)}$ is noisy if $Nd(Ts^{(x)})$ is empty or the direction of $Ts^{(x)}$ does not tally with the top-k most popular directions of its surrounding segments.

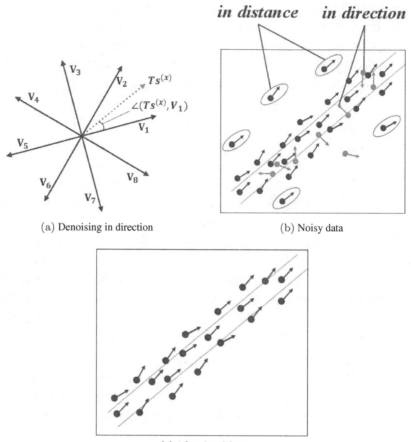

(a) Denoising in direction   (b) Noisy data

(c) After denoising

Figure 6.5.   An example of denoising in distance and direction.

We take the starting point of $Ts^{(x)}$ as the center and the length of $Ts^{(x)}$ as the radius of a circle, and generate a region. For example, in Figure 6.5(a), we divide the region into eight pieces, each representing a sector [Ge *et al.*, 2010]. The distribution is represented as follows:

$$U(Ts^{(x)}) = (C_1, C_2, C_3, C_4, C_5, C_6, C_7, C_8),$$

where C_i records the number of trajectory segments of $Nd(Ts^{(x)})$ that belong to the ith direction. Considering that each road usually has at least two lanes with opposite directions, we determine whether $Ts^{(x)}$ is a noisy trajectory segment by calculating to test whether $Ts^{(x)}$ belongs to the top two most popular directions. For example, in Figure 6.5(a), for a trajectory segment $\mathrm{Ts}^{(x)}$, we can determine which direction the trajectory segment, $\mathrm{Ts}^{(x)}$, belongs to in terms of the angle range between $\mathrm{Ts}^{(x)}$ and V_1, denoted as $\angle(\mathrm{Ts}^{(x)}, V_1)$.

Besides, each inferred road can be represented by a road centerline.

Definition 6.5 (Road Centerline). A road centerline, denoted as Rc, is represented by a polyline. It consists of a sequence of continuous positional points, $(p_1, p_2, \ldots, p_n)$, where p_i is the geographical position.

Finally, we summarize the problem as: given a road network, G, and sets of trajectories in multiple time periods, our goal is to infer the missing roads using the trajectories as early as possible, and then update the road network, G, by utilizing the inferred missing roads.

6.2.2 Hybrid map updating mechanism

In this section, we introduce a novel framework called Hybrid Map Updating (HyMU), which aims to identify missing roads based on trajectory data. As shown in Figure 6.6, HyMU is mainly composed of two phases: *candidates generation* and *missing roads inferring*. During the first phase, we attempt to obtain the unmatched trajectories in each time window by map matching, distance denoising, and direction denoising. Then, through clustering and centerline fitting on the unmatched and denoised trajectories, we derive the road candidates in each time window. During the second phase, we combine the candidates of multiple time windows via continuous observation. Once the number of hybrid candidates related to a certain road reaches the threshold, k, they will be merged to generate a missing road. Finally, through road combination, we update the road network with the inferred roads. Note that our hybrid framework integrates the advantages of *line-based* and *point-based* strategies, including high coverage and greater precision of the missing roads.

6.2.2.1 Candidate generation

As shown in Algorithm 20, the candidate generation phase involves *map matching* (lines 3–5), *denoising* (lines 6–8), *clustering* (lines 9–10), and *centerline fitting* (lines 11–14). First, the trajectories in each time window

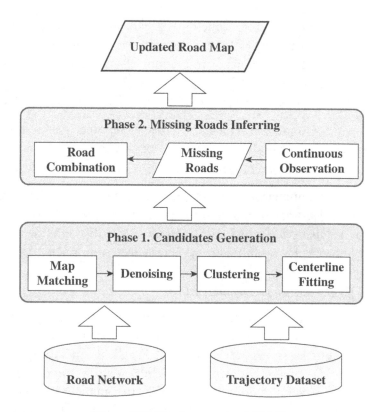

Figure 6.6. The framework of HyMU.

are matched with the road network to obtain unmatched trajectories. Then, after denoising, the denoised and unmatched trajectories are grouped into clusters using both *line-based* and *point-based* clustering methods. Finally, each cluster is fitted into a polyline that represents a road candidate through centerline fitting.

Map matching. The purpose of map matching is to match GPS trajectories to the right roads. Commonly used map matching can be divided into two categories: incremental approach [Mazhelis, 2010; Velaga *et al.*, 2009], which aims to select the best matching candidate only on the basis of the preceding observations, and global methods [Wei *et al.*, 2012; Thiagarajan *et al.*, 2011], the task of which is to observe the entire series to select the best candidate. The Fast Viterbi [Wei *et al.*, 2012], one of the most popular map matching methods, has

---

Algorithm 20: Candidate Generation

Input: A trajectory set, TwS, in the current time window;

Output: RC_l: *Line-based* candidate set; and RC_p: *point-based* candidate set;

1   $RC_l \leftarrow \emptyset$; $RC_p \leftarrow \emptyset$; //*line-based* and *point-based* candidate set

2   $TuS \leftarrow \emptyset$; //unmatched trajectory segment set

3 **foreach** *trajectory* $\mathrm{Tw}^{(i)}$ *in* TwS **do**

4   Tu $\leftarrow$ MapMatching($\mathrm{Tw}^{(i)}$); //unmatched trajectory segments

5   TuS $\leftarrow$ TuS $\cup\, Tu$;

6 **foreach** *trajectory segment* $\mathrm{Ts}^{(x)}$ *in* TuS **do**

7   **if** $\mathrm{Ts}^{(x)}$ *is noisy trajectory segment* **then**

8   TuS $\leftarrow$ TuS $\setminus \{T_s^{(x)}\}$;

9   $\mathrm{CS}_l \leftarrow LClustering(\mathrm{TuS})$; //*line-based* clustering

10   $\mathrm{CS}_p \leftarrow PClustering(\mathrm{TuS})$; //*point-based* clustering

11 **foreach** *cluster* $\mathrm{CS}_l^{(i)}$ *in* CS_l **do**

12    $RC_l \leftarrow RC_l \cup CLFitting(\mathrm{CS}_l^{(i)})$; //*line-based* candidate generation

13 **foreach** *cluster* $\mathrm{CS}_p^{(j)}$ *in* CS_p **do**

14    $RC_p \leftarrow RC_p \cup CLFitting(\mathrm{CS}_p^{(j)})$; //*point-based* candidate generation

15 **return** RC_l and RC_p;

---

been adopted by most of the map updating methods (e.g., CrowdAtlas and Glue) due to its excellent performance. Likewise, our MapMatching method in Algorithm 20 (line 4) also leverages the Viterbi method and derives unmatched trajectory segments by selecting candidates with the maximal weight after calculating the candidate positions within a certain radius. Finally, we will obtain a set of unmatched trajectory segments.

Denoising. GPS samples often have a few noisy data of position or direction. To improve the accuracy of inferred missing roads, the denoising process is required to reduce the noisy samples. For example, there are a few noisy points in Figure 6.5(b). First, the points inside the ellipses can be removed through distance denoising because they are far from most of their surrounding points. Subsequently, as a few GPS points in Figure 6.5(b) are significantly different from most of their surrounding points in directions, they are removed by direction denoising [Ge *et al.*, 2010]. Specifically, we search the nearby segments of each trajectory segment and compare its direction with its neighboring segments. Then, we identify a noisy trajectory segment according to the significant gap between its direction and most of its surrounding segments' directions. The denoising result after going through distance and direction denoising is shown in Figure 6.5(c).

Clustering. After map matching and denoising, the unmatched trajectory segments need to be clustered to infer the road candidates. To enhance the accuracy of inferred missing roads, we combine both *line-based* clustering (abbreviated as *LClustering*) and *point-based* clustering (abbreviated as *PClustering*). *Point-based* clustering takes two endpoints of all the trajectory segments as input, while *line-based* cluster takes the trajectory segments as input. In Algorithm 21 (*LClustering*), each trajectory segment is initialized as a cluster once the number of its similar trajectory segments is greater than a specific threshold, i.e., $Nd(p_i) > th_c$ (lines 2–5). The similar trajectory segment is defined here as follows.

Definition 6.6 (Similar Trajectory Segment). Given two trajectory segments, $Ts^{(x)}$ and $Ts^{(y)}$, a distance threshold, th_{dis}, and a direction threshold, th_{dir}, $Ts^{(x)}$ and $Ts^{(y)}$ are two similar trajectory segments if the distance between $Ts^{(x)}$ and $Ts^{(y)}$ is smaller than th_{dis}, and the angle between $Ts^{(x)}$ and $Ts^{(y)}$ is less than th_{dir}.

Then, for each segment, $Ts^{(x)}$, in one cluster and each segment, $Ts^{(y)}$, in $Nd(Ts^{(x)})$, if they are similar and satisfy $Nd(Ts^{(y)}) > th_c$, we add $Ts^{(y)}$ into the queue. If $Ts^{(y)}$ does not belong to any cluster, it should also be added into the cluster of $Ts^{(x)}$ (lines 7–13). The *PClustering* approach also divides the input points into several clusters according to the similar criterion. The directions of two endpoints of a segment can be seen as the direction of the segment. Due to space limitations, we omit the detail of *PClustering*.

Centerline fitting. The centerline fitting step aims to generate the centerlines to represent road candidates. Since a cluster that consists of the trajectory points or trajectory segments may belong to the same

---

Algorithm 21: LClustering

Input: TuS: Trajectory segment set; th_c: a threshold;

Output: CS: Cluster set;

1 CS $\leftarrow \emptyset$; $l \leftarrow 1$;

2 **foreach** *unvisited segment* $Ts^{(i)}$ *in* TuS **do**

3   Mark $Ts^{(i)}$ as visited;

4   **if** $Nd(Ts^{(i)}) > th_c$ **then**

5          $C_l \leftarrow \{Ts^{(i)}\}$; $Q \leftarrow \emptyset$; $Q.enqueue(Ts^{(i)})$;

6   **while** Q *is not empty* **do**

7              $Ts^{(x)} \leftarrow Q.dequeue()$;

8   **foreach** *segment* $Ts^{(y)}$ *in* $Nd(Ts^{(x)})$ **do**

9   Mark $Ts^{(y)}$ as visited;

10   **if** $Nd(Ts^{(y)}) > th_c$ **and** $Ts^{(x)}$ *and* $Ts^{(y)}$ *are similar* **then**

11                      $Q.enqueue(Ts^{(y)})$;

12   **if** $Ts^{(y)}$ *does not belong to any cluster* **then**

13                      $C_l \leftarrow C_l \cup \{Ts^{(y)}\}$;

14   CS $\leftarrow$ CS $\cup \{C_l\}$; $l \leftarrow l + 1$;

15 **return** CS;

---

road candidate, we need to fit a centerline to represent a road candidate. For the clustering results of the former stage, we use the sweeping line method employed by Lee *et al.* (2007) to realize the centerline fitting process. The *CLFitting* function in Algorithm 20 takes trajectory points or segments as input, and generates the road candidates (lines 11–14). Finally, we obtain *line-based* candidates and *point-based* candidates.

6.2.2.2 *Missing roads inferring*

In this stage, we group the road candidates belonging to the same road based on two kinds of road candidates, RC_l and RC_p, generated in Algorithm 20. To be specific, if k road candidates (at least one *line-based* candidate and one *point-based* candidate) are located on the same road, they are merged to infer a missing road. After that, we strive to connect

---

Algorithm 22: Continuous Observation

Input: RC_p: Road candidate sets; and RC_l: a threshold k ($k \geqslant 3$);

Output: RS $= \{R_1, R_2, \ldots, R_m\}$: A missing road set;

1   RS $\leftarrow \emptyset$; $i \leftarrow 1$;

2   **foreach** *unvisited candidate* $Rc^{(i)}$ *in* $RC_p \cup RC_l$ **do**

3     $Z \leftarrow Rc^{(i)} \cup \{Rc^{(j)} \mid Rc^{(j)} \in RC_p \cup RC_l, Rc^{(i)}$ and $Rc^{(j)}$ are similar\} ;

4   Mark all the road candidates in Z as visited;

5   **if** $|Z| \geqslant k$ **and** *at least exists one* point-based *candidate in* Z **then**

6       $R_i \leftarrow CLFitting(Z)$;

7   RS $\leftarrow$ RS $\cup \{R_i\}$; $i \leftarrow i + 1$;

8   **return** RS;

---

the inferred roads with existing roads in the map. Accordingly, the missing roads inferring phase is composed of two steps: *continuous observation* and *road combination*.

Continuous observation. Since the sparse trajectories in a one time window may be confused with noise, the road candidates derived from them may imply wrong missing roads. To improve the inferring accuracy, we propose a continuous observation strategy to infer the missing roads based on the candidates of multiple time windows. To be specific, as shown in Algorithm 22, we collect the candidates of consecutive time windows so far and take them as input. First, we divide all the road candidates according to the roads that they belong to (line 3). When the number of road candidates exceeds a predefined threshold, k ($k \geqslant 3$), and at least one point-based candidate is involved, we can identify a missing road. Next, we fit them into a missing road by invoking the *CLFitting* function (line 6).

For instance, there are three similar road candidates (highlighted in black polyline) as seen in Figure 6.7. As the number of road candidates reaches the predefined threshold (e.g., $k = 3$), we combine them to generate a new road centerline to represent a missing road. To be specific, given two road candidates, $Rc^{(x)}$ and $Rc^{(y)}$, if $\exists Ts^{(i)} \in Rc^{(x)}$, $Ts^{(j)} \in Rc^{(y)}$, and $Ts^{(i)}$ and $Ts^{(j)}$ are similar, we take $Rc^{(y)}$ as one of the similar road

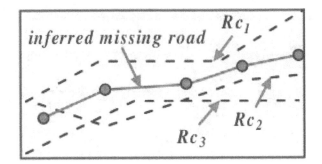

Figure 6.7. An example of a missing road generated in the MBR.

candidates of $Rc^{(x)}$ and regard them as the candidates of the same road. In Figure 6.7, if the number of road candidates reaches k ($k = 3$), a missing road will be inferred through centerline fitting. If $k = 4$, we continue to observe the road candidates in the subsequent time windows until the number of road candidates belonging to the same road reaches 4.

Road combination. After inferring missing roads, we try to update the road network by connecting the inferred roads with their neighboring roads that existed in the map. Given an inferred missing road, $Rc^{(x)}$, we attempt to find a road, $Rc^{(y)}$, in the road network, such that the $Rc^{(y)}$ is close to one of the endpoints of $Rc^{(x)}$ (e.g., smaller than 20 meters). If such a $Rc^{(y)}$ exists, we update the existing road network by connecting $Rc^{(x)}$ with $Rc^{(y)}$.

6.2.3 *Empirical evaluation*

We conduct substantial comparison experiments on real data sets to evaluate the performance of HyMU. Specifically, we compare HyMU with the representative *line-based* method (CrowdAtlas [Wang *et al.*, 2013]) and *point-based* method (Glue [Wu *et al.*, 2015]) to verify the superiority of HyMU. Our codes, written in Java, are conducted on a PC with 16 GB of memory, and an Intel Core CPU 3.2 GHz i7 processor and Windows 10 as its operating system.

6.2.3.1 *Evaluation method*

In order to ensure fairness, we randomly select an area on the existing road map and remove some road segments from this region. The goal is

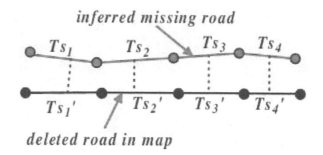

Figure 6.8. An example of two similar road centerlines.

to verify whether the deleted road segments can be inferred by different map updating methods. The evaluation criteria utilizes Precision, Recall, and F-measure [Liu *et al.*, 2012; Wu *et al.*, 2015]. Let *truth* denote the deleted roads, *inferred* denote all the inferred roads, and *tp* denote the correctly inferred roads. Accordingly, we use len(*truth*), len(*inferred*) and len(*tp*) to represent the length of all the deleted roads, the inferred roads, and the correctly inferred roads, respectively. Then, Precision, Recall, and F-measure can be calculated as follows:

$$\text{Precision} = \frac{\text{len}(tp)}{\text{len}(inferred)}, \quad \text{Recall} = \frac{\text{len}(tp)}{\text{len}(truth)},$$

$$F\text{-measure} = \frac{2 \times \text{Precision} \times \text{Recall}}{\text{Precision} + \text{Recall}}.$$

As shown in Figure 6.8, the deleted roads and their corresponding inferred missing roads are split into small segments with fixed length. Then, *tp* can be denoted as follows:

$$tp = \{si(\text{Ts}^{(x)}, \text{Ts}^{(y)}) \mid \forall \text{Ts}^{(x)} \in inferred, \ \forall \text{Ts}^{(y)} \in truth\}.$$

The function $si(\text{Ts}^{(x)}, \text{Ts}^{(y)})$ returns $\text{Ts}^{(x)}$ if $\text{Ts}^{(x)}$ and $\text{Ts}^{(y)}$ are similar. Otherwise, it returns *null*.

Data sets and map. We use two real data sets to evaluate the effectiveness of the HyMU method, including a taxi trajectory data set of 2015 in *ShanghaiOpen Data Apps*[2] (hereafter termed *Taxi*2015) and a high-sampling Shanghai taxi data set in 2013 (hereafter

---

[2]http://soda.datashanghai.gov.cn/.

termed *Shanghai*2013). In addition, we choose an open source map *OpenStreetMap(OSM)*[3] as our map data.

*Taxi*2015 contains GPS logs of taxis from 1 to 30 April 2015. It involves about 10,000 trajectories every day (about 115 million points). Each GPS log, represented by a sequence of timestamped points, contains attributes like vehicle ID, time, longitude and latitude, speed, etc.

*Shanghai*2013 contains the GPS logs of taxis for 2 days (from 1 to 2 October). It involves about 50,000 trajectories every day (about 107 million points). The average sampling rate of the taxis is about 60 seconds. Besides, each GPS log, represented by a sequence of timestamped points, contains such attributes as vehicle ID, time, longitude and latitude, speed, etc.

6.2.3.2 *Effectiveness evaluation*

Results for Taxi2015. We first implement HyMU on *Taxi*2015 to infer about 150 road segments that have not been described in the OSM map. The visualization result is shown in Figure 6.9(a), where the lines represent the missing roads detected by HyMU. As compared to the roads in AutoNaviMap[4] (as shown in Figure 6.9(b)), we can find that six roads (R_1-R_6) are correctly inferred by HyMU. This verifies the high precision of our proposal. In addition, we can infer the road, R_7, that is not marked on AutoNaïveMap, which further confirms the superiority of HyMU in discovering missing roads on sparse trajectory data.

Results for Shanghai2013. We compare HyMU with CrowdAtlas and GLUE on *Shanghai*2013 and randomly select a test area consisting of 19 road segments (from North Zhang Yang Road, through Wuzhou Avenue and Shenjiang Road, to Jufeng Road). First, to verify the robustness of HyMU, we evaluate the sensitivity of the parameters (th_{dis}, th_{dir} and k) on *Shanghai*2013, as illustrated in Figure 6.10. Through tuning the parameters repeatedly, we find that HyMU could achieve the best performance on *Shanghai*2013 when $th_{dis} = 20$ m, $th_{dir} = \frac{\pi}{6}$ and $k = 3$.

---

[3] http://wiki.openstreetmap.org/.
[4] http://ditu.amap.com/.

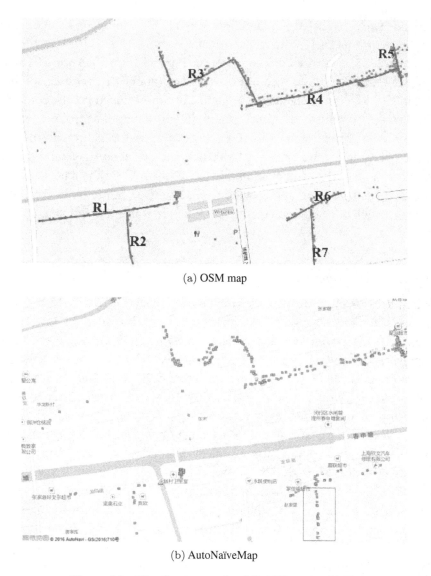

(a) OSM map

(b) AutoNaïveMap

Figure 6.9.   Visualization result of HyMU on *Taxi*2015.

Second, we try to evaluate HyMU, CrowdAtlas and GLUE by varying the sampling interval from 40 s to 160 s. As shown in Figure 6.11, we find that GLUE has the best precision because a *point-based* strategy will not infer the missing roads with wrong directions. But it does not take

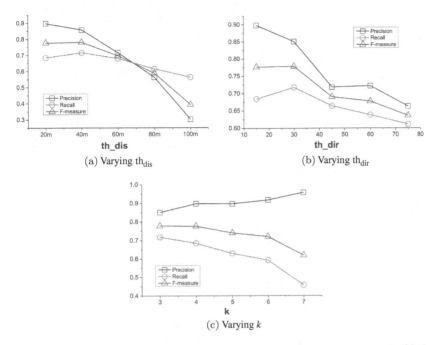

Figure 6.10. Performance of HyMU under different parameters on *Shanghai*2013.

into account inferring roads on a parse region, which results in a lower recall rate. By contrast, HyMU combines the advantage of the *line-based* and *point-based* strategies. It attains almost the same precision as GLUE, and the highest recall as well as F-measure.

Third, we attempt to compare the performance of HyMU with CrowdAtlas and GLUE under various data volume, as shown in Figure 6.12. As data volume becomes larger, we observe that the Precision, Recall, and F-measure values of HyMU increases accordingly, and that the precision approaches that of GLUE. Hence, HyMU has a good scalability. In addition, we observe that HyMU has a higher recall rate than other methods in all situations, which demonstrates that it is capable of inferring the missing roads on sparse trajectory data.

6.2.3.3 *Efficiency evaluation*

Next, we assess the efficiency of HyMU by comparing it with CrowdAtlas and GLUE on *Shanghai*2013. As shown in Figure 6.13(a), HyMU

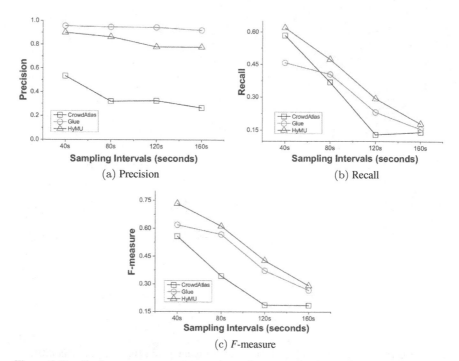

(a) Precision

(b) Recall

(c) *F*-measure

Figure 6.11.   Performance comparison under various sampling intervals on *Shanghai*2013.

runs faster than the other two methods with the increase of trajectory data. It indicates that HyMU is more efficient than other map updating methods. GLUE, by contrast, is extremely time-costing, due to the cost on calculating the direction of each point.

In addition, we evaluate the efficiency of HyMU by varying the time window size N. Figure 6.13(b) shows the processing time comparison when N is set to 3 h, 6 h, and 21 h, respectively. When $N = 6$ h, the execution time is the smallest. This is due to the massive amount of data in a time window requiring to be denoised and clustered, which is relatively time-consuming when the time window size is large. Conversely, when the time window size is small, we need to deal with too many road candidates, which is also time-consuming. So the appropriate window size is 6 h on *Shanghai*2013, and we also use this optimal value to execute effectiveness evaluation on *Shanghai*2013. Consequently, HyMU is efficient and effective to infer the missing roads for a given map.

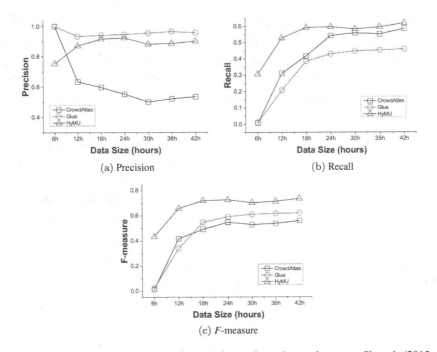

(a) Precision (b) Recall

(c) *F*-measure

Figure 6.12. Performance comparison under various data volume on *Shanghai*2013.

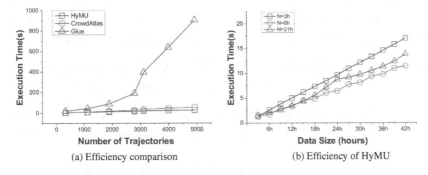

(a) Efficiency comparison (b) Efficiency of HyMU

Figure 6.13. Efficiency evaluation.

6.3   Underground Road Discovering

6.3.1   *Preliminaries*

Definition 6.7 (Trajectory).   Given the trajectory database, D, a trajectory, $T_k \in D$, is a sub-sequence of GPS points affiliated to an object, o_k, denoted as $T_k = \{(p_1, t_1), (p_2, t_2), \ldots, (p_i, t_i), \ldots\}$, where p_i is the location of the object, o_k, at the timestamp, t_i, in 2D space (i.e., $p_i = (x_i, y_i)$). Such records arrive in chronological order, i.e., $\forall i < j$, $t_i < t_j$. A line segment, L_i, refers to a line connecting two adjacent points, i.e., $L_i = (s_i, e_i) = (p_i, p_{i+1})$. Correspondingly, a trajectory is also denoted as $\{L_1, L_2, \ldots\}$.

After analyzing the trajectories, we find many line segments that exist missing sampling points like the pattern shown in Figure 6.2. Our major idea is to cluster this kind of line segments as defined in the following. In addition, we compute the total number of sub-trajectories within the range of a cluster. Our goal is to detect the clusters where underground roads exist.

Definition 6.8 (Line Segment of Missing Sampling Points, LM). An LM, $L_i = (p_i, p_{i+1})$, is a line segment in a trajectory missing sampling points between t_i and t_{i+1}. Correspondingly, the time interval of the LM is denoted as $\Delta t_i = t_{i+1} - t_i$.

Definition 6.9 (Sub-trajectory Passing a certain area, SP). Assuming a certain area has an underground road, an SP for the area is a sub-trajectory that a user goes along the underground road, no matter whether he/she goes through the underground road or remains above ground, denoted as $SP = \{p_{j-n}, \ldots, p_{j-1}, p_j\}$, where p_j is the jth point in one trajectory.

Definition 6.10 (Cluster Feature, CF). CF for a cluster of LMs $\{L_1, L_2, \ldots, L_n\}$ is of the form $(L_{cen}, \Delta t_{max}, N_{LM}, N_{SP})$.

- L_{cen}: The representative line segment of the cluster, denoted as $L_{cen} = (s_{cen}, e_{cen})$, where s_{cen} and e_{cen} are the starting point and the ending point of L_{cen};
- Δt_{max}: The maximal time interval of the set of LMs in the cluster;
- N_{LM}: The number of LMs in the cluster, i.e., $N_{LM} = n$; and
- N_{SP}: The number of SPs for the area of the cluster.

It is difficult to calculate L_{cen} in UNClu and TUClu because the planforms of underpasses and tunnels are different. The planform of an underpass can be expressed as a rectangle and there is no directional limit when going through the underpass. Hence, given a CF, we can

obtain the minimal bounding rectangle (MBR) of all the LMs contained
in the cluster. And s_{cen} and e_{cen} of L_{cen} in UNClu are just the bottom left
vertex and the top right vertex of the MBR. The tunnels are generally
long and the planform of a tunnel can be expressed as a line segment
in a direction. s_{cen} and e_{cen} of L_{cen} in TUClu can be calculated with
$s_{cen} = \frac{\sum_{i=1}^{n} L_i . s_i}{n}$ and $e_{cen} = \frac{\sum_{i=1}^{n} L_i . e_i}{n}$. Note that an LM inserted into a
cluster is also an SP for the area of the cluster.

When clustering LMs, we use the distance function between a line
segment and a cluster, which is defined between the line segment and the
representative line segment of the cluster. It is adapted from similarity
measures in the area of pattern recognition [Chen *et al.*, 2003]. We
assign the longer line segment to L_i and the shorter one to L_j without
losing generality.

Definition 6.11. The distance function is the sum of the perpendicular
distance, the parallel distance, and the angle distance, which is defined as

$$\text{dist}(L_i, L_j) = \frac{d_{\perp 1}^2 + d_{\perp 2}^2}{d_{\perp 1} + d_{\perp 2}} + \frac{d_{\|1} + d_{\|2}}{2}$$
$$+ \begin{cases} \| L_j \| \times \sin(\theta), & 0^o \leq \theta < 90^o, \\ \| L_j \|, & 90^o \leq \theta < 180^o \end{cases} \quad (6.1)$$

where $d_{\perp 1}$ is the Euclidean distance between s_j and p_s, $d_{\perp 2}$ is that
between e_j and p_e, $d_{\|1}$ is the Euclidean distances of p_s to s_i and $d_{\|2}$ is
that of p_e to e_i, supposing that p_s and p_e are the projection points of
the points, s_j and e_j, onto L_i, respectively. $\| L_j \|$ denotes the length of
L_j and θ denotes the smaller intersecting angle between L_i and L_j.

We compute the parallel distance with $\frac{d_{\|1}+d_{\|2}}{2}$ instead of $\min(d_{\|1}, d_{\|2})$,
which can help us distinguish the directions of the two line segments.

6.3.2 *Overview*

Algorithm 23 describes the overall framework. The input is the trajectory
database D. This framework copes with each trajectory, T_k, in D. For
each line segment, L_i, in T_k, it first tries to judge whether L_i is an LM.
If it is an LM, L_i will be inserted into the clusters. Then, it tries to

---

Algorithm 23: FindingUnderpasses

Input: D: The trajectory database;
Output: Z: The set of CFs for generated clusters;

1 $Z \leftarrow \emptyset$;
2 **foreach** *trajectory $T_k \in D$* **do**
3   **foreach** *line segment $L_i \in T_k$* **do**
4   **if** *L_i is an* LM **then**
5          $Z \leftarrow Z.InsertToClusters(L_i)$;
6   **foreach** CF $C_j \in Z$ **do**
7   **if** *$\{L_{i-n}, \ldots, L_i\}$ is an* SP *for C_j* **then**
8             $C_j.N_{SP} \leftarrow C_j.N_{SP} + 1$;

9 $Z \leftarrow FilteringClusters(Z)$;
10 **return** Z;

---

judge whether the sub-trajectory $\{L_{i-n}, \ldots, L_i\}$ is an SP for each CF, C_j. If it is, then the variable N_{SP} of C_j is updated accordingly. Finally, it will filter the clusters and discover the clusters where the underground roads exist.

6.3.2.1 *LM clustering*

This module aims at detecting whether a line segment, L_i, is an LM. If it is, we insert L_i into the existing clusters. The most critical task in detecting an LM is to check whether the sampling rate changes suddenly. As shown in Figure 6.14, no matter which type the situation is, the time interval of the LM is longer than that of normal line segments because of missing sampling points. Assuming that the speed is constant in a short period of time, the length of the LM is also longer than that of normal line segments.

Therefore, a line segment, L_i, is an LM if it satisfies two constraints: the time constraint and the distance constraint. The time constraint is given as follows:

$$\Delta t_i > \alpha_1 \times (\Delta t_{i-1} + \Delta t_{i+1}), \tag{6.2}$$

where Δt_i is the time interval of L_i.

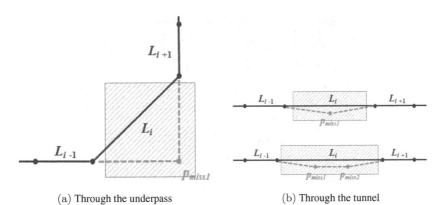

(a) Through the underpass   (b) Through the tunnel

Figure 6.14. LMs through the underground roads.

The distance constraint is given as

$$S_i > \alpha_2 \times (S_{i-1} + S_{i+1}), \tag{6.3}$$

where S_i is the length of the L_i. And α_1 and α_2 are tuning parameters for two constraints that vary with different types of data sets. For instance, α_2 for the underpass data set as in Figure 6.14(a) $\left(\text{approximately } \frac{\sqrt{2}}{2}\right)$ is smaller than α_2 for the tunnel data set as in Figure 6.14(b) (approximately 1).

After finding an LM, L_i, we insert L_i into the existing clusters. The goal of Algorithm 24 is to generate and incrementally maintain the clusters by applying the hierarchical clustering method. It proceeds as follows. For an LM, L_i, we attempt to find its closest CF, C_j. If the distance between L_i and L_{cen} of C_j is shorter than a distance threshold β, L_i will be inserted into C_j. Otherwise, a new CF, C_{new}, will be created for L_i. When the number of CFs exceeds m, which is the maximum number of the CFs kept in memory, we need to merge the two closest CFs to make room for the newly created CF and ensure high efficiency of the algorithm. Note that β is related to the length of L_{cen} for C_j, which is computed as $\min(\text{LENGTH}(C_j.L_{\text{cen}})/2, \beta)$.

6.3.3 *SP detection*

This module aims to detect whether the sub-trajectory, $\{L_{i-n}, \ldots, L_i\}$, is an SP for the CF, C_j. If it is, the variable N_{SP} of C_j will be updated

---

Algorithm 24: InsertToClusters

Input: L_i: An LM extracted from trajectories; Z: the set of CFs for generated clusters; β: the maximum distance limitation, and m: the maximum number of the CFs;

Output: Z: The set of CFs for the generated clusters after inserting the LM;

1 Find the closest $C_j \in Z$ to L_i;

2 $\beta \leftarrow \min(\text{LENGTH}(C_j.L_{\text{cen}})/2, \beta)$;

3 **if** $\text{DISTANCE}(L_i, C_j.L_{\text{cen}}) \leq \beta$ **then**

4 $\quad \lfloor \; C_j \leftarrow C_j \cup \{L_i\}$;

5 **else**

6 $\quad$ **if** $|Z| = m$ **then**

7 $\quad\quad \lfloor$ Merge two closest CFs;

8 $\quad C_{\text{new}} \leftarrow \{L_i\}$;

9 $\quad \lfloor \; Z \leftarrow Z \cup C_{\text{new}}$;

10 **return** Z;

---

accordingly. The sub-trajectory across an underpass is usually distinct from that along a tunnel, which necessitates designing different methods to detect SPs in UNClu and TUClu, respectively.

6.3.3.1 UNClu

Because the underpasses are usually located at the intersections of two roads, we can simply regard an underpass as a rectangle, whose diagonal side is viewed as L_{cen} of a CF. The pedestrians can walk across the road in various directions, so there is no directional limit on the SP. The sub-trajectory, $\{L_{i-n}, \ldots, L_i\}$, is treated as an SP for the CF, C_j, if it meets the following two conditions. First, L_{i-n} and L_i intersect with two different edges of the rectangle. Second, the time interval from L_{i-n} to L_i is shorter than Δt_{max} of C_j. As shown in Figure 6.15(a), ST_1 and ST_2 are both SPs.

TUClu. Since there are usually two tunnels in either opposite direction at the same location, we can limit the direction of the sub-trajectory. Besides that, the time interval from L_{i-n} to L_i is shorter than Δt_{max} of

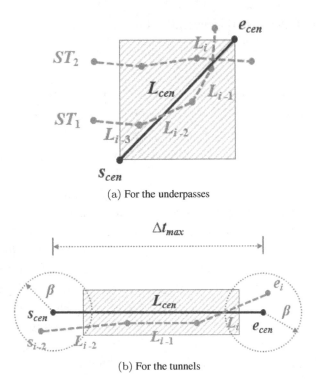

(a) For the underpasses

(b) For the tunnels

Figure 6.15. Two SP detection methods in UNClu and TUClu.

C_j, the starting point and the ending point must be within the circles that are centered at s_{cen} and e_{cen}, with a radius of β, respectively. Then, we can say we find an SP for C_j. Note that β is computed as $\min(\text{LENGTH}(C_j.L_{\text{cen}})/2, \beta)$.

6.3.3.2 *Filtering*

This module aims at filtering the clusters to find the locations where underground roads exist. In general, the area of a cluster containing an underground road may have a greater value of N_{LM} since there are a large number of people going through the underground roads. Once they are traveling underground, it is prone to miss sampling points in their trajectories. However, the value of N_{LM} is associated with the traffic flow in the area of the cluster. Hence, the constraint of N_{LM} for C_i is given as

$$C_i.N_{\mathrm{LM}} > \gamma \times \frac{\sum_j C_j.N_{\mathrm{LM}}}{N}, \tag{6.4}$$

where $C_j \in C_\varepsilon$, the distance between C_i and C_j is shorter than the parameter, ε, and N is the number of CFs in C_ε. So $\frac{\sum_j C_j.N_{\mathrm{LM}}}{N}$ is just the average number of LMs in that area that reflects the density of trajectories. γ is a tuning parameter used to adjust the threshold of N_{LM} of C_i.

Nevertheless, some other locations like urban canyons also have plenty of LMs, where the number of which may be even larger than that in the location of underground roads, because there is a larger flow of people there and more LMs are produced owing to other factors. Therefore, it is not comprehensive to determine whether there is an underground road in the area of one cluster by simply depending on N_{LM}. With N_{LM} and N_{SP} of a CF, we can calculate the proportion of LMs among all the SPs, i.e., $R_{\mathrm{LS}} = \frac{N_{\mathrm{LM}}}{N_{\mathrm{SP}}}$. Since it is more prone to miss sampling points and there are fewer SPs in longer underground roads, we consider the constraint of R_{LS} of C_i, which is given as

$$C_i.R_{\mathrm{LS}} \geq \frac{\delta l_i}{l_{\max}}, \tag{6.5}$$

where l_i is the length of L_{cen} for C_i, $l_{\max}$ is the maximal length of L_{cen} for all the clusters, and δ is a tuning parameter used to adjust the threshold of R_{LS} of C_i.

6.3.3.3 *Performance analysis*

The space complexity of our framework is $O(m)$, where m is the number of CFs and can be set according to the memory of the computer. Concerning the time complexity, the cost of traversing all the line segments of trajectories is $O(n)$, where n is the number of line segments of all the trajectories. For each LM, L_i, the cost of incorporating it into the nearest CF is $O(m)$. If we record the nearest CF for each CF, we can merge the two closest CFs in $O(m)$, and the cost of the SP detection stage takes $O(m)$. The cost of the cluster filtering stage is also $O(m)$. So the total processing cost of our framework is $O(nm)$. When the data set is large, process can be hastened if the CFs are indexed by an R-tree. In our framework, the SPs for a CF before the generation of CFs will be missed, but it is negligible when the data set is large enough. Consequently, our framework can scale to large data sets very well.

6.3.4 Empirical evaluation

In this section, we conduct extensive experiments upon real-life data sets. All the code is written in Java, and run on a computer with 8 GB of memory and an Intel i5 CPU.

6.3.4.1 Data set description

We used four real-life data sets, including *HefeiTraj*, *ShanghaiTraj*, *HefeiUnderpasses*, and *ShanghaiTunnels*.

- *HefeiTraj*: This data set describes the walking records gathered by the volunteers in early 2014 in the city center of Hefei. After deduplication, it has 90,037 trajectories, each containing a sequence of coordinates.
- *ShanghaiTraj*: This data set records the trajectories of the taxis in Shanghai. It contains GPS logs of about 30,000 taxis during three months (October, November, and December) in 2013, covering about 93% of Shanghai's main road network.
- *HefeiUnderpasses*: This data set contains the locations of all the underpasses in the central area of Hefei by using street view maps.
- *ShanghaiTunnels*: This data set contains the locations of all the tunnels in Shanghai by using street view maps.

6.3.4.2 Settings

This section introduces how we evaluate these methods and to which baseline method these were compared with.

Criteria. We used several parameters in our framework, including α_1, α_2, β, ε, γ, and δ. Among them, β is related to the length of L_{cen}. As for ε, the larger the value is, the better and lower its effectiveness and efficiency are, respectively. Hence, we simply try to test the parameters α_1 and α_2 used in the LM clustering stage, and the γ and δ used in the cluster filtering stage.

- *Density Ratio*: We utilize the *Density Ratio* that denotes the ratio between the local LM density and global LM density to measure the performance of LM detection. The local LM density denotes the average number of LMs in the areas where underground roads exist, and the global LM density is that in the whole area. Hence, the larger the density ratio is, the better the performance of LM detection is.
- *F*-measure: We evaluate the effectiveness of the algorithms by using *F*-measure, which is calculated by $\frac{2 \times \text{Precision} \times \text{Recall}}{\text{Precision} + \text{Recall}}$.

Baseline. We compare our methods with the naïve approach that groups line segments that are longer than $d_{\max}$. The baseline methods upon the *HefeiTraj* and *ShanghaiTraj* data sets are shortened as "UBase" and "TBase", respectively. We show that the performance reaches its peak when $d_{\max} = 40$ in UBase and $d_{\max} = 500$ in TBase, respectively. However, the best performance (*F*-measure is 0.182 in UBase and 0.464 in TBase) is still bad, because although Recall is high here, Precision is too low.

6.3.4.3 *Effectiveness*

UNClu. Figure 6.16(a) shows the variation of *Density Ratio* under different values of α_1 and α_2 in UNClu. When the value of α_2 is fixed, the value of *Density Ratio* grows initially, then decreases with the increment of α_1. When $\alpha_1 = 1$, it reaches its peak. When the value of α_1 is fixed, the value of *Density Ratio* also reaches the peak when $\alpha_2 = 1$, since the lengths of the underpasses are not long, and it usually misses only one sampling point when a pedestrian walks through an underpass. We can also find the effect of γ and δ after fixing α_1 and α_2, as shown in Table 6.1. When the value of δ is fixed, the precision initially increases then decreases, while the recall decreases with the increment of γ. When the value of γ is fixed, the precision grows and the recall decreases with the increment of δ. According to *F*-measure, when we set $\gamma = 0.6$ or 0.7 and $\delta = 0.09$, we can obtain the best effectiveness, which is significantly better than that of UBase.

TUClu. Figure 6.16(b) shows the variation of *Density Ratio* under different values of α_1 and α_2 in TUClu. When the value of α_2 is fixed, the value of *Density Ratio* grows with the increment of α_1. When $\alpha_1 = 1$,

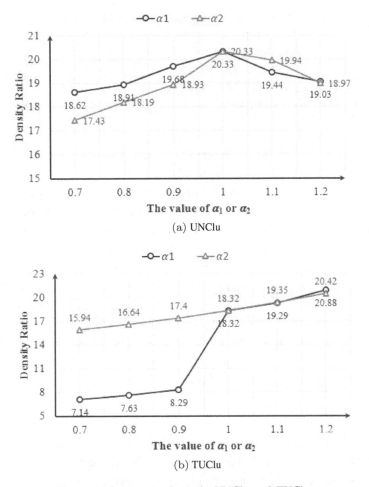

(a) UNClu

(b) TUClu

Figure 6.16. *Density Ratio* in UNClu and TUClu.

Table 6.1. Performance of different parameters (γ, δ) in UNClu.

γ	0.5	0.6	0.7	0.8	0.9	δ	0.07	0.08	0.09	0.10	0.11
Precision	0.667	**0.750**	**0.750**	0.714	0.667	**Precision**	0.583	0.667	**0.750**	0.800	1.000
Recall	0.857	**0.857**	**0.857**	0.714	0.571	**Recall**	1.000	0.857	**0.857**	0.571	0.429
F-measure	0.750	**0.800**	**0.800**	0.714	0.615	**F-measure**	0.737	0.750	**0.800**	0.666	0.600

Table 6.2. Performance of different parameters (γ, δ) in TUClu.

γ	0.8	1.0	1.2	1.4	1.6	δ	1.0	2.0	3.0	4.0	5.0
Precision	0.838	**0.862**	0.859	0.857	0.855	**Precision**	0.862	0.875	**0.930**	0.925	0.930
Recall	0.950	**0.933**	0.917	0.900	0.883	**Recall**	0.933	0.933	**0.883**	0.817	0.667
F-measure	0.890	**0.896**	0.887	0.878	0.869	*F*-measure	0.896	0.903	**0.906**	0.868	0.777

it grows most significantly. When the value of α_1 is fixed, the value of *Density Ratio* grows very slowly with the increment of α_2, since the speeds of the vehicles do not change very frequently compared to the speeds of walkers, and the time constraint is consistent with the distance constraint. We can also observe the same effect of γ and δ as that in UNClu after fixing α_1 and α_2, as shown in Table 6.2. According to *F*-measure, when we set $\gamma = 1$ and $\delta = 3$, we obtain good effectiveness, which is nearly two times better than that of TBase. δ in TUClu is larger than δ in UNClu, since tunnels are generally longer than underpasses. We can find most of these tunnels in Shanghai. The tunnels that could not be found were shorter than 400 m in length or in the areas that have fewer or no trajectories. Areas that we found that had no tunnels were in fact usually underground parking lots.

6.3.4.4 *Efficiency*

Figure 6.17(a) shows the average execution time of TUClu as the number of trajectory points grows. We can observe that the per-record processing time increases with the increment of the number of trajectory points. This is due to the number of clusters increasing, as shown in Figure 6.17(b). However, the efficiency will be steady when the number of clusters reaches the given threshold, m. The efficiency of UNClu is similar to that of TUClu.

6.4 Road Intersection Detection

6.4.1 *Preliminaries*

Definition 6.12 (Road Map). A road map is typically represented by a graph, $G = (V, E)$, where the set of vertexes, V, denotes the junctions,

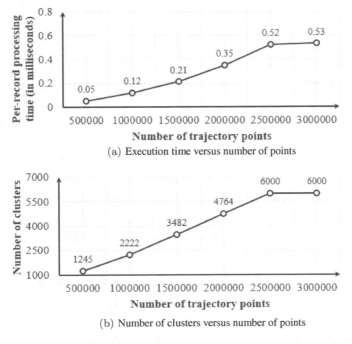

(a) Execution time versus number of points

(b) Number of clusters versus number of points

Figure 6.17. Efficiency of TUClu.

V_{crossing}, or other breakpoints, V_{others}, in the road segments, and the set of edges, E, denotes the road segments linking the vertexes, V.

Distinct from a traditional graph structure, each vertex, $v \in V$, has its geo-location represented by the longitude and latitude coordinates. In this chapter, the junctions (or road intersections) are identified from GPS trajectory data of the vehicles.

Definition 6.13 (GPS Trajectory). A GPS trajectory, Tr, refers to a sequence of GPS points measured by the devices in chronological order, denoted as Tr $= \{p_1, p_2, \ldots, p_n\}$ with $p_i = (\text{lng}_i, \text{lat}_i, t_i)$. Here lng_i and lat_i denote the longitude and latitude of the point at timestamp, t_i, respectively, $\forall i < j$, where p_i arrives earlier than p_j.

Furthermore, velocity and heading can be calculated by the set of longitude and latitude coordinates of consecutive GPS points. As mentioned in Section 6.1, GPS sampling missing and GPS point shifting pose the challenges to accurately identify the intersections. The raw trajectory data cannot be directly used to extract the intersections' locations.

First, to solve the problem of GPS sampling missing, we attempt to split a raw GPS trajectory into partitions where the sampling interval exceeds the average sampling interval and the velocity of any GPS point is significantly lower than the normal velocity. For instance, for a road with only one motorway in the same direction, motor vehicles shall not exceed 70 km/h on urban highways, according to traffic regulations.[5] As illustrated in Figure 6.18, a trajectory, Tr_1, is split into two partitions due to the sampling interval between two adjacent points in it (i.e., p_3 and p_4) being beyond the average sampling interval. Then, to avoid the situation of GPS point shifting, trajectory partitions are resampled to remove noisy GPS points with great directional change within a small range (Figure 6.18(b)).

Definition 6.14 (Noisy GPS Point). Given a GPS trajectory, Tr, and a distance threshold, th_{dis}, a GPS point, p_i ($p_i \in Tr$), is noisy if the distance (denoted as $dist(p_{i-1}, p_i)$) between p_i and its previous point, p_{i-1}, is less than th_{dis}, and the variation between their directions is beyond th_{dir}.

Here, th_{dis} is set to not exceed 1 m, and $th_{dir} \in [60°, 90°]$ based upon empirical observations. To address the difficulty in discriminating the road intersection from road segment that result from driving behaviors like lane changing and overtaking, our solution is to design a heading filter based on distance and angle, defined as follows:

$$h'_i = \eta h_i + (1 - \eta) \left(\frac{d_{i+1} h_{i-1}}{d_{i-1} d_{i+1}} + \frac{d_{i-1} h_{i+1}}{d_{i-1} d_{i+1}} \right),$$

where η denotes the weight that is used to smooth the heading, h'_i denotes the smoothed heading, h_i denotes the heading calculated by any two consecutive GPS points, and d_{i-1} denotes the distance between the current point, p_i, and its previous point, p_{i-1}. The heading filter can smooth the sharp headings of GPS points and eliminate some points with large angle changing on the road segment, as shown in Figure 6.18(c).

---

[5]http://www.122.cn/zcfg/flfl/fg/382759.shtml.

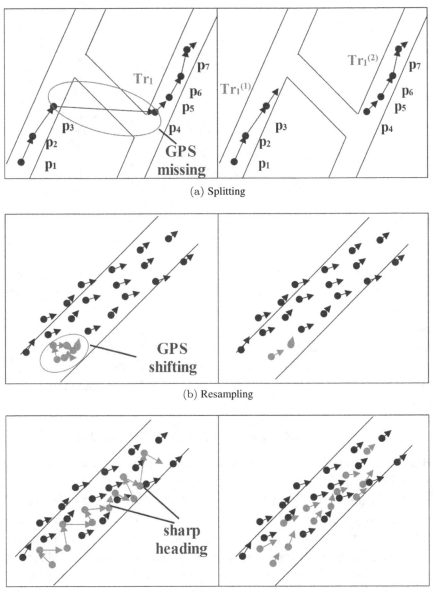

(a) Splitting

(b) Resampling

(c) Filtering

Figure 6.18. An example of improving the trajectory quality.

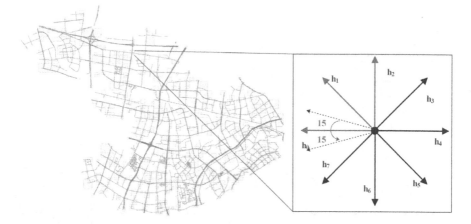

Figure 6.19.   An example of a candidate cell.

After improving the quality of raw GPS trajectory data, a top-down cell-partitioning strategy is harnessed to identify the road intersections with different sizes. It is observed that more points with various directions gather at the road intersections than on the road segments, and these points usually have lower speeds because they slow down when cornering. In view of this, we classify the headings of the trajectory points into eight directions in each cell. The direction distribution (denoted as PH) of a cell, $G^{(x)}$, is represented as follows:

$$\text{PH}(G^{(x)}) = (p_{h_0}, p_{h_1}, p_{h_2}, p_{h_3}, p_{h_4}, p_{h_5}, p_{h_6}, p_{h_7}),$$

where p_{h_i} denotes the percentage of points in ith direction to all the points in $G^{(x)}$.

As illustrated in Figure 6.19, the median heading of all the points' headings in a cell is chosen as the direction, h_0, of the cell, which is based on the consideration that the median heading can represent the orientation of most trajectory points. In addition, we set a direction tolerance of $\pm 15°$ for each direction to obtain a certain number of points that go in this direction. Then, we calculate the standard deviation of the directional proportions in the cell, which would be less than some specified threshold. Since there are generally two opposite directions on the road, the standard deviation of the direction proportion on the road would be much larger than that at the intersection. Along with gradually splitting the cells using the quadtree model, the process of direction ratio statistics analyzing is implemented from the largest to smallest cells. Combining this with the velocity analysis of each cell, the candidate cells containing the intersections are found.

Definition 6.15 (Candidate Cell). Given a collection of cells, $U(G)$, a cell direction threshold, θ, and a cell velocity threshold, β, a cell, $G^{(x)}$ ($G^{(x)} \in U(G)$), is a candidate cell where an intersection exists if it contains at least three distinct directions, the standard deviation of its directions is less than θ and the average velocity of its points does not exceed β. The extracted collection of candidate cells can be represented as follows:

$$\mathrm{CG}(G^{(x)}) = \{G^{(y)} \in U(G) \mid (G^{(y)}.\bar{v} \le \beta)$$
$$\cap (G^{(y)}.\mathrm{std} \le \theta) \cap (p_{h_i} > 0)\}, \tag{6.6}$$

where p_{h_i} denotes the ith direction proportion, β denotes the speed threshold, and θ denotes the standard deviation threshold. With the aid of the hybrid clustering strategy consisting of the DBSCAN and Meanshift method, the locations of the intersections are identified. Here, the DBSCAN method is leveraged to remove the center outliers from the points, and the Meanshift method is harnessed to refine the locations of the intersections.

Problem Definition: Given a collection of raw GPS trajectories, our task is to detect the intersections represented by the set of vertexes, V_{crossing}, where $v_i \in V_{\mathrm{crossing}}$ is the actual geospatial location that is represented as a tuple (latitude, longitude).

6.4.2 Overview

In this section, we present a two-phase framework for road intersection detection, called Road Intersection Detection Framework (RIDF). As the road intersections can be viewed as the influxes of various road segments, the main underlying idea of our solution is that a great number of GPS trajectories with multiple directions usually gather at the road intersections rather than at road segments. To this end, based on the collection of low quality GPS trajectory data, we aim to detect the

---

Algorithm 25: Road Intersection Detection Framework

    Input: A trajectory collection, *Traj_set*;

    Output: The set of intersections' locations, KP_*set*;

1 KP_*set* ← ∅;

2 The set of candidate cells: CG_*set* ← ∅;

3 The set of trajectory segments: *TrajSeg* ← ∅;

4 **for** $T_r^{(i)}$ **in** Traj_*set* **do**

5 | *SubTraj* ← *Splitting*($T_r^{(i)}$);

6 | **for** *each trajectory segment* $\mathrm{Tr}^{(j)}$ **in** *SubTraj* **do**

7 | | $\mathrm{Tr}^{(j)*}$ ← *Resampling*($\mathrm{Tr}^{(j)}$);

8 | | tf ← *Filtering*($Tr^{(j)*}$);

9 | | *TrajSeg* ← *TrajSeg* ⋃ {tf};

10 CG_*set* ← *CandidateCellGenerate*(*TrajSeg*);

11 KP_*set* ← *HybridClustering*(CG_*set*);

12 **return** KP_*set*;

---

road intersections by improving data quality, extracting candidate cells containing the intersections, and refining the locations of intersections.

More specifically, the process involves two phases, as outlined in Algorithm 25: (i) trajectory quality improving (lines 4–9), where raw GPS trajectory data is split into partitions and resampled to remove noisy GPS points, and then smoothed into sharp headings of GPS points to obtain high-quality trajectories, and (ii) road intersection extracting (lines 10–11) where the candidate cells are first extracted according to the direction ratio statistics analysis in a top-down manner, and then the positions of the intersections are refined through hybrid clustering.

6.4.2.1 *Trajectory quality improving*

As analyzed in Section 6.1, the measurement errors made by devices easily result in inaccurate GPS position information. For instance, the large sampling interval between successive GPS points results in two consecutive points being too far apart from each other, especially when the vehicle turns at the road intersection. The interpolation technique attempts to artificially add points between two adjacent points to make the trajectory coherent, but it cannot be utilized to solve our mentioned issue because it would increase the uncertainty of intersection detection. For another example, when a taxi stops at a traffic light or is caught in a traffic jam, its generated continuous GPS points are within a small range but with different directions. The cases mentioned above add difficulties when detecting road intersections from raw GPS traces.

Since the road intersection generally connects multiple road segments in different directions, accordingly, GPS trajectories at the road intersection move in various directions. However, when the vehicles drive on the road, the headings of vehicles' traces also result in a large angular variation because of changing lanes and frequent overtaking. An effective mechanism is required to remove the interference of non-intersections on intersection detection. The trajectory quality improving procedure is detailed in Algorithm 25. The whole procedure consists of *splitting* (line 5), *resampling* (line 7), and *filtering* (line 8).

Splitting. Targeting the issue of GPS point loss due to GPS signal interruption, raw GPS trajectory data is split into partitions according to the average sampling interval and normal velocity to ensure that they are consistent in the direction. It can reduce the interference of the heading distortion inferred by distant successive points. As exemplified in Figure 6.18(a), a vehicle's trajectory is split into several partitions, correspondingly, the headings calculated by the successive points would be derived accurately.

Resampling. The phenomenon of GPS point shifting behaves as the vehicles are still moving slightly with different directions while stopping (as shown in Figure 6.18(b)). To solve the issue of GPS point shifting, GPS points in each trajectory partition are resampled in terms of the gap in distance and direction between adjacent points. Specifically, for any GPS point in a trajectory partition, if the distance between its previous point (it is much smaller than th_{dis}) and the gap of their directions is larger than th_{dir}, it is a directional noisy point (Definition 6.14) and shall be removed from the points.

Filtering. To differentiate the intersection and non-intersection, an indispensable task is to smooth the headings of GPS points. Here, a distance-based heading filter that is similar to the Gaussian filter is employed to smooth the points with sharp heading. For instance, the headings of the points pointed by two lines become smoother after filtering, as illustrated in Figure 6.18(c).

6.4.2.2 *Intersection extracting*

After obtaining the high-quality GPS trajectory data, we need to differentiate the intersection from the road segment and further identify the location of the intersection, which is based on the premise that the trajectories at the intersections have more directions and lower cornering speeds than the other areas. For this purpose, the intersection extracting process is composed of two main steps: candidate cell generation and an intersection's location identification. We extract the candidate cells based on direction and speed analysis from top-down divided cells, and employ the hybrid clustering strategy to refine the locations of the detected intersections.

Candidate cell generation. Frequent direction changing of vehicles' trace on the road segment adds to the difficulty of effective road intersection detection. But the behaviors of directional change on the road do not often occur on the same road segment, and the small size cell can be employed to identify the intersections. In addition, it is observed that various road intersections in urban road networks usually have different sizes. Therefore, we try to divide the road map into various sized cells using a top-down cell division method based on the *quadtree* model. Then, we implement the speed and direction analysis in terms of the specified thresholds (β and θ). The stop condition of cell division is to check whether it satisfies the definition of the candidate cell (Definition 6.15).

Specifically, GPS points would be arranged into the quadtree model where the region of intersection locates, and each node of the quadtree is expressed as a rectangular area containing GPS points that fall into the cell. As illustrated in Algorithm 26, searching for the candidates starts with the penultimate layer of the quadtree, namely, the cells with a large boundary that is generally designed as 200 m in terms of the maximum road width (line 4). As long as the cell meets this rule, we first check whether its parent node exists in the collection of candidate set to eliminate redundancy. Then, we obtain the collection of the candidate

---

Algorithm 26: CandidateCellGenerate

Input: *TrajSeg*: A set of trajectory segments; and the
  minBoundary: minimum side length of the cell;

Output: A set of candidate cells, CG_*set*;

1 CG_*set* ← ∅;

2 *G_set* ← ∅,*tempCell_set* ← ∅;

3 *G_set* ← *Quadtree(TrajSeg, minBoundary)*;//divide the map into
  cells;

4 *i* ← the current depth of the quadtree;

5 **while** *i* ≤ *G_set.maxdepth* **do**

6   **for** $G^{(j)}$ *in* *G_set* **do**

7   **if** $G^{(j)}.depth == i$ **then**

8   *tempCell_set* ← *tempCell_set* ⋃ $G^{(j)}$;

9   **for** $G^{(j)}$ *in* *tempCell_set* **do**

10   **if** *IsCandidate*($G^{(j)}$) **then**

11   **if** $G^{(j)}.parent ∈ CG\_set$ **then**

12   *CG_set.remove*($G^{(j)}.parent$);

13   CG_*set* ← CG_*set* ⋃ {$G^{(j)}$};

14   *tempCell_set* ← ∅;

15   *i* ← *i* + 1;

16 **return** CG_*set*;

---

cells (lines 9–13). We finish the searching procedure until all the leaf nodes of the quadtree are traversed.

Algorithm 27 elaborates the procedure of judging whether the cells contain the intersections. Above all, the velocity of all the points in the cell is calculated to obtain the average velocity (line 6). Then, the median of the smoothed headings is chosen as the initial direction of that cell, which is viewed as a representative value of all the points' directions. Subsequently, we calculate the standard deviation of the directional proportion sorted in descending order (lines 8–16). At last, the candidate cell can be extracted according to the average speed of the points, the number of the directions, and the distribution of the directional ratio of

---

Algorithm 27: IsCandidate

Input: G: A cell; β: cell velocity threshold; and θ: cell direction
        threshold;
Output: Whether the cell, G, is a candidate cell;

1 *Point_set* $\leftarrow \varnothing$, *angle_list* $\leftarrow \varnothing$, *ratio_anglelist* $\leftarrow \varnothing$;
2 **if** *the number of points in G is zero* **then**
3   $\rfloor$ **return** *False*;

4 **for** *point p_i **in** cell G* **do**
5   $\rfloor$ *Point_set* $\leftarrow$ *Point_set* $\bigcup p_i$;

6 *average_speed* $\leftarrow$ *calculateAverageVelocity(Point_set)*;
7 $d_0 \leftarrow$ *median(Point_set.smooth_heading)*;
8 **for** $i = 0$; $i < 8$; $i++$ **do**
9   $|$ *temp_angle* $\leftarrow (d_0 + i * 45)\%360$;
10 $\rfloor$ *angle_list* $\leftarrow$ *angle_list* $\bigcup \{temp\_angle\}$;

11 **for** d_i **in** *angle_list* **do**
12   $|$ *numforangle* $\leftarrow$ the number of points near d_i;
13   $|$ *ratio_angle* $\leftarrow$ *Anumforangle/len(temp_point)*;
14 $\rfloor$ *ratio_anglelist* $\leftarrow$ *ratio_anglelist* $\bigcup \{ratio\_angle\}$;

15 *Sort(ratio_angle)*;//sort the ratio of the direction in descending
    order;
16 *temp_std* $\leftarrow$ *std(ratio_angle)*;
17 **if** *average_speed* $\leq \beta$ **and** *temp_std* $\leq \theta$ **and** $|\text{PH}(G)| > 3$ **then**
18   $\rfloor$ **return** *False*;

19 **else**
20   $\rfloor$ **return** *True*;

---

the cell meeting the specified thresholds (lines 17–20), i.e., it has at least three distinct directions and the standard deviation of its directions is smaller than θ, and the average velocity of its points is not beyond β.

Intersection's location refinement. For the extracted candidate cells containing the road intersections, the next step is to precisely identify the locations of intersections. Density-based clustering approaches, such as Meanshift and DBSCAN, are widely used to map inference from trajectory data. Among them, the Meanshift algorithm is often used to derive the center positions of the road intersections. In our study, we also utilize the Meanshift algorithm to identify the locations where all the adjacent points converge, i.e., the centers of the road intersections. However, there exist some of the points in the candidate cell that are distant from the center of the intersection. They would result in the drift of identified intersection centers and hence reduce the precision of intersection detection results. Given that the DBSCAN method has the capability to identify the noisy points that are far from any class, we leverage the DBSCAN method to pre-eliminate the noisy points before the Meanshift clustering. Through a hybrid clustering strategy consisting of the DBSCAN and Meanshift methods, the locations of road intersections are refined.

6.4.3 *Time complexity analysis*

When m denotes the number of trajectories and $n'(n' < m)$ denotes the number of the trajectory segments, the cost of trajectory quality improving process takes $O(m * n')$. Let T denote the iteration times of the Meanshift algorithm and $n''(n'' \ll m)$ denote the number of trajectory points reserved in the candidate cells, then the cost of the intersection extracting process takes $O(Tn''^2)$. Thus, the time complexity of RIDF is $O(m * n' + Tn''^2)$.

6.4.4 *Empirical evaluation*

In this section, we conduct substantial experiments on real data sets to verify the effectiveness of the RIDF method for road intersection identification. First, we introduce comparative approaches and the data sets for valuation. Then we illustrate a few visualization results to provide initial insights. Subsequently, we compare our proposal with previous works according to some evaluation measures and further demonstrate the usefulness of the RIDF method.

Our code is implemented in Python. All the experiments are run on a computer with an Intel Core i5-6400 CPU (2.70 GHz) and 8 GB of memory. The operating system used is Windows 10.

6.4.4.1 *Experimental setting*

Comparative approach. To evaluate the benefits of our proposal for the detection of road intersections, we single out several representational approaches and compare the RIDF method with them.

- CBTP [Wang *et al.*, 2017a] is based on the implicit assumption that the road intersections are correlated to *turns*, which aims to group high-density cells where *turns* fall into clusters to find the intersections.
- *Ahmed2012* [Ahmed and Wenk, 2012] implements map-matching and then simply treats the endpoints of unmatched portions as the vertexes of the constructed road map.
- *Kharita* [Stanojevic *et al.*, 2018] attempts to obtain cluster centers through k-means clustering and viewed them as the vertexes in the road network.

Among them, only the first approach focuses on directly finding the road intersections from GPS traces. While the latter two approaches intend to infer road maps, the vertexes obtained generally include the intersections and other breakpoints on the road segments.

Data sets. As shown in Table 6.3, we use two real-world data sets for evaluation. The first data set is a shuttle bus trace data set introduced by Stanojevic *et al.* (2018) (hereafter termed *Bus2012*) and the second one is the Shanghai taxi trace data set of 2015 (hereafter termed *Taxi2015*). In addition, the ground truth is obtained by manual labeling, according to the map data from *OpenStreetMap*.[6] Note that the regions with no vehicles' traces are discarded because none of the methods could infer them in the road map. The manually labeled result contains 53 intersections for *Bus2012* and 180 intersections for *Taxi2015*.

Bus2012 is a collection of 889 shuttle bus GPS traces from the campus bus shuttle service in the University of Illinois. Since this collection lacks the attributes like heading and speed, we use the positional information of consecutive GPS points to infer heading and speed information of trajectories.

---

[6]https://www.openstreetmap.org/.

Table 6.3. Statistics of data sets.

Data set	Area	Number of points	Sampling rates(s)	Average speed
Chicago	10.8 km^2	118364	3.6	11 km/h
Shanghai large	22.5 km^2	179112	20	33 km/h

Table 6.4. Parameter setting for intersection detection.

	Intersection extracting					
	Candidate cell generating			Intersection's location identifying		
Data set	β (km/h)	θ	minBoundary	eps	minSample	Bandwidth
Chicago	11.52	0.2	25	18	20	60
Shanghai large	30.6	0.3	25	27	20	60

Taxi2015 contains GPS logs of taxis from 1 to 30 April 2015. It involves about 10,000 trajectories daily (about 115 million points). We use the GPS traces of one week as experimental data, and randomly select a region covering between E121°364′ and E121°421′ longitude and N31°206′ and N31°244′ latitude.

Parameter setting. As shown in Table 6.4, most of the parameters are identical for both data sets, except for the different sampling rates in each data set, and a discrepant limit of velocity due to the laws of different countries. Unless mentioned otherwise, the values of parameters are set for each data set based on our experimental tuning. th$_{dir}$ is set to 90°, and th$_t$ is set to approximately three times of the sampling interval, and β is set to the average speed of each data set. Since there are two opposite directions on the road segments, it would result in the value of standard deviation of the road segment being greater than that of the intersection. Observations in real scenarios suggest that the standard deviation of each direction proportion on the cell for road segments is around 0.4, thus θ is set to 0.2 for *Bus2012* and 0.3 for *Taxi2015*. In addition, the setting of minBoundary for each cell is based on the average road width.

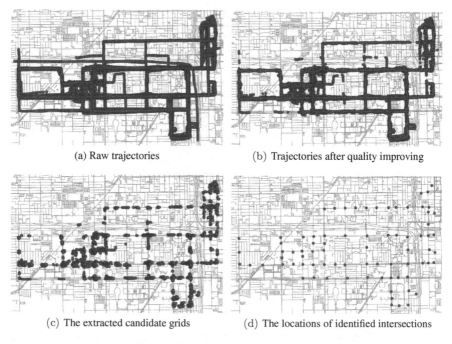

(a) Raw trajectories   (b) Trajectories after quality improving

(c) The extracted candidate grids   (d) The locations of identified intersections

Figure 6.20.   Processing on *Bus2012*.

6.4.4.2 *Visualization*

We first present visual results on *Bus2012* to illustrate the whole procedure of RIDF, and reveal the quality distinctions of the detection results by RIDF and the comparative methods on both data sets.

Procedure of RIDF. Through improving the quality of data by splitting, resampling, and filtering, some GPS points (depicted in Figure 6.20(a)) on the roadway are screened out, accordingly, our method obtains a higher quality trajectory data set, as illustrated in Figure 6.20(b). Then, we leave GPS points in the candidate cells that is derived by the analysis of the velocity and standard deviation of directions according to the specified thresholds (β and θ), as shown in Figure 6.20(c). After hybrid clustering, we obtain about 40 correct intersections, as depicted in Figure 6.20(d). We can see that the road intersections found by our proposal is visually close to the actual map.

Visual comparison. We implement a visual comparison evaluation on *Bus2012* and *Taxi2015*, as shown in Figure 6.21. The detected

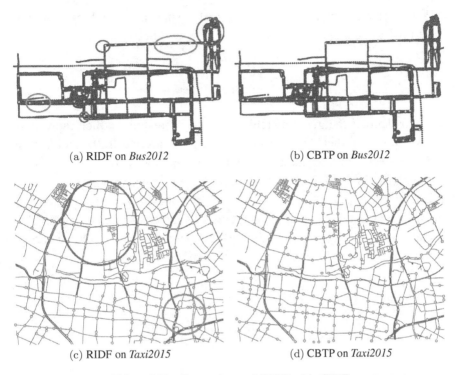

(a) RIDF on *Bus2012*   (b) CBTP on *Bus2012*

(c) RIDF on *Taxi2015*   (d) CBTP on *Taxi2015*

Figure 6.21. Comparison of RIDF with CBTP.

intersections' locations are depicted in small solid circles, which overlay the corresponding road network (marked with light lines). As can be seen from Figure 6.21, for both data sets, neither of the two approaches can completely eliminate the impacts of turning behavior on the road segments, and inevitably neither is accurate to some extent, e.g., several wrongly detected intersections on the highway (marked with ellipses). Nevertheless, owing to the direction ratio statistics analysis within different-sized cells, our proposal is more robust than CBTP, as marked by the circles in Figure 6.21.

6.4.4.3 *Quantitative results*

Evaluation methodology. In our study, we use the Euclidean distance to measure the distance between any two vertexes, denoted as $\text{dist}(v, v')$, where $v \in V_{gt}$ and $v' \in V_{\text{crossing}}$ represent the ground-truth intersection and the detected intersection, respectively. Then the matching function is defined as follows:

$$\mathrm{match}(v, v') = \begin{cases} \mathrm{true}, & \mathrm{if}\ \mathrm{dist}(v, v') \le \alpha \\ \mathrm{false}, & \mathrm{otherwise}, \end{cases}$$

where α denotes the given matching distance threshold, which represents the maximum allowable distance between the ground-truth intersection and the detected one. In addition, we use Precision, Recall, and F-measure as the evaluation criteria. Let I_{truth} denote the number of the ground truth intersections, $I_{\mathrm{extracted}}$ denote the total number of the detected intersections, and I_{cp} denote the number of the correctly detected intersections. The higher the F-measure is, the better the detection approach performs. Precision, Recall, and F-measure are defined as follows:

$$\mathrm{Precision} = \frac{I_{\mathrm{cp}}}{I_{\mathrm{extracted}}}, \quad \mathrm{Recall} = \frac{I_{\mathrm{cp}}}{I_{\mathrm{truth}}},$$

$$F\text{-measure} = \frac{2 * \mathrm{Precision} * \mathrm{Recall}}{\mathrm{Precision} + \mathrm{Recall}}.$$

Comparison. The core task of our empirical evaluation is to verify the robustness and effectiveness of our proposed approach for finding the road intersections from GPS traces. As a result, we compare RIDF with comparative methods on *Bus2012* and *Taxi2015*. Figure 6.22 presents

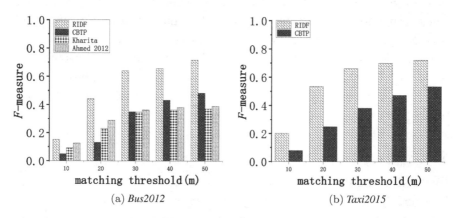

Figure 6.22. Performance comparison.

F-measure obtained by different approaches using different matching thresholds on two data sets.

Analysis on *Bus2012*. As can be observed from Figure 6.22(a), with the increment of matching threshold, α, the F-measure's value of all the approaches rises proportionately. However, *Ahmed2012* and *Kharita* achieve poor precision on *Bus2012*, the reason being that the vertexes found by them not only contain the road intersections, but also include some possible breakpoints in the road segments. By contrast, the detecting results of our proposal and CBTP are more close to the ground truth because they intend to identify the road intersections instead of simply extracting the vertexes of the road map.

Analysis on *Taxi2015*. Subsequently, we compare our proposal with CBTP on a selected region from *Taxi2015*, as illustrated in Figure 6.22(b). As compared to *Bus2012*, the selected region in *Taxi2015* is larger and has a more complicated topological structure. Therefore, the values of F-measure of both approaches on *Taxi2015* are lower than that on *Bus2012*. Notwithstanding, our proposal still achieves higher F-measure than CBTP. The reason for this is that our method could find different sizes of cells where the road intersections exist, and effectively discern the road intersections from the road segments. While CBTP aims to detect the intersections based on the extracted curved parts, which is easily influenced by the curved parts on the road segments. In addition, CBTP does not focus on finding different-sized intersections. Therefore, our proposal is more robust and has higher quality detection results. In our future works, we will focus on adaptive adjustment of parameters according to the density of trajectory points to improve the accuracy of intersection identification.

6.4.4.4 *Execution overhead of RIDF*

In this section, we not only validate the quality of intersection detection when more data is available, but also look into the computational scalability of our algorithm. As illustrated in Table 6.5, we run the RIDF method on slices of 1, 5, and 20 days of the *Taxi2015* data set, respectively. It is clearly seen that execution time grows linearly with the size of the input data set, which demonstrates the high scalability of our proposed algorithm.

Table 6.5. RIDF at scale.

Days	1	5	20
GPS points	33384	179112	802633
Trajectories	1517	5726	34356
Time performance(s)	185	368	1617

6.5 Related Work

In the past decades, much research has been conducted on map inference and map updating. Notwithstanding, there exist few researches on underground road identification, which needs to extract specific features of that type of road such as the line segments of missing sampling points. Although Stockx *et al.* (2014) could detect subway stations when a user was taking a subway, it detected them by using the accelerometer and the gyroscope embedded in a smartphone instead of analyzing trajectory data.

Next, we briefly conduct a systematic review over the related work in the following areas: map inference, map updating, and road intersection detection.

6.5.1 *Map inference*

Based on the trajectory data set or satellite images, map inference aims to infer the entire road map. Image processing technology is mainly applied to infer the road map from satellite images [Mokhtarzade and Zoej, 2007; Seo *et al.*, 2012]. But it is costly to obtain high-resolution satellite images data. Therefore, most researches on map inference are based on the trajectories of vehicles. Early in 1999, Rogers *et al.* (1999) firstly attempted to make a road map from GPS traces. It used an initial map to refine the centerline of the road by a hierarchical agglomerative clustering algorithm. Guo *et al.* (2007) presented initial simulation work with a similar goal of finding the centerline of the road through the statistical analysis. Without using any prior road map, Cao and Krumm (2009) clarified and then merged GPS traces to create a routable road map. Chen and Krumm (2010) found traffic lanes by modeling the spread of GPS traces across multiple lanes as a mixture of Gaussians.

Biagioni and Eriksson (2012) presented an extensible map inference pipeline, designed to mitigate GPS error and admit less-frequently traveled roads.

Most of the map inference methods apply three kinds of techniques, including K-means [Agamennoni *et al.*, 2011; Edelkamp and Schrödl, 2003; Schrödl *et al.*, 2004], KDE algorithm [Biagioni and Eriksson, 2012; Davies *et al.*, 2006] and the trace merging algorithm [Cao and Krumm, 2009; Liu *et al.*, 2012]. But in the actual applications, the aforementioned methods have poor performance in handling trajectory data with excessive random noise, nonuniform distribution and uneven sampling rate. Additionally, they are too time-consuming to fit online map inference.

6.5.2 *Map updating*

Compared with the time overhead of inferring the whole map, it is more realistic to simply add on to or modify the roads for a given map. Map updating methods aim to discover the missing roads based on unmatched trajectories and then update the given map with the newly found roads, including CrowdAtlas [Wang *et al.*, 2013], Glue [Wu *et al.*, 2015] and COBWEB [Shan *et al.*, 2015]. CrowdAtlas consists of four stages: trajectory clustering, centerline fitting, connection, and iteration. When the number of unmatched trajectory segments reaches the specified quantity criterion, CrowdAtlas implements clustering and polyline fitting to generate the centerlines that represent the missing roads. Nevertheless, CrowdAtlas may infer the missing roads with false directions when unmatched trajectory segments cross over two or more roads, as illustrated in Figure 6.1(a). In addition, CrowdAtlas easily obtain poor detection accuracy when dealing with low sampling rate data.

To improve the precision of inferred roads on low sampling rate trajectory data, Glue attempts to cluster the unmatched trajectory points to infer the missing roads. Similarly, COBWEB organizes GPS points using a COBWEB data structure and reduces the vertices and edges from COBWEB to generate Road-Tree, and finally finishes map updating. However, both Glue and COBWEB aim to cluster unmatched trajectory points and can easily infer incomplete road segments instead of intrinsically long roads, as illustrated in Figure 6.1(b). Moreover, all the above mentioned approaches cannot infer the missing roads based on sparse trajectory data. Thus, it becomes necessary to devise a map updating mechanism with high precision and noise tolerance to infer the missing roads on the trajectory data of various sampling rate and density.

6.5.3 *Road intersection detection*

As a vital component of map construction, the issue of road intersection detection has also attracted wide attention and interest of researchers. Numerous methods (Cao and Krumm, 2009; Ahmed and Wenk, 2012; Karagiorgou and Pfoser, 2012; Liu *et al.*, 2012; Wang *et al.*, 2013; Ahmed *et al.*, 2015; Wang *et al.*, 2015; Wu *et al.*, 2015; Li *et al.*, 2016; Chen *et al.*, 2016; Wang *et al.*, 2017b; Stanojevic *et al.*, 2018) have been put forward to construct the road maps from GPS traces of vehicles. However, the vertexes extracted usually not only contain the real road intersections, but also include possible breakpoints on the road segments. As a result, they cannot ensure high-quality intersection detecting result in actual scenarios.

Several approaches (Wang *et al.*, 2017a; Xie *et al.*, 2017; Xie and Philips, 2017; Fathi and Krumm, 2010; Karagiorgou and Pfoser, 2012; Wu *et al.*, 2013) attempted to find the road intersections based on the premise that the intersections are the regions where the majority of vehicles change driving directions. Fathi and Krumm (2010) trained a classifier using a *shape descriptor* based on sub-trajectories features to distinguish intersections from non-intersections. Karagiorgou and Pfoser (2012) put forward an intersection detection method by extracting *turn samples* in terms of the specified speed threshold and direction threshold. Wu *et al.* (2013) presented an intersection recognizing algorithm by *turn points* searching and *converging points* clustering. Xie and Philips (2017) tried to find the longest common subsequences using dynamic programming and then derive the connecting points from partitioned subsequences to further extract the intersections. Li *et al.* (2017) identified the intersections by extracting dominant orientations and merging similar orientations while maintaining independent conflicting orientations. Based on the assumption that *turns* occur at intersections rather than on roadways,

Wang *et al.* (2017a) identified the intersections by extracting curved parts (*turns*) of trajectories, grid density analysis of turns, and density-based clustering.

However, the aforementioned intersection detection methods typically rely on the trajectories with high sampling rate, low noise, and uniformly distribution. The real-world scenario is often not the case, e.g., trajectory data is of low precision and the densities of trajectories in various areas are heterogeneous. In addition, the roads has many curves except the intersections and many trajectories with frequent heading changing occur on the road segment, etc. Therefore, the precision of the existing detection approaches is limited, especially when using uniform threshold.

6.6 Conclusion

In this chapter, we leverage the clustering technique to identify several kinds of roads in the map, including missing roads inferring, underground road identification, and road intersection detection. First, we solve the issue of inferring missing roads on sparse trajectory data of vehicles. On the basis of the sliding-window model, we propose a hybrid framework called HyMU to infer the missing roads. HyMU is mainly composed of two phases: road candidates generation and missing roads inferring. Owing to the advantages of the hybrid mechanism, HyMU attains a better performance as compared to the other map updating methods. Substantial experimental results demonstrate the superiority of HyMU, especially in dealing with sparse trajectory data.

Second, we put forward a novel framework to detect underground roads from raw trajectories without a road network. To the best of our knowledge, we are the first to address the issue of detecting both underpasses and tunnels. We find underground roads mainly using three steps: (1) we first detect whether the line segments that belong to different trajectories are LMs and then group the identified LMs into clusters, (2) we judge whether the present sub-trajectory is an SP for a cluster while we update two critical variables, N_{LM} and N_{SP}, accordingly, and (3) we filter the clusters and obtain the clusters satisfying two constraints. The experimental results show that our approach can find the underground roads effectively and efficiently.

Third, we present an effective two-phase framework called RIDF to detect road intersections from GPS trajectory collections. The key idea of our method is to improve low quality trajectories through splitting, resampling, and filtering, and then identifying different sizes of intersections based on the direction ratio statistics and speed analysis for the split cells. Finally, we refine the locations of intersections through a hybrid clustering strategy. We demonstrate its effectiveness and robustness by comparing it with state-of-the-art methods by conducting comprehensive experiments on two real data sets.

Chapter 7

Summary and Future Trends

7.1 Summary

The proliferating deployment of positioning devices and surveillance equipments have expedited exponential growth of position stream data. It is necessary to analyze the trajectory streams in a centralized or distributed manner due to the demands of various time-critical applications. However, it is not necessary to develop efficient solutions to analyze the trajectory streams. The main challenge lies in the strict space and time complexities of processing the continuously arriving trajectory data, combined with the difficulty of concept drift. In addition, the analysis technique must satisfy the requirements like real-time response, noise tolerance and being able to track the evolutionary property of skewed trajectory data. For distributed streams, it is even more difficult to design a highly scalable two-phase mechanism, which includes parallel analyses on the remote sites and then consolidating these analyses on the coordinator afterwards, while ensuring the minimization of transmission overheads among the nodes.

In this book, we are primarily concerned with the problems of clustering and outlier detection upon the trajectory streams. First, we addressed the problem of online clustering streaming trajectories using the sliding-window model. We design a two-phase framework that incrementally summarizes clusters and safely eliminates the expired tuples, and present two clustering methods (TSCluWin and OCluST) based on the two defined synopsis data structures.

Then, aiming at identifying the outlier that behaves significantly from its neighbors, on the basis of the *feature grouping* mechanism, we propose a two-phase trajectory outlier detection framework and provide two outlier detection solutions upon trajectory streams, i.e., TODS and OTODS.

Furthermore, in order to solve the issues of efficient clustering and outlier detection upon distributed trajectory streams, we first put forward an online clustering algorithm that includes parallel clustering on the incoming trajectory data, as well as re-clustering on all the local clustering results. We then propose a distributed outlier detection framework to identify outliers upon the trajectory streams. It is comprised of parallel outlier detection (including the trajectory fragment outlier and fragment cluster outlier) at the remote sites, and evolving abnormal object detection at the coordinator site.

Finally, based on the techniques of trajectory clustering and trajectory outlier detection, we solve a few problems in the actual applications like traffic safety management and road map updating. We first improve the effectiveness of cloned vehicle identification by incorporating the *feature grouping*-based outlier detection mechanism. Then, we leverage the technique of trajectory clustering to give solutions for missing road inferring, underground road identification, and road intersection detection.

7.2 Future Trends

There remains a few interesting topics to be studied in the future.

First, in order to keep the analysis close to data and provide timely detection results, the analysis shall be implemented in a distributed manner among the nodes where trajectory streams are produced. An intuitive solution would be to analyze the sets of trajectories at each remote site and then integrate these local analysis results to obtain the global result. However, the analysis for a local trajectory data set on a single remote site usually cannot ensure accurate results, which may need the help of data from neighboring remote sites. For instance, in the case of outlier detection upon distributed trajectory streams, for the trajectory fragment cluster that is located at the border of some regions, local neighbors cannot always be found together on the same remote site, i.e., only a few neighbors on the same remote site while most of the rest belong to neighboring sites. As a result, it is worthwhile studying how one can analyze distributed trajectory streams based upon all the possible data collected by different nodes and then further scaling up the analysis's accuracy.

Second, although a great number of trajectories have offered us unprecedented information to understand the behavior characteristics of moving objects, other data aside from the trajectories of objects can be utilized to help us learn about the events behind the moving patterns and even reveal the reasons why they happen. According to the actual application requirements, it may include POI data, weather data, rainfall monitoring data, air pollution data, social media data, internet data, house pricing data, etc. How to effectively fuse these data and analyzing them to provide in-depth insight or semantic meaning is another topic worthy of study.

Third, trajectory clustering and trajectory outlier detection have already been widely applied in actual applications. Nevertheless, to solve all kinds of actual problems, the implementations of these techniques not only involve the setting of various thresholds for distinct clustering or the outlier detection method, but also requires a restructuring of the methods. For example, to the question of road intersection detection, trajectory clustering can be utilized to decide the locations of the intersections. In addition, trajectory clustering can be used to determine the shape of the road intersection by grouping the turning behaviors of various trajectory within the coverage of that intersection into different classes. To tackle the above two issues, the data needed to process and the chosen clustering techniques may be distinct, which fits within our saying of "one size does not fit all". Thus, customizing an effective analysis method using trajectory clustering or trajectory outlier detection for different application scenarios is an issue worthy of research.

References

Agamennoni, G., Nieto, J. I., and Nebot, E. M. (2011). Robust inference of principal road paths for intelligent transportation systems, *IEEE Trans. Intelligent Transportation Systems*, **12**(1), pp. 298–308.

Aggarwal, C. C., Han, J., Wang, J., and Yu, P. S. (2003). A framework for clustering evolving data streams, in *VLDB* (Morgan Kaufmann, Berlin), pp. 81–92.

Aggarwal, C. C. and Yu, P. S. (2008). A framework for clustering uncertain data streams, in *ICDE*, IEEE (IEEE, Cancún), pp. 150–159.

Agrawal, R. and Srikant, R. (1994). Fast algorithms for mining association rules in large databases, in *VLDB*, pp. 487–499.

Agrawal, R. and Srikant, R. (1995). Mining sequential patterns, in *Proceedings of the Eleventh International Conference on Data Engineering*, pp. 3–14.

Ahmed, M., Karagiorgou, S., Pfoser, D., and Wenk, C. (2015). A comparison and evaluation of map construction algorithms using vehicle tracking data, *GeoInformatica*, **19**(3), pp. 601–632.

Ahmed, M. and Wenk, C. (2012). Constructing street networks from GPS trajectories, in *Algorithms — ESA 2012 — 20th Annual European Symposium*, Ljubljana, Slovenia, September 10–12, 2012, pp. 60–71.

Anagnostopoulos, A., Vlachos, M., Hadjieleftheriou, M., Keogh, E. J., and Yu, P. S. (2006). Global distance-based segmentation of trajectories, in *KDD*, ACM (ACM, Philadelphia), pp. 34–43.

Assent, I., Wichterich, M., Krieger, R., Kremer, H., and Seidl, T. (2009). Anticipatory DTW for efficient similarity search in time series databases, *PVLDB*, **2**(1), pp. 826–837.

Babcock, B., Datar, M., Motwani, R., and Callaghan, L. (2003). Maintaining variance and k-medians over data stream windows, in *PODS*, ACM (ACM, San Diego), pp. 234–243.

Barnett, V. (1994). *Outliers in Statistical Data*, Wiley, ISBN 978-0-471-93094-5, doi:10.1016/0169-2070(95)00625-7.

Biagioni, J. and Eriksson, J. (2012). Map inference in the face of noise and disparity, in *SIGSPATIAL*, ACM (ACM, Redondo), pp. 79–88.

Breunig, M. M., Kriegel, H., Ng, R. T., and Sander, J. (2000). LOF: identifying density-based local outliers, in *SIGMOD*, ACM (ACM, Dallas), pp. 93–104.

Bu, Y., Chen, L., Fu, A. W., and Liu, D. (2009). Efficient anomaly monitoring over moving object trajectory streams, in *SIGKDD*, ACM (ACM, Paris), pp. 159–168.

Cao, H., Mamoulis, N., and Cheung, D. W. (2005). Mining frequent spatio-temporal sequential patterns, in *ICDM*, pp. 82–89.

Cao, L. and Krumm, J. (2009). From GPS traces to a routable road map, in *GIS*, ACM (ACM, Seattle), pp. 3–12.

Cao, L., Yan, Y., Kuhlman, C., Wang, Q., Rundensteiner, E. A., and Eltabakh, M. Y. (2017). Multi-tactic distance-based outlier detection, in *33rd IEEE International Conference on Data Engineering, ICDE 2017*, San Diego, CA, USA, April 19–22, 2017, pp. 959–970.

Castro, P. S., Zhang, D., and Li, S. (2012). Urban traffic modelling and prediction using large scale taxi GPS traces, in *Pervasive*, Springer (Springer, Newcastle), pp. 57–72.

Chakka, V. P., Everspaugh, A., and Patel, J. M. (2003). Indexing large trajectory data sets with SETI, in *CIDR 2003, First Biennial Conference on Innovative Data Systems Research*, Asilomar, CA, USA, January 5–8, 2003, Online Proceedings.

Chawla, S., Zheng, Y., and Hu, J. (2012). Inferring the root cause in road traffic anomalies, in *ICDM*, IEEE (IEEE, Brussels), pp. 141–150.

Chen, B., Sun, W., and Vodacek, A. (2014). Improving image-based characterization of road junctions, widths, and connectivity by leveraging openstreetmap vector map, in *IGARSS*, pp. 4958–4961.

Chen, C., Chen, X., Wang, Z., Wang, Y., and Zhang, D. (2017). Scenicplanner: planning scenic travel routes leveraging heterogeneous user-generated digital footprints, *Frontiers of Computer Science*, **11**(1), pp. 61–74.

Chen, C., Lu, C., Huang, Q., Yang, Q., Gunopulos, D., and Guibas, L. J. (2016). City-scale map creation and updating using GPS collections, in *SIGKDD*, pp. 1465–1474.

Chen, C., Zhang, D., Castro, P. S., Li, N., Sun, L., and Li, S. (2011). Real-time detection of anomalous taxi trajectories from GPS traces, in *MobiQuitous*, Springer (Springer, Copenhagen), pp. 63–74.

Chen, C., Zhang, D., Castro, P. S., Li, N., Sun, L., Li, S., and Wang, Z. (2013). iBoat: Isolation-based online anomalous trajectory detection, *IEEE Transactions Intelligent Transportation Systems*, **14**(2), pp. 806–818.

Chen, J., Leung, M. K. H., and Gao, Y. (2003). Noisy logo recognition using line segment hausdorff distance, *Pattern Recognition*, **36**(4), pp. 943–955.

Chen, L. and Ng, R. T. (2004). On the marriage of lp-norms and edit distance, in *VLDB* (Morgan Kaufmann, Toronto), pp. 792–803.

Chen, L., Özsu, M. T., and Oria, V. (2005). Robust and fast similarity search for moving object trajectories, in *SIGMOD*, ACM (ACM, Baltimore), pp. 491–502.

Chen, Y. and Krumm, J. (2010). Probabilistic modeling of traffic lanes from GPS traces, in *18th ACM SIGSPATIAL International Symposium on Advances in Geographic Information Systems, ACM-GIS 2010*, November 3–5, 2010, San Jose, CA, USA, pp. 81–88.

Christensen, R., Wang, L., Li, F., Yi, K., Tang, J., and Villa, N. (2015). STORM: spatio-temporal online reasoning and management of large spatio-temporal data, in *Proceedings of the 2015 ACM SIGMOD International Conference on Management of Data*, Melbourne, Victoria, Australia, May 31–June 4, 2015, pp. 1111–1116.

Chu, S., Keogh, E. J., Hart, D. M., and Pazzani, M. J. (2002). Iterative deepening dynamic time warping for time series, in *SIAM*, SIAM (SIAM, Arlington), pp. 195–212.

Cormode, G., Shkapenyuk, V., Srivastava, D., and Xu, B. (2009). Forward decay: A practical time decay model for streaming systems, in *ICDE* (IEEE, Shanghai), pp. 138–149.

Costa, G., Manco, G., and Masciari, E. (2014). Dealing with trajectory streams by clustering and mathematical transforms, *Journal of Intelligent Information Systems*, **42**(1), pp. 155–177.

Dai, C. (2016). *Data Analysis to the Traffic Checkpoint Based on Cloud Computing*, Ph.D. thesis, South China University of Technology.

Das, S., Mirnalinee, T. T., and Varghese, K. (2011). Use of salient features for the design of a multistage framework to extract roads from high-resolution multispectral satellite images, *IEEE Transactions Geoscience and Remote Sensing*, **49**(10), pp. 3906–3931.

Datar, M., Gionis, A., Indyk, P., and Motwani, R. (2002). Maintaining stream statistics over sliding windows, in *SODA*, ACM (ACM, San Francisco), pp. 635–644.

Davies, J. J., Beresford, A. R., and Hopper, A. (2006). Scalable, distributed, real-time map generation, *IEEE Pervasive Computing*, **5**(4), pp. 47–54.

Deng, C., Xue, L., Li, W., and Zhou, Z. (2010). The real-time monitoring system for inspecting car based on rfid, gps and gis, in *International Conference on Environmental Science and Information Application Technology*, pp. 772–775.

Deng, Z., Hu, Y., Zhu, M., Huang, X., and Du, B. (2015). A scalable and fast OPTICS for clustering trajectory big data, *Cluster Computing*, **18**(2), pp. 549–562.

Duan, X., Jin, C., Wang, X., Zhou, A., and Yue, K. (2016). Real-time personalized taxi-sharing, in *DASFAA*, Springer (Springer, Dallas), pp. 451–465.

Edelkamp, S. and Schrödl, S. (2003). Route planning and map inference with global positioning traces, in *Computer Science in Perspective, Essays Dedicated to Thomas Ottmann*, pp. 128–151.

Ester, M., Kriegel, H., Sander, J., and Xu, X. (1996). A density-based algorithm for discovering clusters in large spatial databases with noise, in *KDD*, AAAI Press (AAAI Press, Portland), pp. 226–231.

Faloutsos, C., Ranganathan, M., and Manolopoulos, Y. (1994). Fast subsequence matching in time-series databases, in *Proceedings of the 1994 ACM SIGMOD*, pp. 419–429.

Fathi, A. and Krumm, J. (2010). Detecting road intersections from GPS traces, in *Geographic Information Science*, (Springer, Zurich), pp. 56–69.

Gaffney, S. and Smyth, P. (1999). Trajectory clustering with mixtures of regression models, in *SIGKDD*, ACM (ACM, San Diego), pp. 63–72.

Ge, Y., Xiong, H., Liu, C., and Zhou, Z. (2011). A taxi driving fraud detection system, in *ICDM* (IEEE, Vancouver), pp. 181–190.

Ge, Y., Xiong, H., Zhou, Z., Ozdemir, H. T., Yu, J., and Lee, K. C. (2010). Top-eye: top-k evolving trajectory outlier detection, in *CIKM* (ACM, Toronto), pp. 1733–1736.

Giannotti, F., Nanni, M., and Pedreschi, D. (2006). Efficient mining of temporally annotated sequences, in *SIAM*, pp. 348–359.

Giannotti, F., Nanni, M., Pinelli, F., and Pedreschi, D. (2007). Trajectory pattern mining, in *SIGKDD* (ACM, San Jose), pp. 330–339.

Guo, T., Iwamura, K., and Koga, M. (2007). Towards high accuracy road maps generation from massive GPS traces data, in *IEEE International Geoscience & Remote Sensing Symposium, IGARSS 2007*, July 23–28, 2007, Barcelona, Spain, pp. 667–670.

Han, B., Liu, L., and Omiecinski, E. (2015). Road-network aware trajectory clustering: Integrating locality, flow, and density, *IEEE Transactions on Mobile Computing*, **14**(2), pp. 416–429.

Hawkins, D. M. (1980). *Identification of Outliers* (Springer), ISBN 978-94-015-3994-4, doi:10.1007/978-94-015-3994-4.

Hönle, N., Großmann, M., Reimann, S., and Mitschang, B. (2010). Usability analysis of compression algorithms for position data streams, in *SIGSPATIAL*, ACM (ACM, San Jose), pp. 240–249.

Iqbal, U., Zamir, S. W., Shahid, M. H., Parwaiz, K., Yasin, M., and Sarfraz, M. S. (2010). Image based vehicle type identification, in *International Conference on Information and Emerging Technologies*, pp. 1–5.

Jensen, C. S., Lin, D., and Ooi, B. C. (2007). Continuous clustering of moving objects, *IEEE TKDE*, **19**(9), pp. 1161–1174.

Jeung, H., Yiu, M. L., Zhou, X., Jensen, C. S., and Shen, H. T. (2008). Discovery of convoys in trajectory databases, *PVLDB*, **1**(1), pp. 1068–1080.

Jin, C., Yu, J. X., Zhou, A., and Cao, F. (2014). Efficient clustering of uncertain data streams, *Knowledge and Information Systems*, **40**(3), pp. 509–539.

Karagiorgou, S. and Pfoser, D. (2012). On vehicle tracking data-based road network generation, in *SIGSPATIAL*, ACM (ACM, Redondo), pp. 89–98.

Knorr, E. M. and Ng, R. T. (1998). Algorithms for mining distance-based outliers in large datasets, in *VLDB*, Morgan Kaufmann (Morgan Kaufmann, New York), pp. 392–403.

Knorr, E. M. and Ng, R. T. (1999). Finding intensional knowledge of distance-based outliers, in *VLDB*, Morgan Kaufmann (Morgan Kaufmann, Edinburgh), pp. 211–222.

Knorr, E. M., Ng, R. T., and Tucakov, V. (2000). Distance-based outliers: Algorithms and applications, *VLDB J.*, **8**(3–4), pp. 237–253.

Lange, R., Dürr, F., and Rothermel, K. (2011). Efficient real-time trajectory tracking, *VLDB J.*, **20**(5), pp. 671–694.

Lee, J., Han, J., and Li, X. (2008a). Trajectory outlier detection: A partition-and-detect framework, in *ICDE*, IEEE (IEEE, Cancún), pp. 140–149.

Lee, J., Han, J., Li, X., and Gonzalez, H. (2008b). *TraClass*: trajectory classification using hierarchical region-based and trajectory-based clustering, *PVLDB*, **1**(1), pp. 1081–1094.

Lee, J., Han, J., and Whang, K. (2007). Trajectory clustering: a partition-and-group framework, in *SIGMOD*, ACM (ACM, Beijing), pp. 593–604.

Lei, P. (2016). A framework for anomaly detection in maritime trajectory behavior, *Knowledge and Information Systems*, **47**(1), pp. 189–214.

Li, H., Kulik, L., and Ramamohanarao, K. (2016). Automatic generation and validation of road maps from GPS trajectory data sets, in *CIKM*, ACM (ACM, Indianapolis), pp. 1523–1532.

Li, L., Li, D., Xing, X., Yang, F., Rong, W., and Zhu, H. (2017). Extraction of road intersections from GPS traces based on the dominant orientations of roads, *International Journal of Geo-Information*, **6**(12), p. 403.

Li, X., Ceikute, V., Jensen, C. S., and Tan, K. (2013). Effective online group discovery in trajectory databases, *IEEE Transactions on Knowledge and Data Engineering*, **25**(12), pp. 2752–2766.

Li, X., Han, J., Kim, S., and Gonzalez, H. (2007). ROAM: rule- and motif-based anomaly detection in massive moving object data sets, in *SDM*, SIAM (SIAM, Minneapolis), pp. 273–284.

Li, X., Li, Z., Han, J., and Lee, J. (2009). Temporal outlier detection in vehicle traffic data, in *ICDE*, IEEE (IEEE, Shanghai), pp. 1319–1322.

Li, Y., Han, J., and Yang, J. (2004). Clustering moving objects, in *SIGKDD*, ACM (ACM, Seattle), pp. 617–622.

Li, Y. and Liu, C. (2015). An approach to instantly detecting fake plates based on large-scale ANPR data, in *WISA*, pp. 287–292.

Li, Z., Lee, J., Li, X., and Han, J. (2010). Incremental clustering for trajectories, in *DASFAA*, Springer (Springer, Tsukuba), pp. 32–46.

Liu, H., Jin, C., and Zhou, A. (2016). Popular route planning with travel cost estimation, in *DASFAA*, Springer (Springer, Dallas), pp. 403–418.

Liu, S., Ni, L. M., and Krishnan, R. (2014). Fraud detection from taxis' driving behaviors, *IEEE Transactions Vehicular Technology*, **63**(1), pp. 464–472.

Liu, W., Zheng, Y., Chawla, S., Yuan, J., and Xing, X. (2011). Discovering spatio-temporal causal interactions in traffic data streams, in *SIGKDD*, ACM (ACM, San Diego), pp. 1010–1018.

Liu, X., Biagioni, J., Eriksson, J., Wang, Y., Forman, G., and Zhu, Y. (2012). Mining large-scale, sparse GPS traces for map inference: comparison of approaches, in *KDD*, ACM (ACM, Beijing), pp. 669–677.

Lloyd, S. P. (1982). Least squares quantization in PCM, *IEEE Transactions Information Theory*, **28**(2), pp. 129–136.

Ma, Q., Yang, B., Qian, W., and Zhou, A. (2009). Query processing of massive trajectory data based on mapreduce, in *CIKM*, ACM (ACM, Hong Kong), pp. 9–16.

Mao, J., Jin, C., Zhang, Z., and Zhou, A. (2017a). Anomaly detection for trajectory big data: Advancements and framework, *Journal of Software*, **28**(1), pp. 17–34.

Mao, J., Wang, T., Jin, C., and Zhou, A. (2017b). Feature grouping-based outlier detection upon streaming trajectories, *IEEE Transactions on Knowledge and Data Engineering*, **29**(12), pp. 2696–2709.

Mazhelis, O. (2010). Using recursive bayesian estimation for matching gps measurements to imperfect road network data, in *Intelligent Transportation Systems, International IEEE Conference*, pp. 1492–1497.

Mokhtarzade, M. and Zoej, M. J. V. (2007). Road detection from high-resolution satellite images using artificial neural networks, *International Journal of Applied Earth Observation and Geoinformation*, **9**(1), pp. 32–40.

Nanni, M. and Pedreschi, D. (2006). Time-focused clustering of trajectories of moving objects, *Journal of Intelligent Information Systems*, **27**(3), pp. 267–289.

Nascimento, M. A. and Silva, J. R. O. (1998). Towards historical r-trees, in *Proceedings of the 1998 ACM symposium on Applied Computing, SAC'98*, Atlanta, GA, USA, February 27–March 1, 1998, pp. 235–240.

Nehme, R. V. and Rundensteiner, E. A. (2006). SCUBA: scalable cluster-based algorithm for evaluating continuous spatio-temporal queries on moving objects, in *EDBT*, Springer (Springer, Munich), pp. 1001–1019.

Pan, B., Zheng, Y., Wilkie, D., and Shahabi, C. (2013). Crowd sensing of traffic anomalies based on human mobility and social media, in *SIGSPATIAL*, ACM (ACM, Orlando), pp. 334–343.

Panagiotakis, C., Pelekis, N., Kopanakis, I., Ramasso, E., and Theodoridis, Y. (2012). Segmentation and sampling of moving object trajectories based on representativeness, *IEEE Transactions on Knowledge and Data Engineering*, **24**(7), pp. 1328–1343.

Papadias, D., Zhang, J., Mamoulis, N., and Tao, Y. (2003). Query processing in spatial network databases, in *VLDB 2003*, pp. 802–813.

Pei, J., Han, J., and Hsu, M. (2001). Prefixspan: Mining sequential patterns by prefix-projected growth, in *ICDE*, pp. 215–224.

Pelekis, N., Kopanakis, I., Kotsifakos, E. E., Frentzos, E., and Theodoridis, Y. (2009). Clustering trajectories of moving objects in an uncertain world, in *ICDM*, IEEE (IEEE, Miami), pp. 417–427.

Pfoser, D., Jensen, C. S., and Theodoridis, Y. (2000). Novel approaches to the indexing of moving object trajectories, in *VLDB 2000, Proceedings of 26th International Conference on Very Large Data Bases*, September 10–14, 2000, Cairo, Egypt, pp. 395–406.

Ramaswamy, S., Rastogi, R., and Shim, K. (2000). Efficient algorithms for mining outliers from large data sets, in *SIGMOD* (ACM, Dallas), pp. 427–438.

Rogers, S., Langley, P., and Wilson, C. (1999). Mining GPS data to augment road models, in *Proceedings of the Fifth ACM SIGKDD International Conference on Knowledge Discovery and Data Mining*, San Diego, CA, USA, August 15–18, 1999, pp. 104–113.

Roh, G. and Hwang, S. (2010). Nncluster: An efficient clustering algorithm for road network trajectories, in *DASFAA*, Springer (Springer, Tsukuba), pp. 47–61.

Sacharidis, D., Patroumpas, K., Terrovitis, M., Kantere, V., Potamias, M., Mouratidis, K., and Sellis, T. K. (2008). On-line discovery of hot motion paths, in *EDBT*, ACM (ACM, Nantes), pp. 392–403.

Schrödl, S., Wagstaff, K., Rogers, S., Langley, P., and Wilson, C. (2004). Mining GPS traces for map refinement, *Data Mining and Knowledge Discovery*, **9**(1), pp. 59–87.

Seo, Y., Urmson, C., and Wettergreen, D. (2012). Exploiting publicly available cartographic resources for aerial image analysis, in *SIGSPATIAL*, ACM (ACM, Redondo), pp. 109–118.

Shan, Z., Wu, H., Sun, W., and Zheng, B. (2015). COBWEB: a robust map update system using GPS trajectories, in *UbiComp*, ACM (ACM, Osaka), pp. 927–937.

Song, Z. and Roussopoulos, N. (2003). Seb-tree: An approach to index continuously moving objects, in *Mobile Data Management, 4th International Conference, MDM 2003*, Melbourne, Australia, January 21–24, 2003, pp. 340–344.

Stanojevic, R., Abbar, S., Thirumuruganathan, S., Chawla, S., Filali, F., and Aleimat, A. (2018). Robust road map inference through network alignment of trajectories, in *SDM*, pp. 135–143.

Stockx, T., Hecht, B. J., and Schöning, J. (2014). Subwayps: Towards smartphone positioning in underground public transportation systems, in *Proceedings of the 22nd ACM SIGSPATIAL International Conference on Advances in Geographic Information Systems*, Dallas/Fort Worth, TX, USA, November 4–7, 2014, pp. 93–102.

Tang, L., Niu, L., Yang, X., Zhang, X., Li, Q., and Xiao, S. (2017). Urban intersection recognition and construction based on big trace data, *Acta Geodaetica et Cartographica Sinica*, **46**(6), pp. 770–779.

Tang, L. A., Zheng, Y., Yuan, J., Han, J., Leung, A., Hung, C., and Peng, W. (2012). On discovery of traveling companions from streaming trajectories, in *ICDE*, IEEE (IEEE, Washington), pp. 186–197.

Tang, M., Yu, Y., Malluhi, Q. M., Ouzzani, M., and Aref, W. G. (2016). Locationspark: A distributed in-memory data management system for big spatial data, *PVLDB*, **9**(13), pp. 1565–1568.

Tang, X. (2013). Analysis on the detection method of cloned vehicle, *Journal of Chinese People's Public Security University (Science and Technology)*, **19**(2), pp. 76–79.

Tao, Y. and Papadias, D. (2001a). Efficient historical R-trees, in *Proceedings of the 13th International Conference on Scientific and Statistical Database Management*, July 18–20, 2001, George Mason University, Fairfax, Virginia, USA, pp. 223–232.

Tao, Y. and Papadias, D. (2001b). Mv3r-tree: A spatio-temporal access method for timestamp and interval queries, in *VLDB 2001, Proceedings of 27th International Conference on Very Large Data Bases*, September 11–14, 2001, Roma, Italy, pp. 431–440.

Thiagarajan, A., Ravindranath, L., Balakrishnan, H., Madden, S., and Girod, L. (2011). Accurate, low-energy trajectory mapping for mobile devices, in *NSDI*.

Tong, Y., Zeng, Y., Zhou, Z., Chen, L., Ye, J., and Xu, K. (2018). A unified approach to route planning for shared mobility, *Proceedings of the VLDB Endowment*, **11**(11), pp. 1633–1646.

Velaga, N. R., Quddus, M. A., and Bristow, A. L. (2009). Developing an enhanced weight-based topological map-matching algorithm for intelligent transport systems, *Transportation Research Part C Emerging Technologies*, **17**(6), pp. 672–683.

Vlachos, M., Gunopulos, D., and Kollios, G. (2002). Discovering similar multidimensional trajectories, in *ICDE*, IEEE (IEEE, San Jose), pp. 673–684.

Vlachos, M., Hadjieleftheriou, M., Gunopulos, D., and Keogh, E. J. (2006). Indexing multidimensional time-series, *The VLDB Journal*, **15**(1), pp. 1–20.

Wang, J., Rui, X., Song, X., Tan, X., Wang, C., and Raghavan, V. (2015). A novel approach for generating routable road maps from vehicle GPS traces, *International Journal of Geographical Information Science*, **29**(1), pp. 69–91.

Wang, J., Wang, C., Song, X., and Raghavan, V. (2017a). Automatic intersection and traffic rule detection by mining motor-vehicle GPS trajectories, *Computers, Environment and Urban Systems*, **64**, pp. 19–29.

Wang, T., Mao, J., and Jin, C. (2017b). Hymu: A hybrid map updating framework, in *DASFAA*, Springer (Springer, Suzhou), pp. 19–33.

Wang, W., Yang, J., and Muntz, R. R. (1997). STING: A statistical information grid approach to spatial data mining, in *VLDB*, Morgan Kaufmann (Morgan Kaufmann, Athens), pp. 186–195.

Wang, Y., Liu, X., Wei, H., Forman, G., Chen, C., and Zhu, Y. (2013). Crowdatlas: self-updating maps for cloud and personal use, in *MobiSys* (ACM, Taipei), pp. 27–40.

Wei, H., Wang, Y., Forman, G., Zhu, Y., and Guan, H. (2012). Fast viterbi map matching with tunable weight functions, in *SIGSPATIAL*, ACM (ACM, Redondo), pp. 613–616.

Won, J., Kim, S., Baek, J., and Lee, J. (2009). Trajectory clustering in road network environment, in *CIDM*, IEEE (IEEE, Nashville), pp. 299–305.

Wu, H., Tu, C., Sun, W., Zheng, B., Su, H., and Wang, W. (2015). GLUE: a parameter-tuning-free map updating system, in *CIKM*, ACM (ACM, Melbourne), pp. 683–692.

Wu, J., Zhu, Y., Ku, T., and Wang, L. (2013). Detecting road intersections from coarse-gained GPS traces based on clustering, *Journal of Computers*, **8**(11), pp. 2959–2965.

Xie, D., Li, F., Yao, B., Li, G., Zhou, L., and Guo, M. (2016). Simba: Efficient in-memory spatial analytics, in *Proceedings of the 2016 International Conference on Management of Data, SIGMOD Conference 2016*, San Francisco, CA, USA, June 26–July 01, 2016, pp. 1071–1085.

Xie, X., Liao, W., Aghajan, H. K., Veelaert, P., and Philips, W. (2017). Detecting road intersections from GPS traces using longest common subsequence algorithm, *International Journal of Geo-Information*, **6**(1), p. 1.

Xie, X. and Philips, W. (2017). Road intersection detection through finding common sub-tracks between pairwise GNSS traces, *International Journal of Geo-Information*, **6**(10), p. 311.

Yan, Y., Cao, L., Kuhlman, C., and Rundensteiner, E. A. (2017). Distributed local outlier detection in big data, in *Proceedings of the 23rd ACM SIGKDD International Conference on Knowledge Discovery and Data Mining*, Halifax, NS, Canada, August 13–17, 2017, pp. 1225–1234.

Yang, W., Gao, Y., and Cao, L. (2013). TRASMIL: A local anomaly detection framework based on trajectory segmentation and multi-instance learning, *Computer Vision and Image Understanding*, **117**(10), pp. 1273–1286.

Yi, B., Jagadish, H. V., and Faloutsos, C. (1998). Efficient retrieval of similar time sequences under time warping, in *ICDE*, IEEE (IEEE, Orlando), pp. 201–208.

You, S., Zhang, J., and Gruenwald, L. (2015). Large-scale spatial join query processing in cloud, in *31st IEEE International Conference on Data Engineering Workshops, ICDE Workshops 2015*, Seoul, South Korea, April 13–17, 2015, pp. 34–41.

Yu, J., Wu, J., and Sarwat, M. (2015). Geospark: a cluster computing framework for processing large-scale spatial data, in *Proceedings of the 23rd SIGSPATIAL International Conference on Advances in Geographic Information Systems*, Bellevue, WA, USA, November 3–6, 2015, pp. 70:1–70:4.

Yu, Y., Cao, L., Rundensteiner, E. A., and Wang, Q. (2014). Detecting moving object outliers in massive-scale trajectory streams, in *SIGKDD*, ACM (ACM, New York), pp. 422–431.

Yu, Y., Wang, Q., Wang, X., Wang, H., and He, J. (2013). Online clustering for trajectory data stream of moving objects, *Computer Science and Information Systems*, **10**(3), pp. 1293–1317.

Yuan, M., Deng, K., Zeng, J., Li, Y., Ni, B., He, X., Wang, F., Dai, W., and Yang, Q. (2014). OceanST: A distributed analytic system for large-scale spatiotemporal mobile broadband data, *Proceedings of the VLDB Endowment*, **7**(13), pp. 1561–1564.

Zaki, M. J. (2001). SPADE: an efficient algorithm for mining frequent sequences, *Machine Learning*, **42**(1/2), pp. 31–60.

Zeinalipour-Yazti, D., Laoudias, C., Costa, C., Vlachos, M., Andreou, M. I., and Gunopulos, D. (2013). Crowdsourced trace similarity with smartphones, *IEEE Transactions on Knowledge and Data Engineering*, **25**(6), pp. 1240–1253.

Zeinalipour-Yazti, D., Lin, S., and Gunopulos, D. (2006). Distributed spatio-temporal similarity search, in *CIKM*, ACM (ACM, Arlington), pp. 14–23.

Zhang, D., Li, N., Zhou, Z., Chen, C., Sun, L., and Li, S. (2011). ibat: detecting anomalous taxi trajectories from GPS traces, in *UbiComp*, ACM (ACM, Beijing), pp. 99–108.

Zhang, J., Xu, J., and Liao, S. S. (2013). Aggregating and sampling methods for processing GPS data streams for traffic state estimation, *IEEE Transactions Intelligent Transportation Systems*, **14**(4), pp. 1629–1641.

Zhang, T., Ramakrishnan, R., and Livny, M. (1996). BIRCH: an efficient data clustering method for very large databases, in *SIGMOD*, ACM (ACM, Montreal), pp. 103–114.

Zhang, Z., Wang, Y., Mao, J., Qiao, S., Jin, C., and Zhou, A. (2017). DT-KST: distributed top-k similarity query on big trajectory streams, in *DASFAA*, Springer (Springer, Suzhou), pp. 199–214.

Zheng, K., Zheng, Y., Yuan, N. J., and Shang, S. (2013). On discovery of gathering patterns from trajectories, in *ICDE*, IEEE (IEEE, Brisbane), pp. 242–253.

Zhou, A., Cao, F., Qian, W., and Jin, C. (2008). Tracking clusters in evolving data streams over sliding windows, *Knowledge and Information Systems*, **15**(2), pp. 181–214.

Zhou, P., Zhang, D., Salzberg, B., Cooperman, G., and Kollios, G. (2005). Close pair queries in moving object databases, in *13th ACM International Workshop on Geographic Information Systems, ACM-GIS 2005*, November 4–5, 2005, Bremen, Germany, pp. 2–11.

Zhu, Y., Wang, Y., Forman, G., and Wei, H. (2015). Mining large-scale GPS streams for connectivity refinement of road maps, *The Computer Journal*, **58**(9), pp. 2109–2119.

Index

East China Normal University Scientific Reports
Subseries on Data Science and Engineering

Published (continued from page ii)